MATHEMATICAL DIFFICULTIES

This is a volume in the Academic Press
EDUCATIONAL PSYCHOLOGY SERIES

*Critical comprehensive reviews of research knowledge, theories,
principles, and practices*

Under the editorship of Gary D. Phye

MATHEMATICAL DIFFICULTIES: PSYCHOLOGY AND INTERVENTION

EDITED BY ANN DOWKER

AMSTERDAM • BOSTON • HEIDELBERG • LONDON • NEW YORK • OXFORD
PARIS • SAN DIEGO • SAN FRANCISCO • SINGAPORE • SYDNEY • TOKYO
Academic Press is an imprint of Elsevier

Academic Press is an imprint of Elsevier
525 B Street, Suite 1900, San Diego, CA 92101-4495, USA
30 Corporate Drive, Suite 400, Burlington, MA 01803, USA
32, Jamestown Road, London NW1 7BY, UK
Radarweg 29, PO Box 211, 1000 AE Amsterdam, The Netherlands

First edition 2008

Library of Congress Cataloging-in-Publication Data
A catalog record for this book is available from the Library of Congress

British Library Cataloguing in Publication Data
A catalogue record for this book is available from the British Library

ISBN: 978-0-12-373629-1

For information on all Academic Press publications
visit our website at books.elsevier.com

Typeset by Charon Tec Ltd., A Macmillan Company
www.macmillansolutions.com

Printed and bound in the United States of America

08   09   10   9   8   7   6   5   4   3   2   1

Working together to grow
libraries in developing countries
www.elsevier.com | www.bookaid.org | www.sabre.org

ELSEVIER   BOOK AID   Sabre Foundation
                International

To the memory of Bill Parry

CONTENTS

1

NEURAL CORRELATES OF NUMBER PROCESSING AND CALCULATION: DEVELOPMENTAL TRAJECTORIES AND EDUCATIONAL IMPLICATIONS

LIANE KAUFMANN

2

TOWARD A DEVELOPMENTAL COGNITIVE NEUROSCIENCE APPROACH TO THE STUDY OF TYPICAL AND ATYPICAL NUMBER DEVELOPMENT

DANIEL ANSARI, IAN D. HOLLOWAY, GAVIN R. PRICE, AND LUCIA VAN EIMEREN

3

A NUMBER SENSE ASSESSMENT TOOL FOR IDENTIFYING CHILDREN AT RISK FOR MATHEMATICAL DIFFICULTIES

NANCY C. JORDAN, JOSEPH GLUTTING, AND CHAITANYA RAMINENI

4

THE ESSENCE OF EARLY CHILDHOOD MATHEMATICS EDUCATION AND THE PROFESSIONAL DEVELOPMENT NEEDED TO SUPPORT IT

BARBRINA B. ERTLE, HERBERT P. GINSBURG, MARIA I. CORDERO, TRACY M. CURRAN, LESLIE MANLAPIG, AND MELISSA MORGENLANDER

5

PROGRESSION IN NUMERACY AGES 5–11: RESULTS FROM THE LEVERHULME LONGITUDINAL STUDY

MARGARET BROWN, MIKE ASKEW, JEREMY HODGEN, VALERIE RHODES, ALISON MILLETT, HAZEL DENVIR, AND DYLAN WILLIAM

6

AN ANALYSIS OF CHILDREN'S NUMERICAL DIFFICULTIES WITH THE AID OF A DYSCALCULIA TEST BATTERY AND A PRESENTATION OF REMEDIAL APPROACHES TO FACILITATE ASPECTS OF NUMERICAL DEVELOPMENT

CHRISTINE LAWSON

7

CHILDREN WITH AND WITHOUT MATHEMATICS DIFFICULTIES: ASPECTS OF LEARNER CHARACTERISTICS IN A DEVELOPMENTAL PERSPECTIVE

SNORRE A. OSTAD

8

NUMBER DEVELOPMENT AND CHILDREN WITH SPECIFIC LANGUAGE IMPAIRMENT

RICHARD COWAN, CHRIS DONLAN, ELIZABETH J. NEWTON, AND DELYTH LLOYD

9

THE PERFORMANCE OF DYSLEXIC AND NON-DYSLEXIC BOYS AT DIVISION SUMS

S.A. TURNER ELLIS, T.R. MILES, AND T.J. WHEELER

10

NUMERACY RECOVERY WITH CHILDREN WITH ARITHMETICAL DIFFICULTIES: INTERVENTION AND RESEARCH

ANN DOWKER

11

MATHEMATICS RECOVERY: AN EARLY NUMBER PROGRAM FOCUSING ON INTENSIVE INTERVENTION

ROBERT J. WRIGHT

12

MAKING INTERVENTION IN NUMERACY MORE EFFECTIVE IN SCHOOLS

MARGARET HASELER

AFTERWORD

HELPING CHILDREN WITH NUMERACY DIFFICULTIES IN SCHOOL: A TEACHER'S NOTES

JILL HANNINGTON

LIST OF CONTRIBUTORS

Daniel Ansari (13) Numerical Cognition Laboratory, Department of Psychology, University of Western Ontario, Ontario, Canada N6A 5C2

Mike Askew (85) Professor of Mathematics, King's College London, University of London, The Strand, London WC2R 2LS, UK

Margaret Brown (85) Professor of Mathematics, King's College London, University of London, The Strand, London WC2R 2LS, UK

Maria I. Cordero (59) New York City's Administration for Children's Services, New York, NY 10038, USA

Richard Cowan (155) Institute of Education, Department of Psychology and Human Development, University of London, London WC1H 0AA, UK

Tracy M. Curran (59) Department of Human Development, Teachers College, Columbia University, New York, NY 10027, USA

Hazel Denvir (85) Professor of Mathematics, King's College London, University of London, The Strand, London WC2R 2LS, UK

Chris Donlan (155) Department of Human Communication Science, University College London, London WC1N OPD, UK

Ann Dowker (181) Department of Experimental Psychology, University of Oxford, Oxford, OX1 3UD, UK

Lucia van Eimeren (13) Numerical Cognition Laboratory, Department of Psychology, University of Western Ontario, Ontario, Canada N6A 5C2

Barbrina B. Ertle (59) Department of Human Development, Teachers College, Columbia University, New York, NY 10027, USA

Herbert P. Ginsburg (59) Department of Human Development, Teachers College, Columbia University, New York, NY 10027, USA

Joseph Glutting (45) School of Education, University of Delaware, Newark, DE, 19716-2922, USA

Margaret Haseler (225) Specialist Teacher, Personalised Learning Team, London Borough of Bromley, Bromley, BR1 3UH, UK

Jeremy Hodgen (85) Professor of Mathematics, King's College London, University of London, The Strand, London WC2R 2LS, UK

Ian D. Holloway (13) Numerical Cognition Laboratory, Department of Psychology, University of Western Ontario, Ontario, Canada N6A 5C2

Nancy C. Jordan (45) School of Education, University of Delaware, Newark, DE 19716-2922, USA

Liane Kaufmann (1) Department of Pediatrics, IV, Division Neuropediatrics, Innsbruck Medical University, Anichstrasse 35, A-6020 Innsbruck, Austria

Christine Lawson (109) CAMHS, IoM/Independent, UK

Delyth Lloyd (155) Department of Psychology, University of Melbourne, Melbourne, Victoria 3010, Australia

Leslie Manlapig (59) Department of Human Development, Teachers College, Columbia University, New York, NY 10027, USA

T. R. Miles (167) Professor Emeritus of Psychology, School of Psychology, University of Bangor, Wales, UK

Alison Millett (85) Professor of Mathematics, King's College London, University of London, The Strand, London WC2R 2LS, UK

Melissa Morgenlander (59) Department of Human Development, Teachers College, Columbia University, New York, NY 10027, USA

Elizabeth J. Newton (155) Department of Psychology, London South Bank University, London SE1 6LN, UK

Snorre A. Ostad (143) Department of Special Needs Education, University of Oslo, PP1140 0317 Oslo, Norway

Gavin R. Price (13) Numerical Cognition Laboratory, Department of Psychology, University of Western Ontario, Ontario, Canada N6A 5C2

Chaitanya Ramineni (45) School of Education, University of Delaware, Newark, DE, 19716-2922, USA

Valerie Rhodes (85) Professor of Mathematics, King's College London, University of London, The Strand, London WC2R 2LS, UK

S. A. Turner Ellis (167) Formerly of the Universities of Bangor and currently visiting Research Fellow, University of Chester, Chester CH1 4BJ, Cheshire, UK

T. J. Wheeler (167) Department of Psychology, University of Chester, Parkgate Road, Chester, United Kingdom, CHJ1 4BJ, UK

Dylan William (85) Institute of Education, University of London, London WC1H OAL, UK

Robert J. Wright (203) School of Education, Southern Cross University, NSW Australia

INTRODUCTION

Mathematical difficulties are a big problem. Many children demonstrate significant difficulties in learning mathematics (Dowker, 2004, 2005; Geary, 1993; Ginsburg, 1977; Jordan et al., 2003; Ostad, 1998). It is estimated that up to 6% have severe specific difficulties that may be described as 'dyscalculia' (Butterworth, 2005; Gross-Tsur et al., 1996). Many more have problems that are less severe or less specific. Nor are mathematical difficulties restricted to childhood. For example, Bynner and Parsons (1997) found that nearly one-quarter of a British sample of 37-year-olds had 'very low' skills in basic numeracy, and that their employment and earning power were significantly affected.

In recent years, there has been a greatly increased emphasis on mathematics and mathematical difficulties in (especially developmental) psychology (e.g., Baroody and Dowker, 2003; Dowker, 2005; Geary and Hoard, 2005; Gersten et al., 2005; Mazzocco, 2005); in neuroscience (e.g., Butterworth, 1999; Dehaene, 1997; Delazer, 2003; Lochy et al., 2005); and in education (Chinn, 2004; Department for Education and Skills, 2005; Dowker, 2004; Gifford, 2005; Wright et al., 2002). The British Government is currently in process of setting up an 'Every Child Counts' program for providing interventions for children with mathematical difficulties. However, there is still much less research on learning difficulties in mathematics than in some other areas such as language and reading.

Moreover, if we are to gain a greater understanding of mathematical difficulties and of ways to prevent or ameliorate them, it is important to obtain converging evidence from as many fields as possible. At present, there is still a tendency for research in different disciplines to proceed independently, so that neuroscientists, developmental psychologists and educationists may not even be aware of mutually relevant work: a situation which limits the scope of such research.

This book includes chapters by a variety of authors, looking at mathematical, especially arithmetical, difficulties in both typical and atypical populations. These discuss the behavioural, educational and neuropsychological characteristics of children with mathematical difficulties, and educational interventions to prevent, diagnose, treat or ameliorate such difficulties. A particular aim of the book is to bring together studies from different disciplines, including developmental psychology, neuroscience and education, and to include perspectives from practitioners, including teachers and clinical/educational psychologists.

This book follows on from an international conference held in Oxford in September 2002, which included chapters from leading researchers in psychology, neuroscience and education. This book will include new and updated papers by most of the speakers at the conference and by a few others. There has already been significant change in the field – notably in the increasing application of neuroscience to the study of early arithmetical development, and in the increasing emphasis on early intervention for children with arithmetical difficulties.

This book begins with two chapters about current research on the psychology and neuroscience of arithmetic and arithmetical development. The first chapter by Liane Kaufmann discusses research on the neuroscience of number processing and arithmetic, and its applications to our understanding of mathematical development and difficulties in children. It is followed by a chapter by Daniel Ansari, Ian D. Holloway, Gavin R. Price and Lucia van Eimeren on research on early numerical development in typical and atypical populations, from several perspectives, including neuroscience. The subsequent chapters discuss applications of such research. Nancy Jordan discusses applications of the study of early number development to the creation of an assessment technique for identifying children at risk of mathematical difficulties, and Barbrina Ertle, Herbert Ginsburg and their colleagues discuss its applications to early childhood mathematics education, especially for children from groups at social risk for mathematical underachievement.

The next chapters look at mathematical development and difficulties in somewhat older, primary school children. Margaret Brown discusses the extensive data from the Leverhulme Numeracy Research Program, concerning individual differences in children's perfomance in different aspects of arithmetic. Most children remain in a similar position (whether arithmetically strong or weak) with respect to their contemporaries, over a period of time. However, a significant number show either improvement or deterioration in their relative position over their school career. The author discusses possible reasons for such improvements and deteriorations, and their implications for education.

The chapters that follow on from Brown's look more directly at the characteristics of children with learning difficulties in mathematics. Christine Lawson describes her Dyscalculia Test Battery, and analyzes the nature of children's numerical difficulties, observed in a clinical practice, and proposes remedial approaches. Snorre Ostad reports comparative data on children with and without mathematical difficulties, and discusses the features that tend to characterize children with such difficulties. Two chapters follow, which discuss the mathematical strengths and weaknesses that are associated with *language* difficulties in children. Richard Cowan reports research on number development in children with specific language impairment. Sula Ellis and Tim Miles discuss a particular arithmetical skill – division – in children with dyslexia.

The following chapters discuss intervention programs for children with mathematical difficulties. Ann Dowker describes her Numeracy Recovery program, which was based on previous research suggesting a multi-component theory of arithmetical ability. The chapter looks at the nature of the program, its effectiveness, and at ways in which results of the assessments used in the program give further support to such a multi-component theory. Thus, research and intervention influence and inform each other. Bob Wright describes his intensive Mathematics Recovery program for children with mathematical difficulties.

The final chapters provide perspectives from teachers as to how research on mathematical development and difficulties can be, and is being, applied in the school context. Margaret Haseler of Bromley Local Education Authority proposes ways of making interventions in numeracy more effective in schools.

Thus, this book brings together converging international research from several fields, including developmental psychology, neuroscience and education, which aims to add to our knowledge about how numerical and other mathematical abilities develop in children; what problems can arise in their development; what psychology and neuroscience can tell us about the nature of such difficulties; and how this knowledge can be applied to educational practice, and especially to interventions for children who are experiencing such difficulties.

I am grateful to the British Psychological Society, the Mathematical Association and the McDonnell Foundation for financial support for the conference that inspired this book.

REFERENCES

Baroody, A. & Dowker, A. (Eds.) (2003). *The Development of Arithmetical Concepts and Skills* (pp. 385–407). Mahwah, NJ: Erlbaum.

Butterworth, B. (1999). *The Mathematical Brain*. London: Macmillan.

Butterworth, B. (2005). Developmental dyscalculia. In Campbell, J. I. D. (Ed.), *Handbook of Mathematical Cognition* (pp. 455–467). Hove: Psychology Press.

Bynner, J. & Parsons, S. (1997). *It Doesn't Get Any Better: The Impact of Poor Numeracy Skills on the Lives of 37-Year-Olds*. London: Basic Skills Agency.

Chinn, S. J. (2004). *The Trouble with Maths: A Practical Guide to Helping Learners with Numeracy Difficulties*. London: Routledge.

Dehaene, S. (1997). *The Number Sense*. London: Macmillan.

Delazer, M. (2003). Neuropsychological findings on conceptual knowledge of arithmetic. In Baroody, A. & Dowker, A. (Eds.), *The Development of Arithmetical Concepts and Skills* (pp. 385–407). Mahwah, NJ: Erlbaum.

Department for Education and Skills (2005). *Targeting Support: Implementing Interventions for Children with Significant Difficulties in Mathematics*. London: DfES.

Dowker, A. D. (2004). *Children with Difficulties in Mathematics: What Works?* London: DfES.

Dowker, A. D. (2005). *Individual Differences in Arithmetic: Implications for Psychology, Neuroscience and Education.* Hove: Psychology Press.

Geary, D. C. (1993). Mathematical disabilities: Cognitive, neuropsychological and genetic components. *Psychological Bulletin, 114,* 345–362.

Geary, D. C. & Hoard, M. K. (2005). Learning difficulties in arithmetic and mathematics: Theoretical and empirical perspectives. In Campbell, J. I. D. (Ed.), *Handbook of Mathematical Cognition* (pp. 253–268). Hove: Psychology Press.

Gersten, R., Jordan, N., & Flojo, J. (2005). Early identification and intervention for students with mathematics difficulties. *Journal of Learning Disabilities, 38,* 293–304.

Gifford, S. (2005). *Young Children's Difficulties in Learning Mathematics: Review of Research in Relation to Dyscalculia.* London: Qualifications and Curriculum Agency.

Ginsburg, H. P. (1977). *Children's Arithmetic: How They Learn It and How You Teach It.* New York: Teachers' College Press.

Gross-Tsur, V., Manor, O., & Shalev, R. (1996). Developmental dyscalculia: Prevalence and demographic features. *Developmental Medicine and Child Neurology, 38,* 25–33.

Jordan, N. C., Hanich, L., & Uberti, H. Z. (2003). Mathematical thinking and learning difficulties. In Baroody, A. & Dowker, A. (Eds.), *The Development of Arithmetical Concepts and Skills* (pp. 359–383). Mahwah, NJ: Erlbaum.

Lochy, A., Domahs, F., & Delazer, M. (2005). Rehabilitation of acquired calculation and number processing disorders. In Campbell, J. I. D. (Ed.), *Handbook of Mathematical Cognition.* Hove: Psychology Press (pp. 469–485).

Mazzocco, M. (2005). Challenges in identifying target skills for mathematical disability screening and intervention. *Journal of Learning Disabilities, 38,* 318–331.

Ostad, S. (1998). Developmental differences in solving simple arithmetic problems and simple number fact problems: A comparison of mathematically normal and mathematically disabled children. *Mathematical Cognition, 4,* 1–19.

Wright, R., Martland, J., Stafford, A., & Stanger, G. (2002). *Teaching Number: Advancing Children's Skills and Strategies.* London: Chapman.

1

NEURAL CORRELATES OF NUMBER PROCESSING AND CALCULATION

DEVELOPMENTAL TRAJECTORIES AND EDUCATIONAL IMPLICATIONS

LIANE KAUFMANN

Department of Pediatrics, IV, Division Neuropediatrics, Innsbruck Medical University, Anichstrasse 35, A-6020 Innsbruck, Austria

INTRODUCTION

During the last two decades, our understanding of children's emerging numerical competencies has been considerably refined. For instance, already preschool children demonstrate an almost intuitive knowledge about magnitudes and numbers. It has been repeatedly shown that already before explicitly taught in school; children are able to recite the counting words and more than that, they also seem to have an inherent knowledge of counting principles (Fuson, 1988; Gelman & Gallistel, 1978). However, it is currently still debated whether the principles precede the counting knowledge or not: proponents of the 'principles first' view are Gallistel and Gelman (1992), while Fuson (1988) suggests that the acquaintance of the verbal counting routines is a prerequisite for developing knowledge about counting principles. Nonetheless, it is noteworthy that (non-verbal) magnitude processing per se seems to be independent from language processing (Brannon, 2005b; Gelman & Butterworth, 2005).

While it is not very surprising to learn that preschoolers exhibit magnitude and numerical skills before they enter formal mathematics education, somewhat more astonishing are findings suggesting that already infants might have an innate capacity to discriminate object sets based on their numerical distinctness and moreover, seem to demonstrate expectancy behavior in response to violations of addition and subtraction (e.g., Wynn, 1992). While the findings of Wynn (1992) were restricted to small object sets implicating that babies as young as 5 to 6-month-old are capable to discriminate objects sets up to three or four items only, the follow-up work by Xu and Spelke (2000) showed that 6-month-old infants may also discriminate larger object sets provided the ratio between the to-be-discriminated sets is large enough (i.e., infants succeeded in discriminating 8 from 16 objects, but failed on a ratio of 8–12). Moreover, infants as young as 9–11 months exhibit a sense of ordinality (i.e., of greater than/less than relationships; Brannon, 2002).

Interestingly, infants are not the only preverbal species demonstrating a sense for magnitude. There is accumulating evidence from the animal literature that also non-human species are capable of manipulating – concrete and abstract – magnitudes (the vast majority of respective studies being done with monkeys; e.g., Brannon & Terrace, 1998; Dehaene et al., 1998; Hauser et al., 2000; Matsuzawa, 1985). The latter findings thus corroborate assumptions proposing that (abstract) magnitude processing might be an innate capacity of human beings, possibly shared by non-human species (for controversial views, see Clearfield & Mix, 1999; Mix et al., 2002; Tan & Bryant, 2000).

NEUROANATOMICAL CORRELATES OF NUMBER PROCESSING AND CALCULATION: ARE THEY IDENTICAL IN DEVELOPING AND MATURE BRAIN SYSTEMS?

With the avenue of new technologies enabling us to visualize the human brain 'in action' exciting possibilities for cognitive research emerged. More specifically, brain imaging techniques enable us to trace the neural correlates of the cognitive effort associated with the task of interest. The following section will be devoted to findings obtained from studies implementing functional magnetic resonance imaging (fMRI) and event-related potentials (ERP) as the latter two techniques are the most widely used brain imaging methods and furthermore, up to date seem to be the most advanced from a methodological point of view.[1] Nonetheless, regarding the current debate as to whether number processing is an innate capacity of the human brain, fMRI is not the method of choice because it's applicability is restricted to children aged five and older (however, one recent study investigated magnitude processing in 4-year-olds successfully, Cantlon et al., 2006). This is so because the fMRI technique requires participants to be awake and respond to stimuli presented in the (narrow and very noisy) scanner environment while simultaneously task-processing related changes in the blood oxygen consumption in different brain regions are recorded. Hence, fMRI studies provide both behavioral and brain imaging data by measuring the so called BOLD (blood oxygen level dependent) responses. Though this method renders exciting possibilities to image the neural activity of 'verbal' individuals (i.e., those being capable of comprehending and responding to task requirements), it is generally not suitable for children below age four or five (however, for a study investigating language processing/phoneme discrimination in babies, see Dehaene-Lambertz et al., 2002).

An often cited review of the adult literature on number processing and calculation has been provided by Dehaene et al. (2003). The latter authors propose a neurofunctional three-partitioning within the parietal lobe with respect to number processing and calculation: (i) numerical magnitude processing per se is thought to be modulated by the horizontal segment of the intraparietal sulcus (IPS) bilaterally; (ii) language and phonologically mediated numerical processing (e.g., verbal recitation of counting sequences, verbal retrieval of number facts) is thought to be supported by the left angular gyrus and adjacent perisylvian structures; and (iii) attentional and spatial orientation on the mental number line is supposed to be mediated by posterior superior parietal lobes (PSPL) bilaterally. Moreover, Dehaene et al. propose that more complex arithmetical skills depend on the interplay between parietal and extra-parietal regions (e.g., prefrontal brain areas being essential for monitoring and updating information upon multi-step arithmetic procedures; occipital regions such as the fusiform gyrus subserving the identification of Arabic numerals).

Considering behavioral studies suggesting that numerosity/magnitude discrimination abilities might be an innate capacity inherent to infants and non-human species (see above), the question arises whether the latter magnitude discrimination abilities are supported by identical brain regions in infants and adults. Unfortunately, developmental brain imaging studies in the field of numerical cognition are scarce and moreover, difficult to compare to each other because the methodological approaches employed are not readily comparable.

One of the first studies investigating the neural basis of number processing in children was undertaken by Temple and Posner (1998). The latter authors used the ERP method to compare the electrophysiological correlates of adults and 5-year-old children upon making magnitude classifications. Their findings suggest that children and adults alike recruit parietal brain regions upon making symbolic and non-symbolic magnitude judgments (i.e., picking the larger of two simultaneously presented one-digit numerals [symbolic task]; selecting the more numerous of two simultaneously presented dot patterns [non-symbolic task]). Further support for the hypothesis that (intra)parietal regions play a crucial role in the acquaintance of arithmetical skills was provided by Isaacs et al. (2001) who compared prematurely born adolescents with and without dyscalculia. More specifically, Isaacs et al. (2001) found structural abnormalities in (intra)parietal regions (reduced gray matter densities) in children with, but not in those without, dyscalculia.

Interestingly, a recent fMRI study of 4-year-old children partially corroborates the latter findings. Cantlon et al. (2006) studied magnitude processing by implementing an event-related fMRI adaptation paradigm in adults and 4-year-old children. By using a habituation paradigm requiring participants to indicate the presence of deviant stimuli (the ratio by which the deviant differed from the standard was 2:1); the results of the latter authors reveal that the significant IPS activations upon detecting numerically deviant non-symbolic stimuli were independent of age. Hence, Cantlon et al. (2006) suggest that the IPS plays a crucial role in non-symbolic magnitude processing in both adults and 4-year-old children. Finally, the latter authors propose that the significant IPS activations in 4-year-olds might be '...first evidence that the neural locus of adult numerical cognition takes form early in development, prior to sophisticated symbolic numerical experience' (Abstract, p. e125). Moreover, Cantlon et al. (2006) were able to show that non-symbolic (dot patterns) stimuli elicit significant IPS activations also in adult participants and interpret their findings as supporting the – up to date controversially discussed – notion of a neurophysiologic link between non-symbolic and symbolic number processing. Nonetheless, it has to be noted that up to date our understanding of the developmental processes and mechanisms bridging the gap between non-symbolic and symbolic arithmetic are still undeveloped.

Moreover, the latter findings (demonstrating a link between IPS and the formation of arithmetical skills) are opposed by others demonstrating age-related changes in activation patterns. For example, upon investigating symbolic arithmetic (addition and subtraction with one- and two-digit operands) in healthy participants aged 8–19, Rivera et al. (2005) report a positive correlation between age and parietal activation and a negative correlation between age and frontal activation. In other words, with increasing age children rely more on parietal, but less on frontal brain regions upon solving simple addition and subtraction problems. Importantly, the latter authors were able to demonstrate that this increasing functional specialization of parietal regions was not associated with structural changes (i.e., the gray matter density in parietal regions remained rather stable within this age span). Likewise, the findings of Kaufmann et al. (2005, 2006) suggest that relative to adults, children seem to rely more on (pre)frontal (and cerebellar) regions upon making magnitude classifications. More specifically, parietal activations in 9 to 12-year-old children upon making magnitude classifications were not found to be as strong and consistent than in adults (Kaufmann et al., 2006). Upon extending their study group to individuals aged above 60, Kaufmann et al. (in press) report that both elderly with and without minimal cognitive impairment recruit fronto-parietal networks upon processing number magnitude thus suggesting that the functional specialization of (intra)parietal regions for number magnitude remains stable in the mature brain and even in early phases of deteriorating diseases.

The consistent finding that relative to young adults, children, and elderly seem to recruit additional prefrontal regions in response to magnitude processing has been interpreted as reflecting compensatory efforts such as increased demands on monitoring, working memory or interference control (children: Kaufmann et al., 2006; Rivera et al., 2005; elderly: Kaufmann et al., in press; Wood et al., submitted). Furthermore, a direct comparison between three age groups (children, young adults, and elderly; Wood et al., submitted) revealed a non-linear age trend in parietal activations: Relative to old adults, children and young adults had to recruit the smallest network upon making number magnitude judgments. As children displayed the highest error rates, it is plausible to assume that compared with children the magnitude representations of elderly and young adults are better established (and hence more accurate). Overall, the stronger parietal activations found in elderly have been interpreted as being associated to compensatory mechanisms allowing for very accurate responses (Kaufmann et al., in press; see also Rypma et al., 2006 for similar results in prefrontal regions).

The latter hypothesis is compatible with preliminary findings from children with developmental dyscalculia (Kaufmann & Vogel, 2008). In a group of carefully selected 9-year-old children we found a negative correlation between magnitude processing deficiency and parietal activation extents. In other words: parietal activations of children with extremely poor magnitude skills were weak (i.e., not reaching predefined significance thresholds), while children with relatively better established – but nevertheless deficient – number skills exhibited stronger (and more distributed) parietal activations. Certainly, these preliminary results need to be replicated with larger sample sizes before drawing any strong conclusions. Nonetheless, our results are interesting because they further confirm the notion that the relationship between behavioral performance and cerebral activation is a very complex one and researchers should take a closer look into individual data sets (because group data are likely to mask any individual differences). Moreover and most importantly, our findings clearly show that the activation extent of parietal BOLD responses may vary considerably according to competence level. Hence, instead of merely classifying participants into those with and without dyscalculia (i.e., reflecting a dichotomous disease approach) future research endeavors are encouraged to quantify competence levels, thus enabling us to study the link between behavioral performance and functional activation patterns in more detail (for a similar approach in adults, see also Grabner et al., 2007)."

Though there is converging evidence that magnitude processing is modality independent, at least concerning non-verbal mental magnitudes (numerical magnitudes: Barth et al., 2003; Brannon, 2005a; action: Wynn, 1996; auditory perception: Bijeljac-Babic et al., 1993), a still unresolved issue concerns the domain-specificity of number processing. While in the adult literature, the empirical data leads to quite controversial views (pros: e.g., Cohen-Kadosh et al., 2005; cons: e.g., Shuman & Kanwisher, 2004), respective systematic investigations in the development literature still need to be published. A popular theory challenging the notion that the IPS is domain-specific for numbers was put forward by Walsh (2003). By referring to empirical findings from quite different fields of cognition (i.e., spatial, time and numerical processing) Walsh (2003) proposed the so called 'ATOM' theory (A Theory Of Magnitude) suggesting that numbers are only one manifestation of magnitude and therefore, the repeatedly reported (intra)parietal activations in response to number processing should not be mistaken as reflecting domain-specific activations but rather should be interpreted as indicating the involvement of one kind of magnitude system. According to the latter view, parietal involvement is also to be expected in tasks tapping spatial and time processing as the latter domains are characterized by an inherent magnitude system, too (see also Fias et al., 2003). Likewise, the findings of a recent review detailing empirical evidence from both animal and human studies strongly support the notion of a neurofunctional association between spatial and numerical cognition (Hubbard et al., 2005).

ARE NEUROIMAGING STUDIES APT TO HAVE ANY EDUCATIONAL IMPLICATIONS?

Considering the quickly growing body on imaging studies investigating number processing and calculation, the question whether and how the findings of these studies could be beneficial and/or applicable to educational sciences clearly is warranted. A frequent critique concerns the issue that experimental studies in general and neuroimaging studies specifically tend to investigate isolated skills rather than complex abilities (as required in everyday life and/or academic settings). The latter criticism surely has to be taken seriously, but at the same time it has to be acknowledged that the field of neuroimaging is based on very recent technological advances and the vast majority of respective research is targeted at basic research. Before aiming at investigating complex cognitive abilities, it is essential to gain an understanding of the basic skills that constitute and/or contribute to the complex behaviors of interest.

"A first step toward such an endeavor has been taken by investigating the potential link between fingers and number processing. Children's reliance on finger-based number representations is a universal phenomenon and even in adults fingers may serve as a back-up calculation strategy (Butterworth, 1999). Recently, we asked elementary school children and adults to make number magnitude classifications by judging which of two simultaneously presented finger patterns showed more fingers (Kaufmann et al., 2008).[2] Results revealed that relative to adults, parietal activations of children extended to anterior intraparietal regions as well as to post- and pre-central gyri. Interestingly, the very same regions were deactivated in adults. Upon acknowledging that the anterior IPS and adjacent regions including the post-/pre-central gyri support finger use (and gnosis), it is plausible to argue that children – even though exhibiting a flawless and adult-like performance on this easy task – recruit finger-relevant regions when asked to solve simple number tasks (Kaufmann et al., 2008). Overall, the latter results suggest that finger-based number representations are still important for elementary school children's number processing skills. Clearly, future research is needed to investigate whether the explicit use of fingers (i.e., finger-based counting and calculation) in early mathematics may be beneficial for typically developing children and/or may support the formation of abstract number representations in children with and without dyscalculia.

Nonetheless, the above mentioned critics are justified insofar, as the main interest of professions dealing with the teaching (educational sciences) and re-teaching (rehabilitation sciences) of skills and abilities concern complex and adaptive functions rather than islets of skills. Remarkably, one line of cognitive neuroscience indirectly supports these concerns by questioning the validity and applicability of modular views of cognition.

PROS AND CONS REGARDING A MODULAR VIEW OF NUMERICAL SKILLS

In the adult literature, many insights into the neurofunctional calculation system were gained from patients with acquired calculation disorders (acalculia). There is converging evidence from numerous neuropsychological case studies that specific components of the calculation system might be selectively impaired as a consequence of focal brain injury (mostly affecting left posterior brain regions, for an overview, see Dehaene et al., 2003). These selective impairments in formerly normally functioning brain systems, sometimes leading to so called 'double dissociations' (i.e., function A being deficient in the presence of a spared function B in one patient, while the opposite performance profile, namely function A being spared in the presence of an impaired function B, is found in another patient), have led researchers to suggest that number (magnitude) processing is modularly organized. Furthermore, it has been argued that numerical magnitude representations are quite independent from other cognitive domains such as language, memory, attention, and visual-spatial skills (for overviews, see Butterworth, 1999; Dehaene et al., 2003).

Likewise, a similar approach has been adopted in the developmental literature. Most researchers investigating developmental dyscalculia agree on the modularity hypothesis of number processing or at least, take the assumption of modularity as a starting point. Recent attempts to disentangle language and numerical processing at both functional and neuroanatomical levels (Brannon, 2005b; Gelman & Butterworth, 2005) seem to justify such a view.

However, there are some problems inherent in the modularity view (see also Aslin & Fiser, 2005; Pennington, 2006). As a thorough discussion of the latter issue goes far beyond the scope of this article, I would like to focus on an issue that is intimately linked to the conceptualization of developmental dyscalculia. In the absence of an empirically tested *developmental* calculation model, it has to be noted that the most widely adopted current conceptualization of developmental dyscalculia implicates a single-deficit model. For instance, Butterworth (2005) (see also Landerl et al., 2004; Wilson & Dehaene, 2007) proposes deficient numerosity processing being a core deficit of children suffering from developmental dyscalculia. Others concentrate their investigations on children, who's calculation difficulties are most pronounced regarding the retrieval of simple mental calculations (number fact disorders, Temple & Sherwood, 2002; see also Geary, 2000; Kaufmann et al., 2004; Temple, 1991). However, the mere existence of rather circumscribed functional impairments and/or functional double dissociations (between two individuals or within one individual) in developmental disorders might not be sufficient to conclude that these deficits are indeed causally related to an assumed anatomical substrate mediating this function. This might be somewhat different in adults with acquired calculation disorders, where the assumption that a newly acquired focal lesion is likely to have caused the – previous to the traumatic event not existent – functional deficit which seems rather plausible. However, in developmental disorders the matter is far more complicated.

First, the modular view cannot account for the possibility of cognitive subtypes (e.g., magnitude/numerosity processing deficiencies vs number fact disorder). According to Pennington (2006), who discusses this issue with respect to dyslexia, single deficit models – being fostered by strong modularity views of the cognitive architecture – are neither sufficient nor suitable to explain the symptoms of complex developmental disorders because each subtype possibly has its own distinct single cognitive deficit. Similarly, attempts to link these cognitive deficits to their neuroanatomical and/or genetic underpinnings are far from being straight forward. In a similar vein, Aslin and Fiser (2005) postulate that though neuroimaging techniques may provide valuable insights into the mapping of brain structure and function, they are not sufficient to broaden our understanding of how information is represented and learnt in the brain (unless methods are employed that aim at investigating learning *processes and mechanisms* in a computational framework).

Second, children with developmental dyscalculia very rarely exhibit isolated cognitive deficits in the numerical domain. Rather, even if fulfilling the so-called discrepancy criteria (of age-equivalent intellectual abilities and deficient math achievement), they often have additional difficulties in non-numerical domains such as visual-spatial processing, attention, working memory and motor skills. Despite the scarcity of studies investigating co-morbidities of developmental disorders, there are some studies reporting the co-occurrence of dyscalculia, dyslexia (reading disorder) and attentional disorders. For instance, in a large cohort study incorporating more than 3,000 children, Gross-Tsur et al. (1996) found that in their sample 17% of children with a diagnosis of dyscalculia also met criteria for dyslexia and 26% for ADHD (attention-deficit/hyperactivity disorder). Thus, it is rather surprising that up to date the rather high incidence of co-morbid cognitive difficulties has been little appreciated in the research community investigating developmental dyscalculia.

Third, developmental dyscalculia is a very heterogeneous disorder manifesting itself with very differential performance profiles both between individuals (leading some people to claim the necessity for subtyping) and within individuals (Dowker, 2005). Dowker (2005) devoted a whole book to these individual differences, trying to outline the importance of the appreciation of these inter- and intra-individual differences for both differential diagnosis and intervention planning.

Overall, a major theoretical consequence of acknowledging the complexity of developmental dyscalculia (both with respect to potential subtypes and the frequency of co-morbid disorders and associated, but not yet systematically investigated, processing deficiencies in non-numerical domains) could be a methodological reorientation toward a multiple deficit view of developmental dyscalculia (see Pennington, 2006; for a similar claim regarding dyslexia and ADHD). Multiple deficit models have the advantage that they readily appreciate modulating cognitive abilities (both with respect to numerical and non-numerical components) on the encoding, storing and accessing of mental numerical/magnitude representations, number processing and calculation skills (see also Kaufmann & Nuerk, 2005). Finally, in contrast to single deficit models, multiple deficit models are better apt to account for the up to date rather poorly understood interactions between cognitive (functional), anatomical (structural) and genetic (etiological) factors mediating the acquisition and maintenance of arithmetical skills.

SYNOPSIS

Despite the growing interest and almost exploding number of imaging studies investigating numerical cognition in adults, brain imaging studies in children are scarce. To further complicate the matter, methodological differences between studies make direct comparisons questionable if not impossible.

Up to date, our knowledge regarding the developmental trajectories of the neural underpinnings of number processing and calculation remains undeveloped. Moreover, there is accumulating evidence challenging the view that (intra)parietal regions might be domain-specific for numerical cognition. It is important to note that fronto–parietal network activations are not only a frequent finding in the number processing literature, but also in studies investigating attentional and interference processing. Furthermore, though some components of arithmetic might be modularly organized, calculation abilities on the large are not independent from non-numerical skills such as visual-spatial cognition, language, working memory, motor skills, etc. Similarly, only very small proportions of children with calculation difficulties exhibit a 'pure' dyscalculia but rather are likely to have difficulties in non-numerical domains as well. The latter facts should be taken into account upon developing (behavioral and brain imaging) study paradigms apt for children and adequate for investigating educationally important questions.

Furthermore, experimental paradigms employed in brain imaging studies tap circumscribed skills rather than cognitive processes. Though certainly leading to a better understanding of the association between the neural networks supporting the cognitive task at hand, it has to be stressed that significant activations as reported in imaging studies only identify brain regions that modulate a specific task which is *not* equivalent to regions being necessary to process the task at hand.

Hence, a crucial requirement for future investigations is the development of adequate imaging paradigms tapping ecologically and educationally relevant and process-orientated tasks allowing us to assess *cognitive processes and mechanisms*. Importantly, the quality of future research bridging the gap between educational sciences and neurosciences will critically depend on the quality and intensity of bi-directional knowledge transfer between the two fields. Finally, it has to be noted that imaging studies are only as good as the behavioral paradigms they are implementing. In turn, the development of adequate behavioral paradigms should be based on a sophisticated understanding of the interplay between neurocognitive, genetic and socio-cultural factors determining the development of typical and atypical trajectories of numerical cognition.

REFERENCES

Aslin, R. N. & Fiser, J. (2005). Methodological challenges for understanding cognitive development in infants. *Trends in Cognitive Sciences, 9*(3), 92–98.

Barth, H., Kanwisher, N. & Spelke, E. (2003). The construction of large number representations in adults. *Cognition, 86,* 201–221.

Bijeljac-Babic, R., Bertoncini, J. & Mehler, J. (1993). How do four-day-old infants categorize multisyllabic utterances? *Development Psychology, 29,* 711–721.

Brannon, E. M. (2002). The development of ordinal numerical knowledge in infancy. *Cognition, 83,* 223–240.

Brannon, E. M. (2005a). Number knows no bound. *Trends in Cognitive Sciences, 7*(7), 279–281.

Brannon, E. M. (2005b). The independence of language and mathematical reasoning. *Proceedings of the National Academy of Sciences USA, 102*(9), 3177–3178.

Brannon, E. M. & Terrace, H. S. (1998). Ordering of the numerosities 1 to 9 by monkeys. *Science, 282,* 746–749.

Butterworth, B. (1999). *The Mathematical Brain.* London: Macmillan Publishers Ltd.

Cantlon, J. F., Brannon, E. M., Carter, E. J. & Pelphrey, K. A. (2006). Functional imaging of numerical processing in adults and 4-y-old children. *PLOS Biology, 4*(5), e125.

Clearfield, M. W. & Mix, K. S. (1999). Number versus contour length in infants' discrimination of small visual sets. *Psychological Science, 10,* 408–411.

Cohen-Kadosh, R., Henik, A., Rubinstein, O., Mohr, H., Dori, H., van de Ven, V., Zorzi, M., Hendler, T., Goebel, R. & Linden, D. E. J. (2005). Are numbers special? The comparison systems of the human brain investigated by fMRI. *Neuropsychologia, 43,* 1238–1248.

Dehaene, S., Dehaene-Lambertz, G. & Cohen, L. (1998). Abstract representation of numbers in the animal and human brain. *Nature Neuroscience, 21,* 355–361.

Dehaene, S., Piazza, M., Pinel, P. & Cohen, L. (2003). Three parietal circuits for number processing. *Cognitive Neuropsychology, 20*(3–6), 487–506.

Dehaene-Lambertz, G., Dehaene, S. & Hertz-Panniere, L. (2002). Functional imaging of speech perception in infants. *Science, 298*(5600), 2013–2015.

Dowker, A. (2005). *Individual Differences in Arithmetic: Implications for Psychology, Neuroscience and Education.* Hove, UK: Psychology Press.

Fias, W., Lammertyn, J., Reynvoet, B., Dupont, P. & Orban, G. A. (2003). Parietal representation of symbolic and nonsymbolic magnitude. *Journal of Cognitive Neuroscience, 15*(1), 47–56.

Fuson, K. (1988). *Children's Counting and Concepts of Number.* New York: Springer-Verlag.

Gallistel, C. R. & Gelman, R. (1992). Preverbal counting and computation. *Cognition, 44,* 43–74.

Geary, D. C. (2000). From infancy to adulthood: the development of numerical abilities. *European Child and Adolescent Psychiatry, 9*(2), 11–16.

Gelman, R. & Butterworth, B. (2005). Number and language: how are they related? *Trends in Cognitive Sciences, 9*(1), 6–10.

Gelman, R. & Gallistel, C. R. (1978). *The Child's Concept of Number.* Cambridge, MA: Harvard University Press.

Grabner, R., Ansari, D., Reishofer, G., Stern, E., Ebner, F. & Neuper, C. (2007). Individual differences in mathematical competence predict parietal brain activation during mental calculation. *Neuroimage, 38,* 346–356.

Gross-Tsur, V., Manor, O. & Shalev, R. (1996). Developmental dyscalculia: prevalence and demographic features. *Developmental Medicine and Child Neurology, 38,* 25–33.

Hauser, M. D., Carey, S. & Hauser, L. B. (2000). Spontaneous number representation in wild rhesus monkeys. *Proceedings of the Royal Academy of Sciences, 93,* 1514–1517.

Hubbard, E. M., Piazza, M., Pinel, P. & Dehaene, S. (2005). Interactions between number and space in parietal cortex. *Nature Reviews Neuroscience, 6,* 435–448.

Isaacs, E. B., Edmonds, C. J., Lucas, A. & Gadian, D. G. (2001). Calculation difficulties in children of very low birthweight. *Brain, 124*(9), 1701–1707.

Kaufmann, L., Lochy, A., Drexler, A. & Semenza, C. (2004). Deficient arithmetic fact retrieval – storage or access problem? A case study. *Neuropsychologia, 42,* 482–496.

Kaufmann, L. & Nuerk, H. C. (2005). Numerical development: current issues and future perspectives. *Psychology Science* (Special Issue: Brain and Number), *47*(1), 142–170.

Kaufmann, L., Kaufmann, L., Koppelstaetter, F., Delazer, M., Siedentopf, C., Rhomberg, P., Golaszewski, S., Felber, S. & Ischebeck, A. (2005). Neural correlates of distance and congruity effects in a numerical Stroop task: an event-related fMRI study. *NeuroImage,* 25, 888–898.

Kaufmann, L. (2008). Dyscalculia: Neuroscience and education. *Educational Research, 50*(2), 163–175.

Kaufmann, L. & Vogel, S.E. (2008). Developmental dyscalculia: One or many core deficits? *Paper presented at the International Conference of the British Dyslexia Association,* Harrogate, UK, March 28.

Kaufmann, L., Vogel, S., Wood, G., Kremser, C., Schocke, M., Zimmerhackl, L.-B. & Koten, J. W. (2008). A developmental fMRI study of nonsymbolic numerical and spatial processing. *Cortex, 44,* 376–385.

Kaufmann, L., Ischebeck, A., Koppelstaetter, F., Siedentopf, C., Weiss, E., Gotwald, T., Marksteiner, J. & Wood, G. (in press). An fMRI study of the Numerical Stroop Task in Individuals with and without MCI. *Cortex.*

Kaufmann, L., Koppelstaetter, F., Siedentopf, C., Haala, I., Haberlandt, E., Zimmerhackl, L.-B., Felber, S. & Ischebeck, A. (2006). Neural correlates of a number-size interference task in children. *NeuroReport, 17*(6), 587–591.

Landerl, K., Bevan, A. & Butterworth, B. (2004). Developmental dyscalculia and basic numerical capacities: a study of 8-9-year-old students. *Cognition, 93,* 99–125.

Matsuzawa, T. (1985). Use of numbers by a chimpanzee. *Nature, 315,* 57–59.

Mix, K. S., Huttenlocher, J. & Levine, S. C. (2002). *Quantitative development in infancy and early childhood.* Oxford: Oxford University Press.

Pennington, B. F. (2006). From single to multiple deficit models of developmental disorders. *Cognition , 101*(2), 385–413.

Rivera, S. M., Reiss, A. L., Eckert, M. A. & Menon, V. (2005). Developmental changes in mental arithmetic: evidence for increased functional specialization in the left inferior parietal cortex. *Cerebral Cortex, 15,* 1779–1790

Rypma, B., Berger, J. S., Prabhakaran, V., Bly, B. M., Kimberg, D. Y., Biswal, B. B. & D'Esposito, M. (2006). Neural correlates of cognitive efficiency. *Neuroimage, 33,* 969–979.

Shuman, M. & Kanwisher, N. (2004). Numerical magnitude in the human parietal lobe : tests of representational generality and domain specificity. *Neuron, 44,* 557–569.

Tan, L. S. & Bryant, P. (2000). The cues that infants use to distinguish discontinuous quantities : evidence using a shift-rate recovery paradigm. *Child Development, 71,* 1162–1178.

Temple, C. M. (1991). Procedural dyscalculia and number fact dyscalculia: double dissociation in developmental dyscalculia. *Cognitive Neuropsychology, 8*(2), 155–176.

Temple, E. & Posner, M. (1998). Brain mechanisms of quantity are similar in 5-year-olds and adults. *Proceedings of the National Academy of Sciences USA, 95,* 7836–7841.

Temple, C. M. & Sherwood, S. (2002). Representation and retrieval of arithmetic facts: Developmental difficulties. *Quarterly Journal of Experimental Psychology, 55A,* 733–752.

Walsh, V. (2003). Cognitive neuroscience: numerate neurons. *Current Biology, 13,* 447–448.

Wilson, A. J. & Dehaene, S. (2007). Number Sense and Developmental Dyscalculia. In Coch, D., Dawson, G., & Fischer, K. (Eds.), *Human Behavior, Learning, and the Developing Brain: Atypical Development (pp. 212–238).* New York: Guilford Press.

Wood, G., Ischebeck, A., Koppelstaetter, F., Gotwald, T. & Kaufmann L. (submitted). Developmental trajectories of magnitude processing and interference control: A fMRI study.

Wynn, K. (1992). Addition and subtraction by human infants. *Nature, 358,* 749–750.

Wynn, K. (1996). Infants' individuation and enumeration of actions. *Psychological Science, 7,* 164–169.

Xu, F. & Spelke, E. S. (2000). Large number discrimination in 6-month-old infants. *Science, 7,* 164–169.

NOTE

1. Other frequently used brain imaging methods are SPECT (single photon emission computed tomography) and PET (positron emission tomography). However, the latter methods are not suitable for younger children as its application requires the injection of contrast agents bearing the risk of medical complications. A rather new development is the NIRS (near infrared spectroscopy) which is non-invasive and thus more negligible in developmental studies, but currently not ready for routine clinical investigations.

2. In the control task, identical stimuli were presented but this time, participants had to decide whether the palms of the two hands showed in the same direction or not. The control task is important because by subtracting activation patterns obtained by the control task from those obtained by the experimental task, it is ensured that only relevant activations remain (because task-irrelevant activations such as encoding, decision process, and response selection are partialled out by the subtraction procedure).

2

TOWARD A DEVELOPMENTAL COGNITIVE NEUROSCIENCE APPROACH TO THE STUDY OF TYPICAL AND ATYPICAL NUMBER DEVELOPMENT

DANIEL ANSARI, IAN D. HOLLOWAY,
GAVIN R. PRICE, AND LUCIA VAN EIMEREN

Numerical Cognition Laboratory, Department of Psychology, University of Western Ontario, Ontario, Canada N6A 5C2

INTRODUCTION

The development of methodology to non-invasively measure brain activity and its correlates (such as cerebral blood flow) in humans has led to an explosion in the field of cognitive neuroscience (Albright et al., 2000). Methods such as functional magnetic resonance imaging (fMRI), event-related brain potentials (ERP) and transcranial magnetic stimulation (TMS) have enabled insights into the brain regions that are both correlated with and directly implicated in particular cognitive processes. The field of cognitive neuroscience is concerned with the study of the neural instantiation of cognition, with the principle aim being to develop biologically plausible models of cognitive processes. The cognitive neuroscience approach has been very influential in a host of domains, such as attention (Corbetta & Shulman, 2002), reading (McCandliss & Noble, 2003), social cognition (Ochsner & Lieberman, 2001) and education (Ansari & Coch, 2006) to name a few. Cognitive neuroscience approaches to cognitive functions have helped to constrain existing models based on behavioral data and have lead to the formulation of new hypotheses.

The advent of cognitive neuroscience as a new framework for studying the biological basis of cognition has also lead to significant advances in the understanding of the neural basis of numerical and mathematical cognition. Functional neuroimaging has provided insights into the neural correlates of numerical and mathematical processes ranging from basic numerical magnitude processing (Dehaene et al., 2003) to calculation (Dehaene et al., 1999). In concert with evidence from adult neuropsychological patients, these insights have inspired new models of the systems thought to underlie mathematical processing (Dehaene & Cohen, 1995).

While there continues to be enormous progress in understanding the numerical processes and representations in the adult brain, there are currently only a handful of studies approaching the development of numerical cognition using a cognitive neuroscience approach.

The aim of this chapter is to highlight both the promise and challenges of a developmental cognitive neuroscience approach to the study of both typical and atypical number development and to propose how such an approach can provide insights into the ontogenesis of numerical and mathematical skills not afforded by purely behavioral methods. In order to do this, the chapter will first provide a detailed and critical review of the state-of-the-art of research on number processing in the adult brain, pointing out both the progress that has been made as well as outstanding questions and challenges. While this review aims to reflect the current state of knowledge, it is necessarily selective. In the interest of space and focus, the review focuses on central topics such as numerical magnitude processing and calculation in the adult brain and does not explore more specialized topics, such as the difference between small and large number processing (Piazza et al., 2002, 2003) or the neural basis of the size congruity (numerical stroop) effect (Ansari et al., 2006b; Kaufmann et al., 2005).

This review of the neural correlates of numerical magnitude processing and calculation in adults will provide a resource for the generation of hypotheses relevant to the cognitive neuroscience of number development, and will enable an assessment of the few existing developmental neuroimaging studies of typical and atypical numerical cognition as well as their implications. We will close with a discussion of the methodological and conceptual challenges meeting investigations into the neural basis of the development of numerical cognition as well as what we perceive are the outstanding questions facing a developmental cognitive neuroscience approach to number development.

NUMBER PROCESSING IN THE ADULT BRAIN

Studies exploring the neural substrates of numerical understanding in the adult brain are growing in number and complexity. Over the past 15 years, neuroimaging research has utilized a variety of methodologies and tasks to elicit and characterize aspects of basic numerical processing and representation. The following discussion will highlight some of the key findings from this literature and consider outstanding questions that face the field. The goal, then, is not to give an exhaustive description, but rather to characterize what is currently known and unknown about numerical magnitude in the brain.

NUMERICAL MAGNITUDE PROCESSING IN THE ADULT BRAIN

Many studies exploring basic magnitude processing utilize tasks that involve numerical comparison. In numerical comparison paradigms, individuals are asked to compare which of two numbers is numerically larger or to compare the numerosity of a given number to a target number. The stimuli are varied along the parameter commonly known as numerical distance. Thus, numbers can be separated by a large numerical distance like 7 (e.g., 2 vs. 9) or a relatively small numerical distance such as 2 (e.g., 3 vs. 5). This task is used not simply because it ensures that a participant must access numerical representations necessary for a correct comparison response, but because the task elicits the well-known *distance effect*. The distance effect is characterized by an inverse relationship between numerical distance and reaction time, such that the smaller the numerical distance the longer it takes an individual to subjectively discriminate between the numbers (Moyer & Landauer, 1967). This fundamental relationship between numerical distance and an individual's reaction time is thought to reflect the nature of quantity representations and has therefore inspired a variety of models describing how numbers might be internally represented (Dehaene, 1992; Gallistel & Gelman, 2000; Verguts et al., 2005; Zorzi & Butterworth, 1999). In addition to its theoretical importance to neuroimaging studies of numerical cognition, the distance effect has frequently been utilized in behavioral experiments on quantitative processing and therefore serves as a methodological bridge between behavioral and neuroimaging studies.

One of the fundamental questions about magnitude representation in the brain concerns the degree to which this representation is abstract and therefore invariant to stimulus format and presentation modality. An early neuroimaging study used an additive factors model of Event-related brain potentials, which affords the temporal precision to examine aspects of number comparison, with the goal of determining whether numerical magnitude, independent of surface format, is processed by a stimulus-independent brain mechanism (Dehaene, 1996). Employing a numerical comparison task that presented either two Arabic numerals or two number words, it was shown that the identification and decoding of Arabic numerals and number words had significantly different ERP waveform characteristics. However, the Component of the ERP signal reflecting the effect of numerical distance was similar for both numerals and number words. Furthermore, the distance effect was found to be localized to a right-lateralized parieto-occipito-temporal region of the cerebral cortex. These data were interpreted as evidence for the existence of a dedicated brain area or network involved in the abstract (semantic) representation of numerical magnitude information, located somewhere in the inferior parietal area of the cerebral cortex. This groundbreaking work has led to an influential conceptualization of magnitude representation in the brain.

From this point of departure, a large amount of the subsequent research has attempted better characterize the exact relationship between the *intraparietal lobe* (IPL), particularly the *intraparietal sulcus* (IPS), and abstract numerical magnitude representations (Dehaene et al., 1998, 2003). For instance, Pinel and colleagues utilized a distance effect task that involved either numerals or number words (Pinel et al., 1999). Using fMRI, this study demonstrated that notational effects on the fMRI signal are found to be associated with the right fusiform gyrus. The distance effect, on the other hand, was associated with bilateral parietal activation, including two areas in the left inferior parietal lobule and one at the junction between a right postcentral and inferior parietal region. Importantly, these parietal effects were not affected by the stimulus format (Arabic numerals vs. number words), which was taken as further evidence that these regions are responsible for an abstract (notation independent) representation of numerical magnitude. The findings of these first two studies were replicated in a later study using a combination of fMRI and additive factors model ERPs to examine the distance effect underlying the comparison of Arabic numerals and number words (Pinel et al., 2001).

One of the fundamental assumptions of the above studies is that the activations that are described within them are specific to the activation of *numerical* magnitude representations. However, it is entirely possible, and arguably more likely, that the IPS houses a representational system common to both numerical and non-numerical (e.g., time, space, intensity) magnitudes (see Walsh, 2003, for an alternative theory of magnitude). Several studies have sought to explore the specificity of representation in the IPS. One study asked subjects to determine whether a string of three letters, numbers and shapes were in order (either ascending or descending) or not (Fulbright et al., 2003). In the letter condition 'A, C, H' and 'G, C, B' should both be considered in order and 'F, I, H' considered out of order. A similar condition was created for the numerals 1–9. In the shape condition, three different shapes were presented in three different sizes, which were judged to be in ascending or descending order, or not. Fulbright et al. found that the IPS was involved in judging the relative magnitude for all three types of stimuli. Against this background, Fulbright et al. contended that the parietal regions may instead be reflective of a system for magnitude representation common to both numerical and non-numerical information. The assumption in this design is that an ordinality judgment necessarily involves assignment of a magnitude to the stimuli. The legitimacy of this assumption has been challenged by Turconi and colleagues who, using ERP, demonstrated an important temporal distinction between comparing two numbers along the dimensions of quantity and ordinality (Turconi et al., 2004). This experiment required participants to determine whether a number was smaller or larger than 15 (quantity condition) or whether a number came before or after 15 (order condition). Though they found a behavioral distance effect in both conditions, the characteristics of the ERP waveform were distinct for each condition. The P2 component was found earlier and was left lateralized in the quantity condition, whereas in the order condition this component was later and bilateral. The authors concluded that distinct neural mechanisms are involved in judging the order and quantity of numbers.

In light of the findings by Turconi and colleagues, the conclusion drawn by Fulbright et al. that there exists a shared neural mechanism for numerical and non-numerical ordinality should be interpreted with care. These findings also highlight the importance of using both measures with high temporal resolution (such as ERP) and high spatial resolution (such as fMRI) to assess the neuroanatomical correlates of cognitive processes.

The notion that the IPS houses a representation of both numerical and non-numerical magnitude was supported by a study that analyzed the neural substrate associated with comparison of angles, line length and number. Fias et al. found activation in the left IPS to be associated with magnitude comparison for both the numerical and non-numerical stimuli (Fias et al., 2003). Two subsequent studies presented participants with two numbers that differed along three dimensions: numerical magnitude, physical size and physical luminance (Cohen Kadosh et al., 2005; Pinel et al., 2004). In Pinel et al.'s (2004) study individuals were asked to make judgments along one of the three stimulus dimensions (physical size, numerical magnitude and luminance). The results of this study demonstrated that while distinct regions of the IPS were activated for each type of comparison, these activations overlap for numbers and size comparison in the anterior IPS as well as for size and brightness comparisons in the posterior IPS, but not for number and brightness comparisons. Thus, this study added support to the notion that the IPS activation associated with number comparison is related to both numerical and non-numerical magnitude comparison. Another study addressing the same issue of domain-specific activation in the IPS found similar results (Cohen Kadosh et al., 2005). Using slightly different stimuli, these researchers also found evidence that the bilateral IPS is activated for all three types of magnitude comparison. In addition, however, specific modulation of activity by the numerical distance effect was found exclusively in an area of the left IPS. In sum, these studies support a characterization of the IPS as the seat for the representation of general magnitude, while also indicating there may be some number-specific processing that occurs within this area.

Thus far, the discussion has focused on studies that have utilized numerical comparison as a means to elicit a neural response which is assumed to be caused by the activation of numerical representations. While it is certainly possible that specific areas of the brain are the site of an abstract semantic numerical representation, the use of a comparison task to access these representations is problematic. Specifically, the activations described above could be the result of the comparison and response-selection process rather than anything directly related to magnitude representation. In other words, individuals performing a numerical comparison task are always faced with a forced choice decision. Therefore, activation of representation is always confounded with the process of selecting and performing the proper response. This confound was demonstrated by Göbel et al. (2004) who asked subjects to judge whether a target number was larger or smaller than a reference number. In an additional task, participants were asked to judge whether a line was present or absent in a display of either intact or scrambled numbers. No differences in parietal activation were found in the experimental and control tasks. The authors concluded that insofar as parietal activation is associated with magnitude representation, the activation of quantitative information may be very difficult to disentangle from activation associated with response selection. This study casts doubt upon the role of the IPS as the source of numerical representation.

Eger and colleagues overcame the problem of response selection by presenting subjects with intermixed numbers, letter and colors either in the auditory or visual modality (Eger et al., 2003). In each run, subjects were given a particular target category (numbers, letters or colors) and asked to press a button each time they saw or heard an exemplar of that category. The results revealed that activation in bilateral parietal cortex was significantly greater for number compared to letter and colors regardless of whether they were presented in the visual or auditory modality. Note that this activation was found in the absence of a task that required attention to any semantic information, but simply the detection of a target, which indicated that numerical representations in the IPS could be automatically activated even in the absence of directed attention. This study also asked three of their participants to perform mental subtraction and found that subtraction was associated with a much larger network of areas than number detection. Crucially, however, the intraparietal area found in number detection was also found in subtraction. The authors interpreted this overlap in activation elicited by auditory detection, visual detection and calculation as evidence that the IPS does, indeed, house a representation of numerical magnitude that is independent of both modality and stimulus type. This study is particularly exciting in that it explores the notion of implicit activation of number as a means by which research can bypass response-selection confounds.

Recent studies have utilized the phenomenon of fMRI adaptation (fMRA) to further explore this notion of implicit activation of numerical magnitude representation in the IPS. In adaptation paradigms, individuals are presented with arrays made up of a particular number of items, and that number is invariant across subsequent presentation of stimuli. Simultaneously, these arrays can vary other aspects of the items such as shape, size or color. The neural response to the repeatedly presented number attenuates (*habituation*) after a significant number of repetitions. After a given number of stimuli, a deviant is displayed with a new number of items. Any systematic neural change (*dishabituation*) to this deviant is assumed to result directly from the change in numerosity. Generally, in order to ensure that individuals are attending to the display, participants are asked to make a response to a completely irrelevant aspect of the display, like the appearance of a fixation cross. However, no instructions are given to attend to any particular aspect of the array (for a detailed description of fMRA methodology, see Grill-Spector et al., 2006).

Studies using habituation paradigms have demonstrated automatic activation of numerical magnitude in the IPS, a result which is free from the constraints of response selection (Ansari et al., 2006a; Piazza et al., 2004). Piazza and colleagues habituated individuals to numerosities presented as non-symbolic dots arrays. To rule out the possibility that the dishabituation response could be due to general change detection, the deviants used varied either in number or in shape. The extent to which the numerosity of the number deviant differed from the habituated numerosity was systematically varied to test whether numerical distance would parametrically affect the neural response. These authors found that the right and left intraparietal sulci were the only areas that responded proportionally to the numerical magnitude of the deviants. A parametric effect of numerical distance on neural response in the IPS was also elucidated by Ansari et al. who presented individuals with alternating slides of 8 vs. 8, 8 vs. 12 or 8 vs. 16 squares in separate stimulus blocks. These studies provide evidence to suggest that number may be processed and represented in the parietal cortex independent of response selection. However, the results of these two studies should be tempered by acknowledging the findings of Shuman and Kanwisher who have reported no number-specific activation in the IPS (Shuman & Kanwisher, 2004).

Two very recent studies used fMRA paradigms investigate the issue of stimulus format in the representation of numerical magnitude in the IPS. Piazza and colleagues conducted an experiment in which individuals were habituated to either small (17–19) or large (47–49) numerosities presented as either non-symbolic dot arrays or Arabic numerals (Piazza et al., 2007). The deviants, in addition to being either numerically close or far from the habituated numerosity, could also be the same stimulus format (e.g., Arabic numeral deviants and Arabic numeral habituation stream) or different stimulus format (e.g., Dot arrays deviants and Arabic numeral habituation stream). The results showed that the effect of numerical distance on the dishabituation response was similar for both Arabic numerals and non-symbolic arrays in the right IPS. However, the dishabituation in the left IPS failed to show sensitivity to numerical distance when participants were habituated to Arabic numerals and the deviant used was a dot array. To interpret these subtle findings, the authors argued that the left IPS represents Arabic numerals very precisely compared with the relatively coarse representation of non-symbolic numerosities. Thus, when the non-symbolic numerosity were presented, the IPS dishabituated to all non-symbolic deviants because very little of the numerical magnitude representation between Arabic numerals and non-symbolic magnitudes is shared. This is a very subtle effect that is nonetheless important in its suggestion of hemispheric differences in magnitude representation.

In a separate study habituated individuals using the sequential presentation of two number words and/or Arabic numerals (Cohen Kadosh et al., 2007). Stimulus format and quantity were defined orthogonally to each other such that the two stimuli presented could be different in quantity, format or both. The results demonstrated that the left IPS habituates to the quantity associated with both Arabic numerals and number words, but the right IPS only habituated to the quantity represented by Arabic numerals. Note that these data conflict with those of Dehaene (1996) and Pinel et al. (1999), who both found no notational effects in the IPS response to numerical distance in a comparison task. This conflict is likely due to the differences in methodology. Functional magnetic resonance adaptation (fMRA) affords the explorations of very specific questions, such as the effect of stimulus format that may simply not be possible through the analysis of the number comparison process. Together, these two studies challenge the notion that magnitude representation is entirely abstract, by exposing important hemispheric differences in number representations. The findings of these two studies are relatively disparate, but one interesting possibility for convergence between them is differential activation of the left compared to right IPS when representing culturally defined formats (numerals and words) of numerical representation. However, much more research must be conducted to better characterize the hemispheric differences in and stimulus dependence of number representation.

CALCULATION IN THE ADULT BRAIN

Historically, through neuropsychological studies of brain damaged patients, there exists a long-standing association between the adult parietal lobe and calculation (Henschen, 1919). In particular, damage to the left angular gyrus (AG) has been found to be associated with Gerstmann syndrome, which among other symptoms, causes deficits in calculation (Gerstmann, 1940). Functional neuroimaging studies have also revealed association between calculation and the parietal and frontal lobes. Indeed a review of the functional neuroimaging literature, in particular fMRI, suggests that calculation was one of the first cognitive processes to be studied using this method. In the first neuroimaging study of calculation, Roland and Friberg (1985) using the Xe intra-carotid method for visualization of cerebral blow flow and found activation in left and right AG as well as modulation of prefrontal regions during a subtraction task. In another early neuroimaging study using fMRI, Burbaud et al. (1995) performed fMRI of regions within the frontal lobe to investigate the role of prefrontal cortex in calculation. Activity during sub-vocal calculation was found to be left lateralized in right handed participants. In contrast, left handed participants exhibited more bilateral activation of prefrontal regions during calculation. The authors conclude that similar to language processing, prefrontal activity during calculation is significantly more left lateralized in right compared with left handed individuals.

While Burbaud et al. focused their analyses on the neural correlates of calculation in the prefrontal cortex, Rueckert et al. (1996) used fMRI to investigate brain regions involved in subtraction and found, consistent with the above studies, activation in the angular and supramarginal gyri, with stronger activation on the left compared with the right. In addition to parietal regions, subtraction relative to counting was also found to modulate activation of prefrontal regions. In the same year, Dehaene et al. (1996) used whole brain PET imaging to compare and contrast patterns of activation associated with multiplication and comparison. During the acquisition of PET images participants were presented with two digits and had to either compare these for their relative numerical magnitude (which is larger) or multiply the two digits. When compared against rest, both multiplication and comparison were found to be associated with activation of visual and motor regions. A direct comparison of multiplication and comparison revealed significantly greater activation in bilateral regions of the inferior parietal cortex. In contrast comparison was found to activate frontal and temporal regions more than the multiplication tasks. These results are convergent with the notion that the parietal cortex plays an important role in calculation. However, the absence of significant parietal activation during comparison is somewhat at odds with the data reported above. Furthermore, calculation was not found to significantly modulate the left AG, which has been strongly linked with calculation deficits in studies of neuropsychological patients. However, consistent with the notion that calculation is largely left lateralized, Dehaene et al. report a hemispheric asymmetry in the activation of the parietal lobe during multiplication vs. rest, showing greater activation in left relative to the right parietal lobe. In a more recent fMRI study Rickard et al. (2000) also investigate the brain regions activated by simple arithmetic and number comparison. Convergent with the earlier findings, Rickard et al. found that mental arithmetic (multiplication) yielded significantly greater activity than a control task (detect a one in a string of numbers) and the number comparison task in dorsolateral prefrontal cortex as well as inferior and superior parietal cortex. Furthermore both frontal and parietal activation was found to be greater in the left compared with the right hemisphere. Interestingly the authors found that the angular and supramarginal gyri were significantly deactivated during the arithmetic task in comparison to the control task. Deactivation of the AG has been reported in multiple tasks using both numerical and non-numerical stimuli and the reasons for these patterns of deactivation are largely unknown and are an important topic for further investigation. Rickard et al. interpret this finding as evidence against a strong role of the AG in calculation and go on to suggest that neuropsychological models may have underestimated the effect of lesions to superior regions of the left parietal lobe in causing calculation deficits. What these findings highlight is that it is crucial to explore the sign of activation (whether there are differences in activation or deactivation between conditions) in neuroimaging studies. The absence of AG activation is therefore consistent with the findings of Dehaene et al. (1996) but not those reported by Roland and Friberg (1992) or Rueckert et al. (1996). Furthermore, consistent with the findings reported by

Dehaene et al. (1996), activation during number comparison was found to be less robust in parietal regions and more variable across participants.

These early studies suggest that both prefrontal and parietal regions are involved in mental calculations. Furthermore, they suggest substantial variability in the parietal regions modulated by calculation both between subjects within a single study and between studies. While some studies report activation of superior regions of the parietal lobe such as the IPS and superior parietal lobe during calculation, others have reported activation of the AG. However, variability in functional neuroimaging studies is common, especially when higher-level function are examined, where differences between studies in the paradigms used can lead to differences in the processes of no-interest (e.g., working memory, attention, response selection) and can therefore lead to differences in the areas activated. Furthermore, all the early studies of calculation indicate the involvement of a left lateralized network of prefrontal and parietal regions involved in calculation and thereby provide a good starting point for the investigation of the specific cognitive functions and operations carried out by these brain regions during calculation.

More recently, questions about the neural basis of calculation in adulthood have shifted away from localizing the critical regions involved in calculation to a question of the specific role played by these regions and their relationship to other aspects of number processing. In this vein, Dehaene et al. (1999) in a highly influential study investigated the difference between calculating the exact solution of a simple arithmetic problem vs. performing and approximate calculation. In both fMRI and ERP experiments, participants were presented with single-digit addition (3 + 5) and were instructed to either compute the exact answer or an approximate answer. In order to do this, the presentation of the addition problem was followed by either (a) A slide containing the exact answer together with a close, but wrong answer (8 6) or (b) the presentation of two answers close to the exact answer (6 9). A contrast of brain regions involved in exact vs. approximate calculation revealed that approximate calculation lead to activation of bilateral regions of the IPS, while exact calculation modulated the left AG as well as left frontal regions. Similarly, the ERP data, coupled with source localization techniques, revealed that the time course of the ERP signal varied for exact and approximate calculation in such a way that left inferior frontal electrodes were more strongly modulated by exact compared with approximate calculation, while bilateral parietal electrodes exhibited greater ERP responses during approximate compared with exact calculation. Importantly, these differences were observed very shortly after the presentation of the single-digit addition problem and thus make it unlikely that the difference observed in the fMRI data (which are of substantially lower temporal resolution) can be explained by difference in the decision rather than the calculation stage. These findings highlight the importance of using both measures with relatively high spatial resolution (e.g., fMRI) and those that afford high temporal resolution (e.g., ERP) in cognitive neuroscience research.

The findings reported by Dehaene et al. suggest the existence and neural dissociation of two processes underlying numerical cognition. On the one hand an approximate system of number representation (see previous section on numerical magnitude processing in the adult brain) recruits regions of the bilateral IPS, while exact number processing draws on regions typically associated with verbal processing such as left frontal regions as well as the AG. This dissociation is also interesting in the context of data from neuropsychological patients which suggest that damage to parietal regions impairs approximate calculation while leaving exact calculation intact, while damage to left frontal regions impairs arithmetic fact retrieval while leave approximate number abilities such as number comparison and estimation intact (Dehaene & Cohen, 1995).

It should be noted however, that subsequent fMRI studies using the exact and approximate single-digit addition paradigm have failed to replicate the finding of increased frontal activation during exact but not approximate calculation (Molko et al., 2003; Venkatraman et al., 2005). These studies suggest that the parietal cortex is involved in both exact and approximate calculation. Furthermore, it has been contended that the use of single-digit arithmetic makes it hard for individuals to suppress the exact answer in favor of an approximate strategy. In other words, it is likely the case that during approximate calculation, participants to automatically retrieve the exact answer and then compare this to the two approximate solutions in order to establish which of the solutions is numerically closest to the exact result.

Recently, Venkatraman et al. (2006) compared exact and approximate calculation in English-Chinese participants using a language switching paradigm. Instead of using single-digit arithmetic to compare exact and approximate calculation, Venkatraman et al. trained participants perform exact base-7 addition and percentage estimation. Participants were trained to perform these exact and approximate operations in one of their languages. Subsequent to training, participants were scanned using fMRI while they performed exact (base-7 addition) and approximate calculation (percentage estimation) either in their trained or untrained languages. Comparison of activation during computation of the exact and approximate problems in the trained vs. untrained language served as a way to establish the degree to which language switching would draw on language related areas and therefore suggest the dependence on language processes for either exact or approximate calculation. Consistent with the findings by Dehaene et al. (1999) greater activation for exact problems presented in untrained vs. trained language was found in the left inferior frontal gyrus as well as the left AG (this region showed deactivations for both trained and untrained problems). In contrast, comparison of approximate problems presented in the untrained vs. trained language modulated regions in bilateral posterior parietal cortex.

Taken together there is increasing evidence that exact calculation is functionally dissociated from processes involving approximate number processing. However, there is a need for more studies to address this dissociation using well-matched paradigms to track both associations and dissociations between exact and approximate number processing in the brain. Furthermore, it should be noted that many of the early studies comparing calculation with more basic, approximate numerical processing (e.g., number comparison), reviewed above, found greater engagement of parietal regions for calculation compared to number comparison suggesting that the exact role of the parietal lobes in these processes are as yet unclear.

In addition to the question of how the brain regions involved in calculation differ from and converge with those involved in more basic aspects of number, it is important to dissociate the fronto-parietal network typically revealed in neuroimaging studies of calculation into its subcomponents. Calculation is not process pure. In other words, in addition to processes which are calculation specific, such as the mental manipulation of numerical quantities, calculation draws on processes related to working memory, attention and speed of processing. In this vein it has been argued by numerous authors (Dehaene et al., 1996; Gruber et al., 2001; Rueckert et al., 1996) that the prefrontal activation observed during calculation may reflect processes of working memory, response selection and attention, while parietal activation reflect calculation-specific processes. In order to empirically test this hypothesis, Menon et al. (2000) used a factorial design to manipulate both calculation-dependent and -independent task difficulty. To do this, Menon et al. varied: (a) the number of operands in an arithmetic verification problem (e.g., $3 + 5 = 8$ vs. $6 + 2 - 4 = 4$) or (b) the presentation rate (one problem every 3 or 6 seconds). This enabled an analyses of main effect of rate (3 vs. 6 seconds) and operands (2 vs. 3). While the main effect of rate was found to modulate prefrontal regions, main effects of operand on the fMRI signal were found in left and right IPS and AG. Furthermore, no significant interaction effect of rate and number of operands was found in any brain area. These findings provide empirical support for the notion that while task difficulty which is independent of calculation (such as presentation rate) modulates prefrontal regions, task difficulty related to calculation (such as number of operands) affects activation of regions in the parietal cortex, such as the IPS and AG. These findings therefore strengthen the suggestion of a strong link between calculation and the parietal cortex, while the involvement of prefrontal regions during calculation may be related to domain general factors, such as working memory and response selection.

The above studies treat calculation as a static unitary process. However, adult as well as developmental studies suggest that calculation is underlain by multiple strategies that differ as a function of developmental stage, learning and the particular operation itself. Therefore, in order to understand the neural basis of calculation it is important to understand whether differences in functional brain activation differ as a function of strategy, learning and operation. In a recent series of studies, Delazer and colleagues (Delazer et al., 2003, 2005; Ischebeck et al., 2006) have explored the neural changes associated with learning to calculate. In one study (Delazer et al., 2003) adults were extensively trained on a set of complex multiplication problems. Subsequently, in an fMRI experiment, participants solved both problems they had been trained on as well as novel, untrained problems. Comparison of blocks during which subjects solved untrained vs. trained problems revealed greater activation in left intraparietal as well as left inferior frontal regions. Interestingly, the reverse contrast (trained vs. untrained) revealed greater activation for trained problems in the left AG. These findings therefore suggest a training-related shift in activation from left intraparietal regions to the left AG. Delazer and colleagues suggest that this shift may reflect increasing reliance on automatic fact retrieval with training. Further evidence for a role of the AG in automatic retrieval comes from the comparison of the neural mechanisms underlying multiplication and subtraction. Ischebeck et al. (2006) found that while the AG was more activated by trained compared to untrained multiplication problems, this region did not exhibit training effects for subtraction. Given that training of multiplication leads to increasing fact retrieval, while subtraction requires mental manipulation of quantity and strategies rather than retrieval, these data suggest that the AG plays a crucial role in the efficient retrieval of arithmetic facts.

These training studies are important as they help to reveal the neural processes of learning and can therefore help to formulate developmental predictions. It may be possible in the future to use functional neuroimaging methods to track the changes associated with structured intervention programs for children with mathematical difficulties. In addition to revealing differences in the functional neuroanatomy underlying different operations, Delazer et al. have also investigated the effects of training arithmetic operations by drill or through the use of particular strategies and have been able to reveal different networks underlying these two ways of learning to calculate (Delazer et al., 2005).

NUMBER PROCESSING IN THE TYPICALLY DEVELOPING BRAIN

The above section provides a review of adult cognitive neuroscience research into the neural basis of mature numerical and mathematical processing. We now turn our attention to a critical review of the few existing neuroimaging studies which seek to chart the typical developmental trajectory of number processing in the brain. It should be noted at the outset that there are very few published neuroimaging studies of number development. Hence a cognitive neuroscience approach to the study of number development needs to consider the above discussed adult literature and use this body of literature to generate developmentally sensitive and meaningful predictions and experimental designs.

The first developmental neuroimaging of numerical cognition was conducted by Temple and Posner (1998) and used ERP to investigate developmental differences in the time course underlying symbolic and non-symbolic magnitude comparisons between 5-year-old children and adults. As a measure of magnitude representation the effect of distance on the ERP waveform was investigated. The authors found a significant effect of numerical distance on the ERP waveform as early as 200 milliseconds after the presentation of the pair of Arabic numerals or dots. Most interestingly, the effect of numerical distance on the ERP waveforms was found to be broadly similar between children and adults for both symbolic and non-symbolic comparisons. These findings were therefore interpreted to suggest that the brain circuitry underlying numerical magnitude processing is mature by the age of 5 years. Further evidence for similarity between children and adults brain responses during magnitude comparisons was obtained by means of ERP source localization. Using this method, Temple and Posner were able to demonstrate that the distance effect in the ERP signal for both symbolic and non-symbolic number comparisons in children and adults was maximal over parietal electrodes, similar to those reported by Dehaene (1996), reviewed above.

These findings suggest that there are similarities not only in the time course of brain responses during numerical magnitude processing between children and adults, but that furthermore, the brain region generating this response exhibits developmental continuity. However, it is important to note that while the absence of a developmental difference is certainly suggested by the inspection of their data, it is unclear how ERP responses from children and adults were compared. The paper does not provide a direct statistical comparison between children and adults and it is therefore difficult to ascertain whether or not the profiles of children and adults were in fact similar. Another general constraint of using ERPs is their very limited spatial resolution. Despite the fact that Temple and Posner used source localization, their findings do not represent the same spatial resolution that is afforded by fMRI. It is therefore possible that temporal characteristics of the ERP modulation by numerical distance are similar in children and adults, while the regions generating this response differ as a function of age.

More recently, the neural correlates of arithmetic have been compared between children and adults using fMRI, which affords a greater spatial resolution than ERP (Kawashima et al., 2004; Rivera et al., 2005). Kawashima and colleagues (2004) assessed the neural correlates of addition, subtraction and multiplication. The results suggest that children (9–14 years) and adults (40–49 years) show broadly similar functional activation patterns during each of the three arithmetical operations tested. More specifically, after a direct statistical comparison in a common stereotactic space, areas of overlapping brain activation between children and adults were found in the prefrontal, intraparietal, occipital and occipitotemporal cortices. This is consistent with a large body of adult fMRI studies implicating this network of regions in arithmetic processing (see review of adult studies above). Notwithstanding the broad similarities in the activation profiles of children and adults, some subtle differences were found. More specifically, while activation in the prefrontal cortex was found to be largely left lateralized in the children, the adults exhibited more bilateral activation of prefrontal regions.

Children commonly acquire addition skills before they learn how to subtract and typically start to multiply after they know how to add and subtract. Given this hierarchical developmental pattern it might have been expected that there would be significant differences between the neural networks underlying these three operations in the group of children. However, somewhat surprisingly, no such differences were found, indicating that the behavioral differences typically found between arithmetical operations among children are not reflected in differences in fMRI activation patterns.

Importantly, it should be noted that the behavioral data reported by Kawashima et al. point toward a speed accuracy trade-off. Even though the accuracy levels were comparable between adults and children, the reaction time for each arithmetic operation was significantly longer in children. Thus, the differences in neural activity pointed out by this study and others might in fact be due to differences in cognitive strategies rather than pure numerical processing.

In a more recent study, Rivera et al. (2005) used a cross-sectional approach to investigate how brain activation underlying arithmetic reasoning changes between the ages 8 and 19 years (mean age: 13.67 years). In this study, they only included addition and subtraction and refrained from using multiplication problems as their youngest participants had gained no expertise on this operation yet. The 17 subjects were asked to press a button if the result of an arithmetic equation was correct. The equations were chosen is such a way that all numbers including the resultants were single digits (e.g., $5 - 2 = 4$). The control task was a simple reaction task also including numbers. Here subjects had to respond as soon as a Zero appears in a appeared number string (e.g., '4 0 2 6 9' or '2 4 5 1 3').

One key result of their study was a decrease in activation with age in the prefrontal cortex, namely dorsolateral and ventrolateral prefrontal cortex, in addition to the anterior cingulate cortex. Since these areas are linked to working memory and attentional resources, the authors suggest that younger children use these additional processes to achieve similar levels of arithmetic performance.

Most importantly, Rivera et al. (2005) revealed that activation patterns associated with arithmetic reasoning seem to be subject to an age-related difference in the involvement of left and right parietal cortex. Specifically, while the right parietal cortex showed only little changes in activation, the left parietal cortex, especially the left supramarginal gyrus and adjoining IPS, became gradually more active between the ages of 8 and 19. These regions have been frequently shown to be related to arithmetic processing (e.g., Dehaene et al., 1999). Against this background, Rivera et al. argue that this hemispherical shift should be considered as a functional specialization of these left lateralized structures for arithmetic processing.

A particular strength of Rivera et al.'s study is that in addition to examining age-related changes in functional neuroanatomy, the authors investigated the degree to which these changes were associated with age-related structural changes (measured by gray-matter density, GMD). By comparing functional and structural differences between age groups, Rivera et al. were able to establish that the age-related functional activation changes differed from the age-related GMD changes in the same regions. In other words, this finding suggests that age-related functional changes could be the consequence of a maturing neural network rather than evolving from gray matter changes.

A series of recent neuroimaging studies have sought to reveal developmental differences in brain activation associated with basic numerical processing during symbolic (Ansari et al., 2005) and non-symbolic (Ansari & Dhital, 2006) magnitude comparison. These studies, like the previously discussed study of Temple and Posner, investigated the effect of numerical distance on brain activation patterns. Their findings again support the notion that the IPS has a central role in numerical cognition as it not only plays an active part in number processing in adults, but is already recruited for such processes in early childhood. Ansari et al. (2005) demonstrated age-related shifts in functional activity from reliance on prefrontal regions to increasing recruitment of parietal areas in response to numerical distance in a symbolic number comparison task. In a second study (Ansari & Dhital, 2006) further evidence for such a shift was provided using non-symbolic stimuli. These findings suggest that the functional neuroanatomy underlying the numerical magnitude represented by symbolic (e.g., Arabic numerals) and non-symbolic (e.g., arrays of dots) stimulus formats changes considerably over developmental time.

The finding of greater modulation of parietal regions by numerical distance in adults compared with children has been interpreted as reflecting a shift toward increasingly automatic and efficient processing of numerical magnitude. In this vein, the greater engagement of frontal regions in the group of children may reflect greater recruitment of working memory and attentional resources to operate on representations of numerical magnitude.

These studies leave a number of questions open. First of all, it is unclear whether the increasing recruitment of parietal regions with age represents a number-specific process or a general maturation of parietal structures underlying response selection (Göbel et al., 2004). Similarly, the present findings may suggest that while the processes enabling children to make numerical magnitude comparison mature over developmental time, the representations of numerical magnitudes themselves undergo little ontogenetic change.

Through the use of a passive paradigm Cantlon et al. (2006) have recently been able to address age-related differences in functional neuroanatomy underlying number processing in the absence of response-selection confounds and differences in performance. In their study, subjects passively viewed arrays of visual stimuli that were constant in number (16 or 32) and shape (circles, squares or triangles). Cantlon et al. compared a group of 12 adults (mean age: 25 years) with a group of 4-year-old children. Similar to the fMRA studies discussed above, the prediction here is that repetition of a particular numerosity will lead to adaptation of the fMRI response in number sensitive areas of the brain. The presentation of a deviant (e.g., 16 dots following a long period of repetition of 32 dots) will lead to a recovery of the adapted response. The shape deviants were included to serve as a control for the specificity of number deviant responses. Cantlon et al. predicted that number sensitive regions would exhibit greater responses following number relative to shape deviants.

Consistent with other studies (Ansari et al., 2006a; Piazza et al., 2004, 2007), responses to number deviants (e.g., change from 16 to 32) were found in bilateral regions of the IPS. Furthermore the response to number deviants in these regions was found to be greater than those for shape deviants. On the other hand, shape deviants lead to greater activation than number deviants in the regions within the left lateral occipital cortex. Interestingly, Cantlon et al. found that the response to number and shape deviants in the group of 4-year-old children were very similar to those of the adults. This was particularly true of the right IPS, while left IPS showed greater modulation by number deviants in the adults compared to the children. From these data, Cantlon et al. conclude that the number-specific responses in the IPS develop early and that the non-symbolic processing of numerical magnitude in this region may form the basis for the acquisition of symbolic representation of numerical magnitude (Arabic numerals).

Notwithstanding the significance of these data, one has to keep in mind that passive fMRA paradigms do not address the active processing of numerical quantity in the context of an active task. It is therefore possible that activation in the IPS is associated with low-level processing of numerical magnitude that is similar between children and adults, but that processes that translate these representations into meaningful numerical behaviors differ substantially between children and adults.

Existing developmental neuroimaging studies of number processing provide divergent interpretations of the observed functional differences between children and adults. While for example Kawashima et al. or Cantlon et al. interpret their findings as evidence of a similar activation pattern associated with numerical processing in children and adults, other studies (e.g., Rivera et al., Ansari et al.) argue that the changes are quite substantial across development. The differences in activation patterns – mostly increased frontal activation in children – are usually interpreted as reflecting the recruitment of additional cognitive processes in children when working with numerical quantities. This possible discrepancy between a child's representation of number and how to meaningfully use this information to improve performance should be further examined and disentangled in future research. Furthermore it will be important to investigate the developmental relationship between symbolic and non-symbolic number processing in the brain in an effort to better understand the brain mechanisms involved in mapping numerical magnitude representations onto abstract symbols such as Arabic numerals.

Another important issue is to assess the relationship between age-related changes in both brain structure and function. So far only one study (Rivera et al., 2005) attempted to map out both structural and functional changes and tried to investigate their interaction. Here the authors investigated whether GMD correlates with the functional activations associated with numerical processing in the developing brain. Data from studies looking at age-related changes in structural anatomy using MRI, however, point out that gray-matter volume and density changes have an inverted U-shaped pattern throughout development, whereas white-matter volume and density are roughly linear (for a review see, Amso & Casey, 2006). This suggests that the ongoing myelination process might in fact be a better measure of functionally relevant structural changes than gray-matter volume.

NUMBER PROCESSING IN THE ATYPICALLY DEVELOPING BRAIN

As reviewed above, a wealth of adult neuroimaging literature has investigated the neural correlates of numerical cognition in typically developed adults (Dehaene, 1996; Dehaene et al., 1998, 1999, 2003; Piazza et al., 2004; Pinel et al., 2001) and more recently in comparing typically developing children and adults (Ansari & Dhital, 2006; Ansari et al., 2005). Tasks which require some form of numerical magnitude processing are usually associated with activations in the posterior parietal areas of the brain, typically including the bilateral IPS. An important area that needs to be explored is the association between brain regions and numerical processing across development. Furthermore, how those associations can deviate from typical developmental trajectories will help inform our understanding of behavioral and neurobiological developmental 'checkpoints' and how they underpin successful mathematical learning.

In contrast to research on mathematical disabilities, studies examining the neural correlates of reading, and their dysfunction in dyslexia have been fairly widespread, and have thus been able to identify key differences in brain activation between dyslexics and normal readers, especially in the left occipito-temporal area (e.g., Shaywitz et al., 2002). These findings have been highly relevant in informing theories of developmental dyslexia based on deficits in phonological decoding, for example. In view of this 'success story' it is likely that the study of mathematical learning disabilities would benefit highly from similar neuroimaging contributions. The relatively recent advent of functional imaging studies of numerical cognition in normal populations coupled with the heterogeneity of mathematical learning disabilities and the limited understanding of their root causes have perhaps delayed the approach to this important and exciting area.

An initial pathway into the brain level study of atypical numerical processing has been provided by populations with numerical and visuo-spatial impairments occurring in the context of genetic developmental syndromes, such as Turner Syndrome (TS), Williams Syndrome (WS) and Fragile X syndrome (fraX).

Using both functional and structural neuroimaging methods, Molko et al. (2003) compared 14 TS subjects (Mean age 24.5 years) with 14 controls, in an fMRI design previously reported by Dehaene et al. (1999) that uses exact and approximate calculation to investigate the impact of number size and numerical task demand on brain activation. During exact calculation, subjects had to choose the correct one of two alternative solutions to a visually presented simple calculation. Approximate calculation, on the other hand, required subjects to choose the most plausible of two incorrect candidate solutions. Subjects were told that since one of the incorrect solutions was grossly false they did not have compute the exact solution. The assumption is that participants are able to make the approximate calculation using general estimation mechanisms rather than precise verbally based calculation. While the control subjects showed increased activation in the bilateral IPS as the difficulty of exact calculations increased, the TS subjects did not show the same modulation. In a morphometric analysis, TS subjects also showed abnormal structural organization of the IPS in the right hemisphere. In particular, they showed reduced gray-matter volume and an unusual interruption in the horizontal segment of the IPS, an area which is systematically activated when numbers are manipulated, and which is increasingly activated as the task puts greater emphasis on quantity processing (Dehaene et al., 2003). Interestingly, the behavioral findings showed that TS subjects performed disproportionately worse when the difficulty of exact calculations increased relative to controls. In addition, the brain area associated with supporting the increased level of quantity processing in controls does not respond to increased demand in TS subjects, a pattern also observed in females with fraX in calculation verification tasks (Rivera et al., 2002). Taken together these findings strongly support the crucial role of the IPS in numerical cognition.

Calculation deficits have also been linked to IPS abnormalities by Isaacs et al. (2001), who compared adolescents of very low birth weight who had deficits in numerical operations (including addition, subtraction, multiplication and division, NOD group), those with deficits in mathematical reasoning (including problem solving, numeration and number concepts, MDR group), and typically achieving controls who were matched to the experimental groups for gender, age, IQ and other perinatal variables. The authors found that the NOD group showed significantly less gray matter in the left IPS than matched controls, while the MDR was not found to exhibit significantly different gray-matter volumes from the control group without any mathematical deficits. The region of reduced gray matter was very close to an area described by Dehaene et al. (1999) as being involved in approximate relative to exact calculation (i.e., non-verbal numerical processes).

An important caveat in the interpretation of anatomical studies of atypically performing groups is that the observed structural changes may be either the cause or effect of impaired performance in the cognitive domain with which that brain region is associated, so causal inferences should be treated with caution. However, that does not reduce the importance of observing that region as a correlate of numerical processing, and as our understanding deepens, and theories become more sophisticated, causal relationships will be more clearly elucidated.

A problem in the identification of the neural substrates of numerical processing is the complexity of the cognitive domain being investigated. A wide range of tasks have been used in adult neuroimaging, resulting in theories proposing distinct neural networks subserving various aspects of numerical cognition (Dehaene et al., 2003). This complexity is equally a problem when investigating neural correlates of numerical cognition in atypical populations, but furthermore, the populations themselves increase the complexity of the issue. Groups of atypically developing individuals with different genetic disorders have been compared as though they shared a single deficit in numerical processing. It is dangerous to equate the visuo-spatial and numerical impairments between these groups simply because they share similar behavioral profiles on standardized arithmetic achievement tests. Although the consequences are unknown, the fact that these groups present with these mathematical impairments as part of very different genetic syndromes should not be forgotten when generalizing the results of these studies.

Only one study so far has investigated brain activation during numerical processing in groups of children with developmental dyscalculia that was not part of a wider genetic developmental syndrome. Kucian et al. (2006) conducted an fMRI experiment with developmental dyscalculics in the 3rd and 6th Grades, defined by discrepancy between scores on a battery of mathematical and reading tests and general IQ, and two groups of age matched controls. The experiment included approximate and exact calculation conditions, in the same paradigm used by Molko et al. (2003). Subjects also completed a magnitude comparison task, comparing small sets of different objects (e.g., strawberries vs. nuts). The results of the fMRI showed similar activation patterns, albeit generally weaker and more diffuse, for DD and control groups in all conditions. There was no effect of age on activation pattern. The main difference between groups was found using region of interest analysis in the IPS. In this region DD subjects showed significantly weaker activation in response to approximate calculation in the left IPS, and a non-significant trend in the same direction in the right IPS. However this difference was not observed in direct statistical comparison between groups using repeated measures general linear model analysis on a whole brain level, and so cannot be viewed as a particularly robust finding. It is important to note that in this study no behavioral differences between groups were observed for any of the experimental tasks.

The null results of this study could be the consequence of several factors. The subject selection on the basis of the ICD-10 classification, which is far from precise in characterizing the disorder, leaves open the possibility that the developmental dyscalculic group was comprised of individuals whose mathematical difficulties stemmed from other cognitive domains, or were at least highly variable in their severity. Another possible reason for the absence of group differences may be related to the particular task that was used. Although functional activation differences have been observed between exact and approximate calculation in normal adults (e.g., Dehaene & Cohen, 1995; Dehaene et al., 2003;

Stanescu-Cosson et al., 2000), dissociations between the two tasks have not been replicated in normal and disabled calculators (Molko et al., 2003; Venkatraman et al., 2005), and so it is not clear that they relate directly to behavioral or brain level differences between typically and atypically developing groups. The lack of differences in the magnitude comparison condition can potentially be accounted for by the dramatically different visual properties of the stimuli in comparison sets.

Interesting evidence for the role of impaired development of the parietal area in developmental dyscalculia comes from a single-case study presented by Levy et al. (1999). J.S., a right handed male who at the time of testing was 18 years old, had been diagnosed with acalculia in elementary school. J.S. was in the upper 5th percentile on tests of non-verbal IQ, his full scale IQ was measured at 108, but he exhibited marked impairments in spelling, number computations, and was particularly impaired when the complexity of problems increased or mental computation was required. Levy and colleagues employed magnetic resonance spectroscopy to reveal a 'focal, wedge shaped defect in the left temporo-parietal brain in the region of the AG,' including defects in metabolite amplitudes. Conventional MRI scans showed no abnormalities, and for this reason this case is particularly interesting, because it shows that conventional MRI may not detect functionally relevant impairments in atypically developing brains.

Neuroimaging of basic number processing in atypically developing populations has so far provided variable results. Different experimental designs and populations with highly variable cognitive profiles outside the number domain have made it difficult to apply a uniform interpretation of the findings. However some consistent findings have emerged, in that almost all of these populations, when the task is well controlled, some abnormal functional or structural modulation of parietal regions appear. Given that the role of this area in typically developing populations has yet to be fully resolved, findings linking atypical behavioral profiles in numerical processing to atypical structural and functional properties of specific brain regions may provide a powerful resource in better understand the neural correlates of numerical cognition. This case illustrates the importance of using multiple methods to capture a particular cognitive phenomenon and its developmental trajectory.

When considering directions for future research an important factor emerges from looking at the samples used in most of the studies mentioned above. That is, although they investigate populations whose mathematical deficits are undoubtedly developmental rather than acquired, the majority of subjects are tested during adolescence or early adulthood. It is therefore only possible to say that with a given behavioral developmental trajectory, these subjects do or do not end up to the same neurobiological profile as typically developing groups. Inferences about the association of parietal regions with numerical processing deficits that occur over developmental time cannot yet be made, and hence the exact role of the IPS, for example, in numerical cognition cannot be fully elucidated. Does that region support the development of numerical representation from birth, or is the association formed on the basis of increased frequency of access to numerical semantic information across development? Such questions can only be answered by means of longitudinal studies of typically and atypically developing populations.

FUTURE DIRECTIONS

The above sections represent a critical review of the currently available functional neuroimaging research into the neural correlates of numerical and mathematical processes in adults and children. It is clear that much insight has been gained into the brain processes that enable adults and children to enumerate, estimate and calculate. However, numerous challenges remain. In order to work toward realizing the potential of a developmental cognitive neuroscience approach to the study of typical and atypical number development, it is important to consider both the methodological and conceptual challenges facing this emerging field.

CONCEPTUAL CHALLENGES

On the face of it, a cognitive neuroscience approach is informative simply because it increases our understanding of the neural processes underlying developmental changes in number processing. However, the aim of cognitive neuroscience is not merely to attribute cognitive processes to brain regions but to have neuroscientific and behavioral data mutually constrain one another. In other words, besides the obvious knowledge gain afforded by the new dependent measures (functional neuroimaging methods), the added value of cognitive neuroscience studies must lie in their ability to add to and constrain models of development derived from a behavioral analyses. Seron and Fias (2006) discuss this issue very nicely in the light of numerical research and come to the conclusion that brain imaging in this research area has been valuable for cognitive research since it both tested existing hypothesis and generated new ones. It is important to stress the point that neuroimaging for neuroimaging's sake is not enough. The inferences about cognitive processes that can and cannot be drawn from neuroimaging data are still the subject of significant debate (Henson, 2006; Poldrack, 2006).

With respect to studying the development of cognitive functions, neuroimaging must meet the challenge of providing evidence which will help to construct biologically plausible theories of the development of mental functions. Dowker (2006) distinguishes between three different forms of insight one can gather about child development (typical or atypical) using functional brain imaging. Firstly, functional MRI can be used to diagnose and understand certain neurological disorders in children. Secondly, through fMRI studies with young children we can add to our understanding of children's neurocognitive development and can thus draw conclusions that could not only influence current cognitive models, but might even have implications for intervention or teaching techniques. In gaining insight of how different areas of the brain are differently contributing to certain cognitive processes throughout development, we can deepen our understanding of the connections between cognitive functions. Through this approach we may be able to provide possible educational intervention techniques, which are adapted to the diversity of the different components of cognitive functions and thus facilitate their maturation process.

Thirdly, Dowker (2006) points out that functional neuroimaging studies with adults have had a marked influence on behavioral studies of cognitive development. Even though we are unaware of any direct claims made in adult literature concerning developmental theories, it is certainly evident that results from studies using adults inspire a closer look at, for example, basic number processing in children. For example the notion of approximate, language independent and exact, language-dependent number processing has had an effect on the investigation of number processing in WS. Individuals with WS present with relatively good language skills coupled with strongly impaired visuo-spatial cognitive abilities. This lead Ansari et al. (2003) to investigate approximate vs. exact number abilities in this syndrome.

However, using adult studies to infer developmental processes ignores the fact that the functional and structural organization of the brain differs markedly between infants, children and adults (Karmiloff-Smith, 1998). Therefore activation patterns in the adult brain should be conceptualized as the outcome of a developmental process, that itself needs to be studied. By adopting a developmental perspective, it becomes possible to answer important questions about both development of brain processes underlying the acquisition of numerical skills and the neural correlates of number processing in the mature, adult brain. As developmental changes in neural activation patterns reflect the maturation of cognitive functions, we can answer the important question: how do abilities emerge over developmental time. The answer to this question will deepen our understanding of the nature of higher cognitive functions. In the adult literature we can often only go as far as to understand that certain areas of the brain form a network and are associated with a certain cognitive process. By adopting a developmental approach it is possible to gather more information by finding answers to questions such as: when do certain abilities develop? Which system of a neural network in the adult brain develops first? When do certain parts of the brain come 'online'? Does the connectivity of different systems or the maturation of a network reflect behavioral changes?

METHODOLOGICAL CHALLENGES

In addition to the broad conceptual challenges facing a developmental cognitive neuroscience approach to the study of atypical and typical number development there are numerous methodological challenges.

Developmental neuroimaging studies are subject to the same constraints as behavioral developmental studies. When designing a developmental investigation we have the choice between a cross-sectional and a longitudinal approach, both having advantages and disadvantages. In a cross-sectional approach we have to consider greater unknown between subject variability. In brain imaging this cohort effect means that a certain age group might have certain functional or structural characteristics, which complicates direct comparison. These cohort effects can either be due to cultural or experience-based changes, which were shown to have effects on functional data and brain structure (Maguire et al., 2000; Paulesu et al., 2000). Thus would find differences that are not due to mere development, but are group specific differences.

In a longitudinal approach however it is hard to tease apart whether the changes are due to development or learning, since the same subjects participate multiple times. Also one should not underestimate changes within subjects over time which are unrelated to the cognitive processes assessed. For example the first time in a scanner is a very different experience than the second or third time.

A constraint that cross-sectional and longitudinal studies both share is the potential confound represented by age-related differences in task difficulty. As task difficulty decreases drastically with age and experience, it is hard to distinguish which activations are due to learning processes and which are due to the consequences of learning. Poldrack (2000) suggests that one way to better distinguish performance from age-related changes is to use parametric designs that systematically vary task difficulty, while keeping the variable of interest constant. By comparing regions that show a main effect of task difficulty with those exhibiting an effect of task independent of difficulty it is possible to dissociate areas modulated by the task from those engaged by varying levels of difficulty.

A different approach has been suggested by Schlaggar et al. (2002). These authors suggest that in order to compare the functional neuroanatomy underlying a particular cognitive process between children and adults it is important to match groups on performance. In a design that involved single word reading, Schlaggar et al. divided children and adults into subgroups of children and adults with the same performance level (performance matched) and those who differed in their behavioral performance (non-matched). The authors argue that through this subdivision they can classify regions of activations into being either age related (differences in activation that are revealed in both subgroup analyses) or being performance related (difference in activation is only present in the non-matched subgroup). However, one has to consider the following: this approach is only possible if the two compared age groups are naturally close in performance levels, otherwise the overlap is either too small or meaningless, since the performance-matched group could consist of participants that are not typical of the general population, since slow adults are matched to fast children.

An alternative approach that does not involve matching or parametric modulation of difficulty was put forward by Turkeltaub et al. (2003). These authors used an implicit task to measure the functional neuroanatomy underlying reading. In their task participants were presented with words and false font strings and were instructed to detect the presence of a tall letter. This task is so simple that no age-related performance differences were observed. Against this background, the contrast of words vs. false font strings allowed Turkeltaub et al. to map regions involved in implicit reading without requiring a response directly related to reading. The real strength of their approach is that the authors were able to correlate external reading measures with the functional data and reveal associations between activation related to implicit reading and individual differences in reading competence. This approach is intriguing in the aspect that it tries to connect very basic neural activation patterns to actual behavioral correlates outside of the scanner. However, a slight constraint of this implicit measure is that we actually can not presume that the underlying functions are fundamentally the same. Nor can we be certain about possible interactions between the implicit processing and the explicit task they perform. In other words, the level of difficulty of the primary task may modulate the implicit process functions and this might have a different impact over development.

Another important methodological constraint concerns the possibility that important development differences in the response measured by fMRI exists between children and adults. As mentioned above, fMRI measures changes in local oxygenated and deoxygenated blood flow and the signal is referred to as the Blood Oxygen Level Dependent (BOLD) signal. Recent evidence suggests that when comparing BOLD responses in children to those in adults the shape of the BOLD response changes systematically as a function of age (Richter & Richter, 2003; Thomason et al., 2005) and that furthermore within a child's brain those changes vary depending on the brain region (Schapiro et al., 2004). Against this background, some authors (e.g., Richter & Richter, 2003) suggest using different statistical approaches (e.g., focusing on the peak intensity of the BOLD signal) rather than using a model BOLD signal derived from adult studies to estimate the fit of the data to a given model of activation.

In addition to concerns over differences in the fMRI response between children and adults, there is some controversy over the most accurate way to compare the neuroanatomy of children and adults in the context of functional activation patterns. In adult neuroimaging it is common practice to normalize the brains of individual subjects to a template brain. Such a common space can be associated with a neuroanatomical atlas (Talairach & Tournoux, 1988) or can be a standardized space derived from the averaging of multiple anatomic scans (Evans et al., 1992). This process achieves a degree of structural normalization of the individual brains within a given study and allows for the use of a coordinate system that is common across studies and thereby allows for systematic comparisons of activation patterns between studies. This process of normalization to a template brain may be problematic in the context of comparing children and adults as there are marked anatomical difference between children and even when comparing young and older children. Therefore is it possible to make systematic comparisons of functional activations and to normalize both children and adults to the same template brain? In a series of recent studies no evidence was found that would seriously question the feasibility of direct statistical comparison between different age groups within a common space (Burgund et al., 2002; Kang et al., 2003). Burgund et al. (2002) found that even though there are minor anatomical differences between 7–8 year olds and 18–30 year olds, a computer simulation with the same data revealed that the functional image comparison was not negatively affected by it. Similarly Kang et al. (2003) found that activation location was statistically similar between adults and children. However it has to be mentioned here that their data was restricted to visual and motor cortex region. In the light of investigations into the age-related changes in gray- and white-matter development (e.g., Gogtay et al., 2004) the areas of primary interest the prefrontal and lateral temporal cortices, as these seem to mature late.

Researchers in the field of developmental neuroimaging are constantly struggling with issues related to small sample sizes. While Byars et al. (2002) point out that it is in fact feasible to conduct a large-scale fMRI study with children, they also make quite clear that in order to do so one has to take into consideration that the drop-out/failure rate is inversely related to age. Firstly, very young children usually find the situation estranging. Even for adults scanning sessions can be frightening or at least unpleasant. Preparing young children for fMRI scans is work intensive and time consuming. It usually includes several meetings with the parents and/or the children and if the facilities allow a prior introduction to a so called 'mock scanner,' which simulates the situation in the actual scanner.

CONCLUSIONS

The last 20 years have witnessed tremendous advances in our understanding of the neural correlates of adult numerical cognition. The use of methods such as ERPs, fMRI and TMS have enabled researchers to investigate basic numerical magnitude processing in the brain as well the brain regions underlying calculation. In the present chapter we have reviewed the cognitive neuroscience approach to numerical cognition in an effort to highlight both the promise and challenges facing the emergence of a developmental cognitive neuroscience approach to the study of numerical cognition. To do this we have reviewed and highlighted:

1. The increasing growth of cognitive neuroscience investigations into adult number processing and calculation, which are starting to go beyond simply mapping the neural networks involved in various components of numerical cognition to a finer grained analyses of the specific functions of regions activated by number processing and calculation and the relationship between numerical and non-numerical processes engaged by tasks of basic number processing and calculation.

2. That a cognitive neuroscience approach to number processing, in combination with traditional behavioral measures, can help to constrain models of numerical cognition and provide new levels of analyses that are not afforded by investigations purely based on behavioral measures.

3. Investigations in to the brain circuits underlying the atypical and typical trajectories of number development are lagging behind those into the adult neural correlates of numerical cognition. However, at the same time, these studies are starting to reveal that typical development is marked both by changes in functional neuroanatomy as well as similarities between children and adults. These studies highlight the importance of taking a developmental perspective. Furthermore, the study of atypical development is beginning to show that brain circuits implicated in typical number processing are both structurally and functionally disordered in children suffering from mathematical difficulties.

4. That numerous important conceptual and methodological difficulties are faced by a developmental cognitive neuroscience approach to the study of numerical cognition. These need to be carefully considered in future studies. A consideration of these also highlights the importance of looking toward other fields (e.g., reading research) for ways in which to deal with issues such as performance-related confounds and task design.

In sum, we hope that the present chapter will serve as a resource for researchers taking a developmental cognitive neuroscience approach to the study of numerical cognition. Future studies will help to further characterize the interplay between behavioral, functional and structural neuroanatomical changes that give rise to the ability to enumerate, estimate and calculate as well as the breakdown of these abilities in children with mathematical difficulties. Such information will hopefully contribute to a better understanding of how to both teach mathematics and diagnose and remediate children with mathematical difficulties.

ACKNOWLEDGMENTS

This work was supported by grants from the NSF Science of Learning Center CCEN (Center for Cognitive and Educational Neuroscience, SBE-0354400), the Dickey Center for International Understanding and the Rockefeller Center for Social Sciences at Dartmouth College to DA. We would also like to thank the Numbra Marie Curie Research Training Network for funding to GP.

REFERENCES

Albright, T. D., Kandel, E. R., & Posner, M. I. (2000). Cognitive neuroscience. *Current Opinion in Neurobiology*, *10*(5), 612–624.

Amso, D. & Casey, B. J. (2006). Beyond what develops when: Neuroimaging may inform how cognition changes with development. *Current Directions in Psychological Science*, *15*(1), 24–29.

Ansari, D. & Coch, D. (2006). Bridges over troubled waters: Education and cognitive neuroscience. *Trends in Cognitive Sciences, 10*(4), 146–151.

Ansari, D. & Dhital, B. (2006). Age-related changes in the activation of the intraparietal sulcus during nonsymbolic magnitude processing: An event-related functional magnetic resonance imaging study. *Journal of Cognitive Neuroscience, 18*(11), 1820–1828.

Ansari, D., Donlan, C., Thomas, M. S., Ewing, S. A., Peen, T., & Karmiloff-Smith, A. (2003). What makes counting count? Verbal and visuo-spatial contributions to typical and atypical number development. *Journal of Experimental Child Psychology, 85*(1), 50–62.

Ansari, D., Garcia, N., Lucas, E., Hamon, K., & Dhital, B. (2005). Neural correlates of symbolic number processing in children and adults. *Neuroreport, 16*(16), 1769–1773.

Ansari, D., Dhital, B., & Siong, S. C. (2006a). Parametric effects of numerical distance on the intraparietal sulcus during passive viewing of rapid numerosity changes. *Brain Research, 1067*(1), 181–188.

Ansari, D., Fugelsang, J. A., Dhital, B., & Venkatraman, V. (2006b). Dissociating response conflict from numerical magnitude processing in the brain: An event-related fMRI study. *Neuroimage, 32*, 799–805.

Burbaud, P., Degreze, P., Lafon, P., Franconi, J. M., Bouligand, B., Bioulac, B., Caille, J. M., & Allard, M. (1995). Lateralization of prefrontal activation during internal mental calculation: a functional magnetic resonance imaging study. *Journal of Neurophysiology, 74*(5), 2194–2200.

Burgund, E. D., Kang, H. C., Kelly, J. E., Buckner, R. L., Snyder, A. Z., Petersen, S. E., & Schlaggar, B. L. (2002). The feasibility of a common stereotactic space for children and adults in fMRI studies of development. *Neuroimage, 17*(1), 184–200.

Byars, A. W., Holland, S. K., Strawsburg, R. H., Bommer, W., Dunn, R. S., Schmithorst, V. J., & Plante, E. (2002). Practical aspects of conducting large-scale functional magnetic resonance imaging studies in children. *Journal of Child Neurology, 17*(12), 885–890.

Cantlon, J. F., Brannon, E. M., Carter, E. J., & Pelphrey, K. A. (2006). Functional imaging of numerical processing in adults and 4-year-old children. *PLoS Biology, 4*(5), e125.

Cohen Kadosh, R., Henik, A., Rubinsten, O., Mohr, H., Dori, H., van de Ven, V., Zorzi, M., Hendler, T., Goebel, R., & Linden, D. E. (2005). Are numbers special? The comparison systems of the human brain investigated by fMRI. *Neuropsychologia, 43*(9), 1238–1248.

Cohen Kadosh, R., Cohen Kadosh, K., Kaas, A., Henik, A., & Goebel, R. (2007). Notation-dependent and -independent representations of numbers in the parietal lobes. *Neuron, 53*(2), 307–314.

Corbetta, M. & Shulman, G. L. (2002). Control of goal-directed and stimulus-driven attention in the brain. *Nature Reviews Neuroscience, 3*(3), 201–215.

Dehaene, S. (1992). Varieties of numerical abilities. *Cognition, 44*(1–2), 1–42.

Dehaene, S. (1996). The organization of brain activations in number comparison: Event-related potentials and the additive-factors method. *Journal of Cognitive Neuroscience, 8*, 47–68.

Dehaene, S. & Cohen, L. (1995). Towards an anatomical and functional model of number processing. *Mathematical Cognition, 1*, 83–120.

Dehaene, S., Tzourio, N., Frak, V., Raynaud, L., Cohen, L., Mehler, J., & Mazoyer, B. (1996). Cerebral activations during number multiplication and comparison: A PET study. *Neuropsychologia, 34*(11), 1097–1106.

Dehaene, S., Dehaene-Lambertz, G., & Cohen, L. (1998). Abstract representations of numbers in the animal and human brain. *Trends in Neuroscience, 21*(8), 355–361.

Dehaene, S., Spelke, E., Pinel, P., Stanescu, R., & Tsivkin, S. (1999). Sources of mathematical thinking: Behavioral and brain-imaging evidence. *Science, 284*(5416), 970–974.

Dehaene, S., Piazza, M., Pinel, P., & Cohen, L. (2003). Three Parietal Circuits for Number Processing. *Cognitive Neuropsychology, 20*(3–6), 487–506.

Delazer, M., Ischebeck, A., Domahs, F., Zamarian, L., Koppelstaetter, F., Siedentopf, C. M., Kaufmann, L., Benke, T., & Felber, S. (2005). Learning by strategies and learning by drill – Evidence from an fMRI study. *Neuroimage, 25*(3), 838–849.

Dowker, A. (2006). What can functional brain imaging studies tell us about typical and atypical cognitive development in children? *Journal of Physiology (Paris), 99*(4–6), 333–341.

Eger, E., Sterzer, P., Russ, M. O., Giraud, A. L., & Kleinschmidt, A. (2003). A supramodal number representation in human intraparietal cortex. *Neuron, 37*(4), 719–725.

Evans, A. C., Collins, D. L., & Milner, B. (1992). An MRI-based stereotactic atlas from 250 young normal subjects. *Society for Neuroscience Abstracts, 18*, 408.

Fias, W., Lammertyn, J., Reynvoet, B., Dupont, P., & Orban, G. A. (2003). Parietal representation of symbolic and nonsymbolic magnitude. *Journal of Cognitive Neuroscience, 15*(1), 47–56.

Fulbright, R. K., Manson, S. C., Skudlarski, P., Lacadie, C. M., & Gore, J. C. (2003). Quantity determination and the distance effect with letters, numbers, and shapes: a functional MR imaging study of number processing. *American Journal of Neuroradiology, 24*(2), 193–200.

Gallistel, C. R. & Gelman, I. I. (2000). Non-verbal numerical cognition: from reals to integers. *Trends in Cognitive Science, 4*(2), 59–65.

Gerstmann, J. (1940). Syndrome of finger agnosia, disorientation for right and left, agraphia and acalculia. *Archives of Neurology and Psychiatry, 44*, 398–408.

Göbel, S. M., Johansen-Berg, H., Behrens, T., & Rushworth, M. F. (2004). Response-selection-related parietal activation during number comparison. *Journal of Cognitive Neuroscience, 16*(9), 1536–1551.

Gogtay, N., Giedd, J. N., Lusk, L., Hayashi, K. M., Greenstein, D., Vaituzis, A. C., Nugent, T. F., III, Herman, D. H., Clasen, L. S., Toga, A. W., Rapoport, J. L., & Thompson, P. M. (2004). Dynamic mapping of human cortical development during childhood through early adulthood. *Proceedings of the National Academy of Sciences of the United States of America, 101*(21), 8174–8179.

Grill-Spector, K., Henson, R., & Martin, A. (2006). Repetition and the brain: Neural models of stimulus-specific effects. *Trends in Cognitive Science, 10*(1), 14–23.

Gruber, O., Indefrey, P., Steinmetz, H., & Kleinschmidt, A. (2001). Dissociating neural correlates of cognitive components in mental calculation. *Cerebral Cortex, 11*(4), 350–359.

Henschen, S. E. (1919). Uber Sprach-, Musik- und Rechenmechanismen und ihre Lokalisationen im Großhirn. *Zeitschrift fuer die gesamte Neurologie und Psychiatrie, 52*, 273–298.

Henson, R. (2006). Forward inference using functional neuroimaging: dissociations versus associations. *Trends in Cognitive Science, 10*(2), 64–69.

Isaacs, E. B., Edmonds, C. J., Lucas, A. & Gadian, D. G. (2001). Calculation difficulties in children of very low birthweight: a neural correlate. *Brain, 124*, 1701–1707.

Ischebeck, A., Zamarian, L., Siedentopf, C., Koppelstaetter, F., Benke, T., Felber, S., & Delazer, M. (2006). How specifically do we learn? Imaging the learning of multiplication and subtraction. *Neuroimage, 30*(4), 1365–1375.

Kang, H. C., Burgund, E. D., Lugar, H. M., Petersen, S. E., & Schlaggar, B. L. (2003). Comparison of functional activation foci in children and adults using a common stereotactic space. *Neuroimage, 19*(1), 16–28.

Karmiloff-Smith, A. (1998). Development itself is the key to understanding developmental disorders. *Trends in Cognitive Science, 2*(10), 389–398.

Kaufmann, L., Koppelstaetter, F., Delazer, M., Siedentopf, C., Rhomberg, P., Golaszewski, S., Felber, S., & Ischebeck, A. (2005). Neural correlates of distance and congruity effects in a numerical Stroop task: An event-related fMRI study. *Neuroimage, 25*(3), 888–898.

Kawashima, R., Taira, M., Okita, K., Inoue, K., Tajima, N., Yoshida, H., Sasaki, T., Sugiura, M., Watanabe, J., & Fukuda, H. (2004). A functional MRI study of simple arithmetic – A comparison between children and adults. *Brain Research Cognitive Brain Research, 18*(3), 227–233.

Kucian, K., Loenneker, T., Dietrich, T., Martin, E. & von Aster, M. (2006). Impaired neural networks for approximate calculation in dyscalculic children: a fMRI study. *Behavior and Brain Function, 2*, 31.

Levy, L. M., Reis, I. L., & Grafman, J. (1999). Metabolic abnormalities detected by 1H-MRS in dyscalculia and dysgraphia. *Neurology, 53*(3), 639–641.

Maguire, E. A., Gadian, D. G., Johnsrude, I. S., Good, C. D., Ashburner, J., Frackowiak, R. S., & Frith, C. D. (2000). Navigation-related structural change in the hippocampi of taxi drivers. *Proceedings of the National Academy of Sciences of the United States of America, 97*(8), 4398–4403.

McCandliss, B. D., & Noble, K. G. (2003). The development of reading impairment: a cognitive neuroscience model. *Mental Retardation and Developmental Disabilities Research Review*, *9*(3), 196–204.

Menon, V., Rivera, S. M., White, C. D., Glover, G. H., & Reiss, A. L. (2000). Dissociating prefrontal and parietal cortex activation during arithmetic processing. *Neuroimage*, *12*(4), 357–365.

Molko, N., Cachia, A., Riviere, D., Mangin, J. F., Bruandet, M., Le Bihan, D., Cohen, L., & Dehaene, S. (2003). Functional and structural alterations of the intraparietal sulcus in a developmental dyscalculia of genetic origin. *Neuron*, *40*(4), 847–858.

Moyer, R. S. & Landauer, T. K. (1967). Time required for judgments of numerical inequality. *Nature*, *215*(109), 1519–1520.

Ochsner, K. N. & Lieberman, M. D. (2001). The emergence of social cognitive neuroscience. *American Psychologist*, *56*(9), 717–734.

Paulesu, E., McCrory, E., Fazio, F., Menoncello, L., Brunswick, N., Cappa, S. F., Cotelli, M., Cossu, G., Corte, F., Lorusso, M., Pesenti, S., Gallagher, A., Perani, D., Price, C., Frith, C. D., & Frith, U. (2000). A cultural effect on brain function. *Nature Neuroscience*, *3*(1), 91–96.

Peterson, B. S., Vohr, B., Kane, M. J., Whalen, D. H., Schneider, K. C., Katz, K. H., Zhang, H., Duncan, C. C., Makuch, R., Gore, J. C., & Ment, L. R. (2002). A functional magnetic resonance imaging study of language processing and its cognitive correlates in prematurely born children. *Pediatrics*, *110*(6), 1153–1162.

Piazza, M., Mechelli, A., Butterworth, B., & Price, C. J. (2002). Are subitizing and counting implemented as separate or functionally overlapping processes? *Neuroimage*, *15*(2), 435–446.

Piazza, M., Giacomini, E., Le Bihan, D., & Dehaene, S. (2003). Single-trial classification of parallel pre-attentive and serial attentive processes using functional magnetic resonance imaging. *Proceedings of Biological Science*, *270*(1521), 1237–1245.

Piazza, M., Izard, V., Pinel, P., Le Bihan, D., & Dehaene, S. (2004). Tuning curves for approximate numerosity in the human intraparietal sulcus. *Neuron*, *44*(3), 547–555.

Piazza, M., Pinel, P., Le Bihan, D., & Dehaene, S. (2007). A Magnitude Code Common to Numerosities and Number Symbols in Human Intraparietal Cortex. *Neuron*, *53*(2), 293–305.

Pinel, P., Le Clec, H. G., van de Moortele, P. F., Naccache, L., Le Bihan, D., & Dehaene, S. (1999). Event-related fMRI analysis of the cerebral circuit for number comparison. *Neuroreport*, *10*(7), 1473–1479.

Pinel, P., Dehaene, S., Riviere, D., & LeBihan, D. (2001). Modulation of parietal activation by semantic distance in a number comparison task. *Neuroimage*, *14*(5), 1013–1026.

Pinel, P., Piazza, M., Le Bihan, D., & Dehaene, S. (2004). Distributed and overlapping cerebral representations of number, size, and luminance during comparative judgments. *Neuron*, *41*(6), 983–993.

Poldrack, R. A. (2000). Imaging brain plasticity: conceptual and methodological issues – A theoretical review. *Neuroimage*, *12*(1), 1–13.

Poldrack, R. A. (2006). Can cognitive processes be inferred from neuroimaging data? *Trends in Cognitive Sciences*, *10*(2), 59–63.

Richter, W. & Richter, M. (2003). The shape of the fMRI BOLD response in children and adults changes systematically with age. *Neuroimage*, *20*(2), 1122–1131.

Rickard, T. C., Romero, S. G., Basso, G., Wharton, C., Flitman, S., & Grafman, J. (2000). The calculating brain: An fMRI study. *Neuropsychologia*, *38*(3), 325–335.

Rivera, S. M., Menon, V., White, C. D., Glaser, B., & Reiss, A. L. (2002). Functional brain activation during arithmetic processing in females with fragile X Syndrome is related to FMR1 protein expression. *Human Brain Mapping*, *16*(4), 206–218.

Rivera, S. M., Reiss, A. L., Eckert, M. A., & Menon, V. (2005). Developmental changes in mental arithmetic: Evidence for increased functional specialization in the left inferior parietal cortex. *Cerebral Cortex*, *15*(11), 1779–1790.

Roland, P. E. & Friberg, L. (1985). Localization of cortical areas activated by thinking. *Journal of Neurophysiology*, *53*(5), 1219–1243.

Rueckert, L., Lange, N., Partiot, A., Appollonio, I., Litvan, I., Le Bihan, D., & Grafman, J. (1996). Visualizing cortical activation during mental calculation with functional MRI. *Neuroimage, 3*(2), 97–103.

Schapiro, M. B., Schmithorst, V. J., Wilke, M., Byars, A. W., Strawsburg, R. H., & Holland, S. K. (2004). BOLD fMRI signal increases with age in selected brain regions in children. *Neuroreport, 15*(17), 2575–2578.

Schlaggar, B. L., Brown, T. T., Lugar, H. M., Visscher, K. M., Miezin, F. M., & Petersen, S. E. (2002). Functional neuroanatomical differences between adults and school-age children in the processing of single words. *Science, 296*(5572), 1476–1479.

Seron, X., & Fias, W. (2006). How images of the brain can constrain cognitive theory: the case of numerical cognition. *Cortex, 42*(3), 406–410; discussion 422–407.

Shaywitz, B. A., Shaywitz, S. E., Pugh, K. R., Mencl, W. E., Fulbright, R. K., Skudlarski, P., Constable, R. T., Marchione, K. E., Fletcher, J. M., Lyon, G. R., & Gore, J. C. (2002). Disruption of posterior brain systems for reading in children with developmental dyslexia. *Biological Psychiatry, 52*(2), 101–110.

Shuman, M. & Kanwisher, N. (2004). Numerical magnitude in the human parietal lobe: tests of representational generality and domain specificity. *Neuron, 44*(3), 557–569.

Stanescu-Cosson, R., Pinel, P., van De Moortele, P. F., Le Bihan, D., Cohen, L., & Dehaene, S. (2000). Understanding dissociations in dyscalculia: a brain imaging study of the impact of number size on the cerebral networks for exact and approximate calculation. *Brain, 123 (Pt 11)*, 2240–2255.

Talairach, J. & Tournoux, P. (1988). *Co-planar Stereotaxic Atlas of the Human Brain.* New York: Thieme.

Temple, E. & Posner, M. I. (1998). Brain mechanisms of quantity are similar in 5-year-old children and adults. *Proceedings of the National Academy of Sciences of the United States of America, 95*(13), 7836–7841.

Thomason, M. E., Burrows, B. E., Gabrieli, J. D., & Glover, G. H. (2005). Breath holding reveals differences in fMRI BOLD signal in children and adults. *Neuroimage, 25*(3), 824–837.

Turconi, E., Jemel, B., Rossion, B., & Seron, X. (2004). Electrophysiological evidence for differential processing of numerical quantity and order in humans. *Brain Research Cognitive Brain Research, 21*(1), 22–38.

Turkeltaub, P. E., Gareau, L., Flowers, D. L., Zeffiro, T. A., & Eden, G. F. (2003). Development of neural mechanisms for reading. *Nature Neuroscience, 6*(7), 767–773.

Venkatraman, V., Ansari, D., & Chee, M. W. (2005). Neural correlates of symbolic and non-symbolic arithmetic. *Neuropsychologia, 43*(5), 744–753.

Venkatraman, V., Siong, S. C., Chee, M. W., & Ansari, D. (2006). Effect of language switching on arithmetic: a bilingual FMRI study. *Journal of Cognitive Neuroscience, 18*(1), 64–74.

Verguts, T., Fias, W., & Stevens, M. (2005). A model of exact small-number representation. *Psychonomic Bulletin and Review, 12*(1), 66–80.

Walsh, V. (2003). A theory of magnitude: common cortical metrics of time, space and quantity. *Trends in Cognitive Science, 7*(11), 483–488.

Zorzi, M. & Butterworth, B. (1999). *A computational model of number comparison.* Paper presented at the *Twenty First Annual Conference of the Cognitive Science Society*, Mahwah, NJ.

3

A NUMBER SENSE ASSESSMENT TOOL FOR IDENTIFYING CHILDREN AT RISK FOR MATHEMATICAL DIFFICULTIES

NANCY C. JORDAN, JOSEPH GLUTTING, AND CHAITANYA RAMINENI

School of Education, University of Delaware, Newark, DE, 19716-2922, USA

Poor achievement in math can have serious educational and vocational consequences. Students with weak math skills at the end of middle school are less likely to graduate from college than are students who are strong in math (National Mathematics Advisory Panel, 2007). Competence in advanced math is important for success in college-level science courses and a wide range of vocations in the sciences (Sadler & Tai, 2007). Many students in US elementary schools do not develop foundations for success in algebra, and low-income learners lag far behind their middle-income peers (NAEP, 2007).

Fluency with math operations is a hallmark of mathematical learning in the early grades. Fluency is associated with foundational knowledge of key calculation principles (e.g., reciprocal relations among operations; Jordan et al., 2003a). Calculation fluency is necessary for math achievement at all levels – from solving simple whole number problems, to calculating with fractions, decimals and percentages, to solving algebraic equations. Even success with basic geometry depends on facility with calculation (e.g., calculating the angles of a triangle to add up to 180 degrees).

Dysfluent calculation is a signature characteristic of students with learning disabilities in math (Jordan, 2007). Recent research suggests that calculation deficiencies, from the first year of formal schooling onward, can be traced to fundamental weaknesses in understanding the meaning of numbers and number operations, or *number sense* (Gersten et al., 2005; Malofeeva et al., 2004). Weak number sense can result in poorly developed counting procedures, slow fact retrieval, and inaccurate computation, all characteristics of math learning disabilities (Geary et al., 2000; Jordan et al., 2003a, b). It is difficult to memorize arithmetic 'facts' by rote, without understanding how combinations relate to one another on a mental number line (Booth & Siegler, in press). Accurate and efficient counting procedures can lead to strong connections between a problem and its solution (Siegler & Shrager, 1984). It has been suggested that basic number sense is a circumscribed cognitive function and relatively independent from general memory, language and spatial knowledge (Gelman & Butterworth, 2005; Landerl et al., 2004). Although there is a high rate of co-occurrence between math and reading/language difficulties, specific math difficulties with normal development in other cognitive and academic areas are well documented (Jordan, 2007; Butterworth & Reigosa, 2007).

WHAT IS NUMBER SENSE?

Although number sense has been defined differently and sometimes is used loosely in connection with math (Gersten et al., 2005), researchers generally agree that number sense in the 3- to 6-year-old period involves interrelated abilities involving numbers and operations, such as subitizing (derived from the Latin word subitus, for sudden) quantities of 3 or less quickly, without counting; counting items in a set to at least five with knowledge that the final count word indicates how many are in the set; discriminating between small quantities (e.g., 4 is greater than 3 or 2 is less than 5); comparing numerical magnitudes (e.g., 5 is 2 more than 3) and transforming sets with totals of 5 or less by adding or taking away items. Arguably, number and associated operational knowledge is the most important area of mathematical learning in early childhood (Clements & Sarama, 2007). Weak number sense prevents children from benefiting from formal instruction in math (Baroody & Rosu, 2006; Griffin et al., 1994).

Most children bring considerable number sense to school, although there are clear individual differences often associated with social class and learning abilities (e.g., Dowker, 2005; Dowker, in press; Ginsburg & Russell, 1981; Ginsburg & Golbeck, 2004; Jordan et al., 1992). Nonverbal number sense is present in infancy (Mix et al., 2002). For example, preverbal infants can discriminate between two and three objects and are sensitive to ordinal relations (i.e., more vs. less; Starkey & Cooper, 1980). Infants also can keep track of the results of adding of removing objects from an array, suggesting sensitivity to number operations (Wynn, 1992). Early sensitivities to number have a neurological basis in the intraparietal sulcus

(IPS) regions of the brain and are the roots for learning symbol systems that represent number in preschool (e.g., number names, number symbols, counting; Berger et al., 2006). Atypicalities in IPS brain regions have been associated with specific impairments in mathematical operations (Isaacs et al., 2001).

Knowledge of the verbal number system is heavily influenced by experience or instruction (Geary, 1995; Levine et al., 1992). Case and Griffin (1990) report that number sense development is closely associated with children's home experiences with number concepts. Efforts to teach number sense to high-risk children in early childhood have resulted in significant gains on first-grade math outcomes compared to control groups (Griffin et al., 1994). Engaging young children in number activities (e.g., a mother asking her child to give her 3 spoons) and simple games (e.g., board games that emphasize one-to-one correspondences, counting and number lines) develop foundations and build number knowledge (Gersten et al., 2005).

COMPONENTS OF NUMBER SENSE

Counting: Counting is a crucial tool for learning about numbers and arithmetic operations (Baroody, 1987), and counting weaknesses have consistently been linked to mathematics difficulties (Geary, 2003). Most children develop knowledge of 'how to count' principles before they enter kindergarten (Gelman & Gallistel, 1978), including one-to-one correspondence (each item is counted only once), stable order (count words always proceed in the same order) and cardinality (the final word of a count indicates the number of items in a set). Typically, children learn the count sequence by rote and then map counting principles onto the sequence through their experiences with counting objects (Briars & Siegler, 1984). As children move through early childhood, they learn that items can be counted in any order (e.g., right to left or left to right), that sets do not have to be homogeneous, and that anything can be counted (e.g., the number of promises broken or the number of days in a week). They become increasingly flexible with counting, counting backward and by twos and fives. Children eventually acquire words for decades and learn rules for combining number words (e.g., combining 20 with 5 to make 25) (Ginsburg, 1989). Early difficulties in counting are precursors for later problems with math operations (Geary et al., 1999).

Number knowledge: Children as young as 4 years of age recognize and describe global differences in small quantities (Case & Griffin, 1990; Griffin, 2002, 2004). For example, they can tell which of two sets of objects has more or less. Although younger children rely on visual perception rather than on counting to make these judgments (Xu & Spelke, 2000), by 6 years of age most children incorporate their global quantity and counting schemas into a mental number line (Siegler & Booth, 2004). This overarching structure allows children to make better sense of their quantitative worlds (Griffin, 2002). Children gradually learn that numbers later in the counting sequence have larger quantities than earlier numbers. They come to see that numbers have magnitudes, such that 7 is bigger than 6 or that 5 is smaller than 8. Children use these skills in multiple contexts and eventually construct a linear representation of numerical magnitude, which allows them to learn place value and perform mental calculations. Number knowledge helps children think about mathematical problems, and its development reflects children's early experiences with number (Griffin et al., 1994; Saxe et al., 1987; Siegler & Booth, 2004). Middle-income children enter kindergarten with better-developed number knowledge than low-income children (Griffin et al., 1994; Jordan et al., 2006), and number knowledge is a strong predictor of math achievement in the early school years (Baker et al., 2002; Jordan et al., 2007).

Number Operations: The number knowledge and counting abilities that children acquire in early childhood are relevant to learning conventional math operations involving exact rather than approximate representations. Although preschoolers have limited success in performing verbally presented calculation problems, such as story problems ('Bob had 3 marbles. Jill gave him 2 more marbles. How many pennies does he have now?') and number combinations ('How much is 2 and 3?'), they are successful on nonverbal calculation tasks, which provide physical referents but do not require understanding of words and syntactic structures (Ginsburg & Russell, 1981; Hughes, 1986; Levine et al., 1992; Huttenlocher et al., 1994). Young children's success in solving nonverbal calculations requires children to hold and manipulate mental representations of numbers in working memory (Klein & Bisanz, 2000). Nonverbal calculation ability varies less across social classes than does the ability to solve verbal calculations (which clearly favors middle- over low-income children) (Jordan et al., 1992, 1994, 2006).

PREDICTABILITY OF NUMBER SENSE

Number sense predicts math outcomes in elementary school. A number knowledge test, first developed by Okamoto and Case (1996) and later tested by Baker et al. (2002), revealed strong predictability. The test, which assessed children's understanding of the magnitude concepts of 'smaller than' or 'bigger than' as well as knowledge of math operations, was given in the spring of kindergarten. The correlation with a math achievement criterion at the end of first grade was strong and significant. Clarke and Shinn (2004) also found that the ability to name numbers, to identify a missing number from a sequence of numbers, and to identify which of two numbers is larger predicts math outcomes at the end of first grade. Booth and Siegler (in press) report that the linearity of children's estimates on a number line is highly related to general math outcomes and that visual presentation of the magnitudes of addends and sums improves learning of number operations.

Although much of the research on number sense predictability is concerned with relatively near outcomes (e.g., kindergarten to first grade), we have found in our research lab (see more detailed discussion in the next section of this chapter) that number sense – even at the very beginning kindergarten – retains its predictive validity at least through the end of third grade (Jordan et al., 2007; Jordan et al., under review; Locuniak & Jordan, in press). Moreover, recent work (Duncan et al., 2007) suggests that the connection continues throughout the school years.

DEVELOPING A NUMBER SENSE BATTERY

Many math disabilities are not identified until middle school or later. In US schools, math interventions are much less common for early learners than are reading interventions (Jordan et al., 2002). To improve early identification of math problems, our research group (Jordan et al., 2006, 2007) developed a number sense battery for children from the beginning of US kindergarten to the middle of first grade (from approximately 5 to 6 years of age). The battery, developed as a part of a large longitudinal study of children's math, is based on the premise that number sense is of central importance to math learning and is guided by theoretically valid components of number sense. These components include counting, number knowledge and number operations. As noted earlier in this chapter, the components are closely linked to the skills children will need to acquire in formal math in elementary school. Reliability (alpha coefficient) of our core number sense battery ranged from 0.82 to 0.89 across the six time points. Our battery included the following tasks.

COUNTING AND NUMBER RECOGNITION

Children are assessed on counting skills and principles as well as their ability to recognize numbers. Children are asked to count to at least ten and allowed to restart counting only once but can self-correct at any time. Counting principles were adapted from Geary et al. (1999). For each item (after ruling out color blindness), children are shown a set of alternating yellow and blue dots. Then a finger puppet tells them he is learning how to count. The child is asked to indicate whether the puppet count is 'OK' or 'not OK.' Correct counting involves counting from left to right and counting from right to left. Unusual but correct counts involve counting the yellow dots first and then counting the blue dots or vice versa. For incorrect counts, the puppet counts from left to right but counts the first dot twice. For number recognition, children are asked to name a visually presented Arabic number.

NUMBER KNOWLEDGE

Number knowledge tasks were adapted from Griffin (2002). Given a number (e.g., 7), children are asked what number comes after that number and what number comes two numbers after that number. Given two numbers (e.g., 5 and 4), children are asked, which number is bigger or which number is smaller. Children also are shown visual arrays of three Arabic numbers (e.g., 6, 2 and 5), each placed on a point of an equilateral triangle and asked to identify which number is closer to the target number at the apex (e.g., 5).

NUMBER OPERATIONS

To assess number operations, we used three related tasks: Nonverbal calculation, number combinations and story problems.

On the nonverbal calculation task, adapted from Levine et al. (1992), the tester and child face each other with a 45 × 30 cm white mat in front of each and a box of 20 chips placed off to the side. The tester also has a box lid with an opening on the side. Three warm-up trials are given in which we engage the children in a matching task by placing a certain number of chips on the mat in a horizontal line, in view of the child and then covering the chips with the box lid. The child is asked to indicate how many chips are hidden, either with chips or by saying the number. After the warm-up, addition problems and subtraction problems are presented. The tester places a set of chips on her mat (in a horizontal line) and tells the child how many chips are on the mat. The chips are then covered with the box lid. Chips are either added or removed (through the side opening) one at a time. For each item, the children is asked to indicate how many chips are left hiding under the box, either by displaying the appropriate number of chips or giving a number word.

Addition and subtraction story problems and number combinations are presented orally, one at a time. The addition problems are phrased as follows: 'Jill has m pennies. Jim gives her n more pennies. How many pennies does Jill have now?,' while the subtraction problems are phrased: 'Mark has n cookies. Colleen takes away m of his cookies. How many cookies does Mark have now?' Number combinations are phrased as: 'How much is m and n?' and 'How much is n take away m?'

We used the battery to assess 400 US students in kindergarten (mean age = 5 years, 6 months at the beginning of the year). We followed more than 300 students through first grade and roughly 200 through third grade. About a third of the children were from low-income families. Children's number sense was assessed on six occasions, from the beginning of kindergarten through the middle of first grade. Math achievement was subsequently measured with the *Woodcock–Johnson Tests (WJ) of Achievement* (McGrew et al., 2007) on five occasions, from the end of first grade through the end of third grade.

KEY FINDINGS FROM THE CHILDREN'S
MATH LONGITUDINAL STUDY

Between the beginning of US kindergarten and the middle of first grade, we found three statistically distinct number sense growth trajectories (Jordan et al.,

2006, 2007): Children who start kindergarten at a high level and remain there; children who start kindergarten at a low to moderate level but start showing steep growth in the middle of the year; and children who start kindergarten at a low level and experience little growth. Low-income children were over represented in the latter low performing, low growth group and under represented in the other two groups.

Longitudinal analyses also revealed that number sense performance in US kindergarten, as well as number sense *growth*, accounts for 66% of the variance in first-grade math achievement (Jordan et al., 2007). Background characteristics of income status, gender, age and reading ability did not add explain variance in math achievement over and above number sense. Even at the beginning of kindergarten, number sense is highly related to end first-grade math achievement ($r = 0.70$). Moreover, the predictive value of kindergarten and first-grade number sense holds until at least the end of third grade or 8 to 9 years of age (Jordan et al., under review). Number sense predicted *rate* of math achievement between first and third grades as well as level of math performance at the end of third grade. We also found that least 80% of the time, children who meet state-defined math standards (as required by the US No Child Left Behind Law) have a higher-kindergarten number sense score than children who do not meet the standards.

We were particularly interested in how well early number sense predicts calculation fluency (Locuniak & Jordan, in press). Kindergarten number sense was a significant predictor of calculation fluency in elementary school, over and above age, reading and general cognitive competencies. Although facility with number combinations, number knowledge, and working memory capacity all were uniquely predictive, early facility with number combinations was the strongest single predictor of later calculation fluency.

STREAMLINING THE NUMBER SENSE SCREENING TOOL

As noted above, early number sense is highly predictive of important math outcomes in school. However, the instrument we used for the studies just described was a research tool with a relatively long administration time (more than 30 minutes in most cases). In 2007, we began work on the development of a shortened screening measure of number sense for 5 and 6 year olds. In the initial research battery, a third as many items were developed as the final number in the streamlined version. The final items were selected using Rasch item analyses, as well as a more subjective review of issues related to item bias. The exact number sense test items are presented in the Appendix.

Reliability: Several statistics are useful to describe a test's reliability. Among them are person and item separation indices culled from the Rasch model of Item Response Theory (Hambleton et al., 1991; Thissen & Wainer, 2001). In addition to the Rasch indices, the provision of internal-consistency reliabilities is recommended by the Standards for Educational and Psychological Testing (American Educational Research Association, 1999).

The person and item separation statistics in the Rasch measurement model provide statistical tools by which to evaluate the successful development of a variable and by which to assess the precision of the measurement (Harvey & Hammer, 1999; Wright & Stone, 1979). Respectively, person and item separation reliabilities were 0.80 and 0.99. The person separation statistic gives information on the test's capacity to distinguish among a sample of children on the basis of the total number of items answered correctly. Person separation reliabilities are equivalent to other measures of internal consistency and, accordingly, estimate the amount of error in measurement. Alternatively, item separation reliabilities indicate how well items define the variables being measured. The obtained estimate of 0.99 indicates that the items in the test are sufficiently separated from easy to hard to form variable lines that are complete and well spaced.

Cronbach's (1951) coefficient alpha was used to calculate internal-consistency reliability. Coefficient alpha provides a lower bound value of internal consistency and is considered to be a conservative estimate of a test's reliability (Gregory, 2007). The alpha coefficient was 0.84. As expected, this value exceeds the minimum, accepted internal-consistency level of 0.80 endorsed by leading measurement textbooks (Gregory, 2007; Reynolds et al., 2006; Salvia et al., 2007).

Validity: Strong construct validity is suggested whenever there is an appropriate pattern of convergent and divergent associations between an instrument and an external measure (Campbell, 1960; Reynolds et al., 2006; Thorndike, 1982). Because the number sense screen and the Woodcock–Johnson Achievement Test in math both purport to measure similar qualities, high correlations should occur between the measures. Likewise, scales measuring less similar qualities (e.g., reading achievement) would show lower correlations.

Table 3.1 shows correlations between scores on our number sense screen and the WJ-Math and reading (as measured by the TOWRE, Test of Word Reading Efficiency; Torgesen et al., 1999). Number sense scores were obtained on three occasions in US schools: (1) at the beginning of kindergarten, (2) the end of kindergarten and (3) at the middle of first grade. Criterion scores from the WJ-Math and TOWRE were obtained at the end of third grade.

TABLE 3.1   Correlations Between Scores on the Number Sense Screen and Wj-math (Math Achievement) and TOWRE (Reading Achievement)

Number sense	End of Grade 3 math achievement (WJ-Math)	End of Grade 3 reading achievement (TOWRE)
Beginning of kindergarten	0.65	0.33
End of kindergarten	0.63	0.29
Middle of first grade	0.62	0.40

All of the correlations were statistically significant ($p < 0.01$). With respect to the pattern of associations, the convergent correlations between the number sense screen and the WJ-Math were high, ranging from 0.62 to 0.65. The divergent associations between the number sense screen and the TOWRE were lower than the convergent associations, ranging from 0.29 to 0.40. All three convergent associations (number sense and math achievement) were much higher than the three divergent associations (number sense and reading achievement). Consequently, the pattern of convergent and divergent associations was appropriate and strongly support inferences of construct validity for the number sense screen.

Although the shortened number sense screening tool is still in development and we are collecting normative data in the US, it has good potential for identifying young children who are at risk for developing learning difficulties in math. At present, the measure is reliable, predicts math achievement in the early school years, and can be administered in less than 30 minutes.

INSTRUCTIONAL IMPLICATIONS

Although early interventions in math have received relatively little attention in the literature (Gersten et al., 2005), the available research offers insights for children who may be at risk for struggling in math. Number sense appears to be malleable and young children are likely to benefit from explicit help in representing, comparing and ordering small numbers as well as in joining and separating sets of 5 or less (National Council for Teachers of Mathematics, 2006; Fuson, 1992). Children should manipulate small quantities with sets of objects (e.g., as in the nonverbal calculation task) or their fingers (Jordan et al., in press) and then encouraged to imagine set transformations in their heads and to extract calculation principles (e.g., $2 + 3$ is the same as $3 + 2$ or $4 + 1$). Recent work by Siegler and colleagues (e.g., Booth and Siegler, in press) shows that activities as simple as board games that require children to move up and down a number list help children develop meaningful knowledge of quantities and number magnitudes and increase math achievement. Helping children build number sense early should give them the background they need to achieve in math during the school years. However, this assertion needs to be tested through randomized-controlled studies of number sense interventions. Our number sense instrument should be useful for reliably monitoring progress and responses to targeted interventions.

ACKNOWLEDGMENTS

The research presented in this chapter was supported by a grant US National Institute of Child Health and Human Development (HD36672) to Nancy C. Jordan.

REFERENCES

American Educational Research Association (1999). *Standards for Educational and Psychological Testing*. Washington, DC: American Educational Research Association.

Baker, S., Gersten, R., Flojo, J., Katz, R., Chard, D., & Clarke, B. (2002). *Preventing Mathematics Difficulties in Young Children: Focus on Effective Screening of Early Number Sense Delays (Technical Report No. 0305)*. Eugene, OR: Pacific Institutes for Research.

Baroody, A. J. (1987). The development of counting strategies for single-digit addition. *Journal for Research in Mathematics Education, 18*, 141–157.

Baroody, A. J. & Rosu, L. (2006). Adaptive expertise with basic addition and subtraction combinations – The number sense view. Paper presented at the *Meeting of the American Educational Research Association*, San Francisco, CA.

Berger, A., Tzur, G., & Posner, M. I. (2006). Infant babies detect arithmetic error. *Proceeding of the National Academy of Science USA. 103*(33), 12649–12653.

Booth, J. L. & Siegler, R. S. (in press). Numerical magnitude representations influence arithmetic learning. *Child Development*.

Briars, D. & Siegler, R. S. (1984). A featural analysis of preschoolers' counting knowledge. *Developmental Psychology, 20*(4), 607–618.

Butterworth, B. & Reigosa, V. (2007). Information processing deficits in dyscalculia. In D. Berch & M. Mazzocco (Eds.), *Why Is Math So Hard for Some Children?* (pp. 65–81). Baltimore, MD: Paul H. Brookes Publishing Co.

Campbell, D. L. (1960). Recommendations for APA test standards regarding construct, trait, and discriminant validity. *American Psychologist, 15*, 546–553.

Case, R. & Griffin, S. (1990). Child cognitive development: The role of central conceptual structures in the development of scientific and social thought. In E. A. Hauert (Ed.), *Developmental Psychology: Cognitive, Perceptuo-motor, and Neurological Perspectives* (pp. 193–230). North-Holland: Elsevier.

Clarke, B. & Shinn, M. R. (2004). A preliminary investigation into the identification and development of early mathematics curriculum-based measurement. *School Psychology Review, 33*(22), 234–248.

Clements, D. S. & Sarama J. (2007). Early childhood mathematics learning. In F. K. Lester (Ed.), *Second Handbook of Research on Mathematics Teaching and Learning* (pp. 461–555). New York: Information Age Publishing.

Cronbach, L. J. (1951). Coefficient alpha and the internal structure of tests. *Psychometrika, 16*, 297–334.

Duncan, G. J., Dowsett, C. J., Classens, A., Magnuson, K., Huston, A. C., Klebanov, P., Pagani, L., Feinstein, L., Engel, M., Brooks-Gunn, J., Sexton, H., Duckworth, K., & Japel, C. (2007). School readiness and later achievement. *Developmental Psychology, 43*, 1428–1446

Dowker, A. D. (2005). *Individual Differences in Arithmetic*. Hove: Psychology Press.

Dowker, A. D. (in press). Individual differences in preschoolers' numerical abilities. *Developmental Science*.

Fuson, K. C. (1992). Research on learning and teaching addition and subtraction of whole numbers. In G Leinhardt, R. T. Putnam, & R. A. Harttup (Eds.), *The Analysis of Arithmetic for Mathematics Teaching* (pp. 53–187). Hillsdale, NJ: Erlbaum.

Geary, D. C. (1995). Reflections of evolution and culture in children's cognition: Implications for mathematical development and instruction. *American Psychologist, 50*(1), 24–37.

Geary, D. C. (2003). Learning disabilities in arithmetic: Problem solving differences and cognitive deficits. In H. L. Swanson, K. Harris, & S. Graham (Eds.), *Handbook of Learning Disabilities* (pp. 199–212). New York: Guilford Publishers.

Geary, D. C., Hoard, M. K., & Hamson, C. O. (1999). Numerical and arithmetical cognition: Patterns of functions and deficits in children at risk for a mathematical disability. *Journal of Experimental Child Psychology, 74*, 213–239.

Geary, D. C., Hamson, C. O., & Hoard, M. K. (2000). Numerical and arithmetical cognition: A longitudinal study of process and concept deficits in children with learning disability. *Journal of Experimental Child Psychology, 77*, 236–263.

Gelman, R. & Butterworth, B. (2005). Number and language: how are they related? *Trends in Cognitive Sciences, 9*(1), 6–10.

Gelman, R. & Gallistel, C. R. (1978). *The child's Understanding of Number.* Cambridge, MA: Harvard University Press.

Gersten, R., Jordan, N. C., & Flojo, J. R. (2005). Early identification and interventions for students with mathematics difficulties. *Journal of Learning Disabilities, 38*, 293–304.

Ginsburg, H. P. (1989). *Children's Arithmetic.* Austin, TX: PRO-ED.

Ginsburg, H. P. & Goldbeck, S. L. (2004). Thoughts on the future of research on math and science education and learning. *Early Childhood Research Quarterly, 19*, 190–200.

Ginsburg, H. P. & Russell, R. L. (1981). Social class and racial influences on early mathematical thinking. *Monographs of the Society for Research in Child Development, 46*(6, Serial No. 193).

Gregory, R. J. (2007). *Psychological Testing: History, Principles, and Applications* (5th edn). Boston: Allyn and Bacon.

Griffin, S. (2002). The development of math competence in the preschool and early school years: Cognitive foundations and instructional strategies. In J. M. Roher (Ed.), *Mathematical Cognition* (pp. 1–32). Greenwich, CT: Information Age Publishing.

Griffin, S. (2004). Building number sense with number worlds: A mathematics program for young children. *Early Childhood Research Quarterly, 19*, 173–180.

Griffin, S., Case, R., & Siegler, R. S. (1994). Classroom lessons: Integrating cognitive theory and classroom practice. In K. McGilly (Ed.), *Rightstart: Providing the Central Conceptual Prerequisites for First Formal Learning of Arithmetic to Students at Risk for School Failure* (pp. 25–50). Cambridge, MA: MIT Press.

Hambleton, R. K., Swaminathan, H., & Rogers, H. J. (1991). *Fundamentals of Item Response Theory.* Newbury Park, CA: Sage.

Harvey, R. J. & Hammer, A. L. (1999). Item response theory. *The Counseling Psychologist, 27*, 353–383.

Hughes, M. (1986). *Children and Number.* Oxford: Blackwell.

Huttenlocher, J., Jordan, N. C., & Levine, S. C. (1994). A mental model for early arithmetic. *Journal of Experimental Psychology: General, 123*, 284–296.

Isaacs, E. B., Edmonds, C. J., Lucas, A., & Gadian, D. G. (2001). Calculation difficulties in children of very low birthweight: A neural correlate. *Brain, 124*, 1701–1707.

Jordan, N. C. (2007). Do words count? Connections between mathematics and reading difficulties. In D. Berch & M. Mazzocco (Eds.), *Why Is Math So Hard for Some Children?* (pp. 107–120). Baltimore, MD: Paul H. Brookes Publishing Co.

Jordan, N. C., Huttenlocher, J., & Levine, S. C. (1992). Differential calculation abilities in young children from middle- and low-income families. *Developmental Psychology, 28*, 644–653.

Jordan, N. C., Levine, S. C., & Huttenlocher, J. (1994). Development of calculation abilities in middle- and low-income children after formal instruction in school. *Journal of Applied Developmental Psychology, 15*, 223–240.

Jordan, N. C., Kaplan, D., & Hanich, L. B. (2002). Achievement growth in children with learning difficulties in mathematics: Findings of a two-year longitudinal study. *Journal of Educational Psychology, 94*(3), 586–597.

Jordan, N. C., Hanich, L. B., & Kaplan, D. (2003a). A longitudinal study of mathematical competencies in children with specific mathematics difficulties versus children with comorbid mathematics and reading difficulties. *Child Development, 74*(3), 834–850.

Jordan, N. C., Hanich, L. B., & Kaplan, D. (2003b). Arithmetic fact mastery in young children: A longitudinal investigation. *Journal of Experimental Child Psychology, 85*, 103–119.

Jordan, N. C., Kaplan, D., Olah, L., & Locuniak, M. N. (2006). Number sense growth in kindergarten: A longitudinal investigation of children at risk for mathematics difficulties. *Child Development, 77*, 153–175.

Jordan, N. C., Kaplan, D., Locuniak, M. N., & Ramineni, C. (2007). Predicting first-grade math achievement from developmental number sense trajectories. *Learning Disabilities Research and Practice*, *22*(1), 36–46.

Jordan, N. C., Kaplan, D., Ramineni, C., & Locuniak, M. N. (in press). Development of number combination skill in the early school years: When do fingers help? *Developmental Science*.

Jordan, N. C., Kaplan, D., Ramineni, C., & Locuniak, M. N. (under review). *Early Number Sense Predicts Performance and Growth in Elementary School Math: Results from a Sequential Growth Curve Model.*

Klein, J. S. & Bisanz, J. (2000). Preschoolers doing arithmetic: The concepts are willing but the working memory is weak. *Canadian Journal of Experimental Psychology*, *54*(2), 105–115.

Landerl, K., Bevan, A., & Butterworth, B. (2004). Developmental dyscalculia and basic numerical capacities: A study of 8–9 year old students. *Cognition*, *93*, 99–125.

Levine, S. C., Jordan, N. C., & Huttenlocher, J. (1992). Development of calculation abilities in young children. *Journal of Experimental Child Psychology*, *53*, 72–103.

Locuniak, M. N. & Jordan, N. C. (in press). Using kindergarten number sense to predict calculation fluency in second grade. *Journal of Learning Disabilities*.

Malofeeva, E., Day, J., Saco, X., Young, L., & Ciancio, D. (2004). Construction and evaluation of a number sense test with head start children. *Journal of Educational Psychology*, *96*(4), 648–659.

McGrew, K. S., Schrank, F. A., & Woodcock, R. W. (2007). *Woodcock–Johnson III Normative Update*. Rolling Meadows, IL: Riverside Publishing.

Mix, K. S., Huttenlocher, J., & Levine, S. C. (2002). Multiple cues for quantification in infancy: Is number one of them? *Psychological Bulletin*, *128*(2), 278–294.

NAEP (2007). Retrieved November 15, 2007, from http://nces.ed.gov/nationsreportcard.

National Council for Teachers of Mathematics (2006). *Curriculum Focal Points*. Reston, VA: National Council for Teachers of Mathematics.

National Mathematics Advisory Panel (2007). Strengthening math education through research. Retrieved September 9, 2007 from www.ed.gov/MathPanel.

Okamoto, Y. & Case, R. (1996). Exploring the microstructure of children's central conceptual structures in the domain of number. *Monographs of the Society for Research in Child Development*, *61*, 27–59.

Reynolds, C. R., Livingston, R. B., & Willson, V. (2006). *Measurement and Assessment in Education*. Boston: Pearson.

Sadler, P. M. & Tai, R. H. (2007). The two high-school pillars supporting college science. *Science*, *317*, 457–458.

Salvia, J., Ysseldyke, J. E., & Bolt, S. (2007). *Assessment in Special and Inclusive Education* (10th edn). Boston: Houghton Mifflin.

Saxe, G. B., Guberman, S. R., Gearhart, M., Gelman, R., Massey, C. M., & Rogoff, B. (1987). Social processes in early number development. *Monographs of the Society for Research in Child Development*, *52*(2).

Siegler, R. S. & Booth, J. L. (2004). Development of numerical estimation in young children. *Child Development*, *75*(2), 428–444.

Siegler, R. S. & Shrager, J. (1984). Strategy choice in addition and subtraction: How do children know what to do? In C. Sophian (Ed.), *Origins of Cognitive Skills* (pp. 229–293). Hillsdale, NJ: Erlbaum.

Starkey, P. & Cooper, R. G. (1980). Perceptions of numbers by human infants. *Science*, *210*, 1033–1035.

Thissen, D. & Wainer, H. (Eds.) (2001). *Test Scoring*. Hillsdale, NJ: Lawrence Erlbaum.

Thorndike, R. L. (1982). *Applied Psychometrics*. Boston: Houghton Mifflin.

Torgesen, J. K., Wagner, R. K., & Rashotte, C. A. (1999). *TOWRE, Test of Word Reading Efficiency*. Austin, TX: PRO-ED.

Wright, B. & Stone, M. (1979). *Best Test Design*. Chicago: MESA Press.

Wynn, K. (1992). Addition and subtraction by human infants. *Nature, 27*, 749–750.

Xu, F. & Spelke, E. (2000). Large number discrimination in 6-month-old infants. *Cognition, 74*, B1–B11.

APPENDIX

The streamlined number sense screening tool (N = 33 items).

(Write 1 for correct; 0 for incorrect)

Give the child a picture with 5 stars in a line. Say: '*Here are some stars. I want you to count each star. Touch each star as you count.*' When the child is finished counting, ask, '*How many stars are on the paper?*'

1. Enumerated 5 ____
2. Indicated there were 5 stars were on the paper ____

Say: '*I want you to count as high as you can. But I bet you're a very good counter, so I'll stop you after you've counted high enough, OK?*'

Allow children to count up to 10. If they don't make any mistakes, record '10.' Record the highest-correct number they counted up to without error.

3. Write in last correct number spoken ____
   Child counted up to 10 without error ____

Show the child a line of 5 alternating blue and yellow dots printed on a paper. Say: '*Here are some yellow and blue dots. This is Dino* (show a finger puppet), *and he would like you to help him play a game. Dino is going to count the dots on the paper, but he is just learning how to count and sometimes he makes mistakes. Sometimes he counts in ways that are OK but sometimes he counts in ways that are not OK and that are wrong. It is your job to tell him after he finishes if it was OK to count the way he did or not OK. So, remember you have to tell him if he counts in a way that is OK or in a way that is not OK and wrong. Do you have any questions?*'

Trial type	Response		
4. Left to right	*OK*	Not OK	____
5. Right to left	*OK*	Not OK	____
6. Yellow then blue	*OK*	Not OK	____
7. Double First	*OK*	Not OK	____

For items 8 through 11, point to each number that is printed on a separate card and say: '*What number is this?*'

8. 13 ____
9. 37 ____
10. 82 ____

11. 124 ___
12. What number comes right after 7? ___
13. What number comes two numbers after 7? ___
14. Which is bigger: 5 or 4? ___
15. Which is bigger: 7 or 9? ___
16. Which is smaller: 8 or 6? ___
17. Which is smaller: 5 or 7? ___
18. Which number is closer to 5: 6 or 2? ___

Say: '*We are going to play a game with these chips. Watch carefully.*' Place two chips on your mat. '*See these, there are 2 chips.*' Cover the chips and put out another chip. '*Here is one more chip.*' Before the transformation say, '*Watch what I do. Now make yours just like mine or just tell me how many chips are hiding under the box.*' Add/remove chips one at a time. Items 19 to 22 are the nonverbal calculations.

19. 2 + 1 ___
20. 4 + 3 ___
21. 3 + 2 ___
22. 3 − 1 ___

Say: '*I'm going to read you some number questions and you can do anything you want to help you find the answer. Some questions might be easy for you and others might be hard. Don't worry if you don't get them all right. Listen carefully to the question before you answer.*'

23. Jill has 2 pennies. Jim gives her 1 more penny. How many pennies does Jill have now? ___
24. Sally has 4 crayons. Stan gives her 3 more crayons. How many crayons does Sally have now? ___
25. Jose has 3 cookies. Sarah gives him 2 more cookies. How many cookies does Jose have now? ___
26. Kisha has 6 pennies. Peter takes away 4 of her pennnies. How many pennies does Kisha have now? ___
27. Paul has 5 oranges. Maria takes away 2 of his oranges. How many oranges does Paul have now? ___
28. How much is 2 and 1? ___
29. How much is 3 and 2? ___
30. How much is 4 and 3? ___
31. How much is 2 and 4? ___
32. How much is 7 take away 3? ___
33. How much is 6 take away 4? ___

4

THE ESSENCE OF EARLY CHILDHOOD MATHEMATICS EDUCATION AND THE PROFESSIONAL DEVELOPMENT NEEDED TO SUPPORT IT

BARBRINA B. ERTLE[1], HERBERT P. GINSBURG[1], MARIA I. CORDERO[2], TRACY M. CURRAN[1], LESLIE MANLAPIG[1], AND MELISSA MORGENLANDER[1]

[1]*Department of Human Development, Teachers College, Columbia University, New York, NY 10027, USA*
[2]*New York City's Administration for Children's Services, New York, NY 10038, USA*

Many events occurring over the last 25 years or so have influenced the way in which the field of early childhood education (ECE) views what is meant by 'mathematics' and how it should be taught to young children (usually ages 3, 4, and 5), at least in the US. This chapter begins by describing several social, political, and research influences that have produced a dramatic change in both the perception and the reality of early math education (EME) in the US. Then the paper shows how the new view of EME requires reconceptualizing the mathematics that should be taught to young children and how it should be taught. Implementing the new EME in turn requires new approaches to professional development. We describe one such approach that we employed with a group of teachers who were attempting to implement the *Big Math for Little Kids* curriculum (Ginsburg et al., 2003) at a publicly funded early care and education agency in New York City. We show how that experience affected the group's attitudes, beliefs, and behaviors and discuss the implications for supporting focused professional development.

SOCIAL, POLITICAL, AND RESEARCH INFLUENCES

In 1986, the National Association for the Education of Young Children (NAEYC) issued a position statement on *Developmentally Appropriate Practice in Early Childhood Programs Serving Children from Birth Through Age 8* (Bredekamp & Copple, 1986) that deeply shaped the thinking of ECE policy-makers, administrators and practitioners in the US. The document strongly opposed the 1980's trend of increased formal instruction for young children and instead advocated 'developmentally appropriate' practice (DAP), in which teachers do not lecture or verbally instruct, but instead serve as guides or facilitators. DAP involves providing children with a rich environment and utilizing teachable moments to extend learning. Furthermore, mathematical activities were mostly considered developmentally inappropriate, except when they were integrated with activities such as building with blocks or playing with sand or water.

The NAEYC position statement had a profound impact on ECE in the US (although more explicit early childhood mathematics instruction was employed elsewhere, e.g., Aubrey 1997). The definition of DAP was quickly incorporated into policy. For example, in October 1986, the New York City Agency for Child Development (ACD) used the NAEYC position statement to create a program assessment instrument to assess DAP in over 350 center-based child care centers in New York City.

However, as the century turned, important political and social tensions were brewing in the US that would have a critical effect on ECE. For example, the federal 'No Child Left Behind' legislation (2001) strengthened accountability requirements for the academic achievement of elementary and secondary students. And the country had also become engaged in school reform driven by standards set not only by professional organizations but also by the federal and state governments.

Of equal importance was research on cognition, learning, and child development during the last half of the 20th century. In 1999, the National Research Council commissioned the Committee on Early Childhood Pedagogy to review behavioral and social science research that had clear implications for the education of young children. The findings from this extensive report – *Eager to Learn: Educating our Preschoolers* – indicated that young children were more capable learners than the current practices reflected and that more challenging educational practices in the preschool years could have a positive impact on school learning (Bowman et al., 2001).

For example, considerable research (Ginsburg et al., 2006) has shown that young children develop a relatively powerful 'informal' mathematics before they enter school. They can competently deal with some very abstract ideas

(Ginsburg & Ertle, 2008), such as cardinality (Gelman & Gallistel, 1986) and addition (Brush, 1978; Groen & Resnick, 1977). Indeed, contrary to some interpretations, Piaget did not propose that young children were totally 'concrete' in their thinking. In fact, Piaget claimed that in many respects young children were overly abstract (Piaget & Inhelder, 1969). Taken as a whole, contemporary research suggests that young children are capable of learning more challenging and abstract mathematics than are usually assumed. It is therefore not necessarily developmentally inappropriate to engage in EME (although like anything else, the teaching of early mathematics can be done badly).

Research has shown that not only are children capable of learning challenging mathematics but doing so can be useful, and indeed essential, for subsequent education (Bowman et al., 2001). Recently, Duncan et al. (2007) showed that early mathematics skills are even more powerful predictors of later school success than reading abilities. Research has also shown that early intervention programs can be effective in reducing achievement disparities in mathematics (e.g., Dowker, 2001; Reynolds, 1995), suggesting that beginning instruction as early as possible could potentially reduce or prevent later mathematical difficulties and the need for remediation. EME can play a major role in preparing children for later success in school.

In 2000, the National Council of Teachers of Mathematics (NCTM) responded to research findings like these by including pre-kindergarten (pre-k) in its newest Standards document, *Principles and Standards for School Mathematics*. In 2002, NAEYC partnered with NCTM on a joint position statement which outlined recommendations for the teaching of mathematics in the pre-k classroom (NAEYC/NCTM, 2002). Like earlier NAEYC position papers, the statement endorsed promoting learning through play in rich environments, utilizing teachable moments to extend learning, and even adult-guided learning experiences like theme-based projects. But the document also took the important, and to some, radical position of stating that these types of learning experiences are not enough. The teaching of mathematics needs also to involve an organized curriculum presenting deep mathematical ideas in a coherent, developmental sequence that utilizes and builds on children's prior learning and experiences.

Together, the NAEYC/NCTM position statement and the NCTM preschool standards, based as they were on the research literature, then set the groundwork for the design of developmentally appropriate early mathematics curricula in the US, including *Number Worlds* (Griffin, 2000), *Pre-K Mathematics* (Klein et al., 2002), *Big Math for Little Kids* (Ginsburg et al., 2003), *Building Blocks* (Sarama & Clements, 2004), and a Head Start curriculum (Sophian, 2004). Other countries have also seen the recent emergence of early mathematics curricula and intervention programs (Dowker, 2001; Kaufmann et al., 2003; Van de Rijt & Van Luit, 1998; Young-Loveridge, 2004).

In April 2002, the Good Start, Grow Smart initiative – the early education reform companion of the No Child Left Behind Act (2001) – called for federally funded programs to develop early learning goals that specified the skills and competencies that preschool children should possess before starting school. The initiative is intended to stimulate increased attention to the teaching of mathematics, among other subjects.

But content standards, goals, and curricula exert effects beyond expectations for children. They also change what we require of practitioners. The new policies – which represent a radical shift in perspective for many preschool teachers and ECE professionals – require teachers to engage in a more rigorous, intentional, and organized approach to early childhood mathematics education than was previously employed. This in turn requires extensive professional development: the quality of classroom practice is significantly related to teachers' education and training (Pianta et al., 2005). Yet the educational background of the ECE workforce in the US is weak – only 20–30% of center-based preschool teachers hold a bachelor's degree (Brandon & Martinez-Beck, 2006). Therefore, some federal and state programs now require higher degrees of preparation for their early childhood practitioners (Martinez-Beck & Zaslow, 2006).

In brief, new research on children's abilities and social pressures have resulted in a serious movement in the US to raise standards and expectations for EME, to create new programs of EME, to enhance those already in place, and to provide a teaching force that can implement the programs effectively.

As professionals attempt to implement EME on a wide scale, especially for low-income children, several challenges arise that must be successfully addressed if we are to achieve our goals. This chapter describes those challenges and the means for meeting them. We first discuss the *content* of EME. It is much deeper, wider, and more abstract than ordinarily assumed. Next we examine the several *components* of early mathematics which are now recommended. EME involves far more than letting children play with rich materials. We show how necessary educational activities include free play, the teachable moment, projects, and curriculum. The last of these is the most poorly understood, but potentially the most powerful (and still developmentally appropriate). The nature of *desirable* mathematics *teaching* for little children is also poorly understood. We show that in some ways it is similar to teaching at any grade level. Given our analyses of the mathematics to be taught, the major components of EME, and good teaching, we then examine teachers' *conceptions* about EME. We show that they tend to favor social and emotional development over academic subjects such as mathematics, and many are resistant to the EME movement. But these conceptions are linked to content knowledge and are entangled with socioeconomic status (SES). Then we consider the *quality* of current EME teaching and teachers' readiness to teach mathematics. We show that current teaching practices are often very poor and that considerable professional development is required to improve them. We discuss key features of *professional development* that have been shown to be useful. To illustrate the challenges of creating and implementing a program of professional development for poorly trained early childhood teachers in an inner-city setting, we describe and discuss an example, the *Big Math for Little Kids* professional development program conducted at a city-funded ECE agency in New York City. Finally, we discuss the *implications* of our findings and provide recommendations for helping a district or an agency set up a plan for professional development in EME.

THE CONTENT OF EARLY MATHEMATICS

In many of today's early childhood classrooms and day care centers, children's exposure to mathematics content is fairly narrow, often limited to the learning of small numbers and simple shapes (Balfanz, 1999). However, EME should not be limited to such topics. The leading professional organizations now recommend that EME involve 'big ideas' of mathematics in the areas of number, geometry, measurement, and algebra – particularly pattern (NAEYC/NCTM, 2002; NCTM, 2000). These areas encompass some very deep mathematics, even at the level appropriate for young children (Ginsburg & Ertle, 2008). Number, for example, includes such concepts as the counting words ('one, two, three,...'), the ordinal positions ('first, second, third,...'), the idea of cardinal value (how many are there?), and the various operations on number like addition and subtraction. Even if we examine only elements of number commonly presented in today's early childhood classrooms, the depth of the mathematics can be made evident. Consider the counting words and enumeration (determining how many).

Before we can determine 'how many' are in a group of objects, we first need to know the counting words (in English, 'one, two, three,...'). In most languages, the first ten number words or so are completely arbitrary, but beyond that they assume a pattern, as most languages use a base-ten system to organize numbers. Consequently, despite the need to memorize the first ten numbers, learning to count is not merely an act of memorization. It involves learning the building blocks of an elegant pattern, derived from the base ten system, that once understood, permits counting to very high numbers with little additional memorization. For example, the counting words are organized into groups of tens and ones, and the names for the tens are derived from the names of the units. Once the names for the tens (ten, twenty, thirty,...) are known, the unit words (one, two, three,...) can easily be appended. The result is a simple and elegant pattern, which is even simpler and more elegant in East Asian languages (Miller & Parades, 1996). However, when children first tackle the act of counting, the very elements that make the counting system so simple to adults are not yet known. Children must grapple with memorizing the first set of numbers and with trying to understand why a fixed order is required before its necessity and utility become apparent in the elegance of the system.

Once the counting words are known, they can then be used to enumerate, or 'count' a group of objects. Enumeration also entails a number of underlying complexities that many adults take for granted. One is the idea that a group of things to be counted can contain any variety of things – real or imagined; they do not have to be limited to similar objects, like the set of three red circles that children are commonly presented with. But possibly the most difficult idea for a child to grapple with when counting a set of objects is that the numbers do not specifically name the items being counted; instead they describe the cardinal value of the items. So when counting a set of three objects – a ball, a blue car, and a wood block – you may point to the ball and say 'one,' the car and say 'two', the block and say 'three,' but you could just as easily begin counting with the block. A child must come to understand that pointing to the objects and saying 'one, two, three' is different in a crucial respect from pointing to them and saying 'round,' 'blue,' and 'wood.' Names designate objects; counting words refer to quantity.

And that is just the beginning of the depth of the ideas found within the domain of number. The other areas of mathematics contain equally deep ideas and complexities. Early mathematics is both basic and deep. And as we have seen, young children can deal with ideas like these, even without explicit instruction (Ginsburg et al., 2006).

THE DIFFERENT COMPONENTS OF EARLY MATHEMATICS

If early mathematics is deep, how should it be taught? A new NAEYC guide clarifies guidelines for DAP (Copple & Bredekamp, 2006): 'The idea that there is very little or no structure in a DAP classroom is a misconception. Again, in reality the opposite is true. To be developmentally appropriate, a program must be thoughtfully structured to build on and advance children's competence' (p. 60). The issue then arises as to the form this structure should take.

Drawing in part on the Joint Position Statement (NAEYC/NCTM, 2002), we propose five levels of classroom structure necessary for promoting mathematics learning: a rich environment, play, the teachable moment, projects, and curriculum.

The first is the *environment*. The preschool classroom (or 'day care center' – we use the terms synonymously) should contain a rich variety of materials that can afford mathematics and other learning. It should be divided into areas such as blocks, water table, and science table which encourage children's play, exploration, and discovery. There has never been much controversy about the need for a rich environment. Widespread agreement on this requirement has resulted in the extensive use of the *Early Childhood Environment Rating Scale (ECERS)* (Harms et al., 1998), which mainly provides a rating of the quality of the preschool classroom environment. But a rich environment by itself is not enough. The crucial factor is not just what the environment makes possible, but what children *do* in a rich environment.

The second important component of EME is *play*. We know that children do indeed learn a good deal of everyday mathematics on their own (Seo & Ginsburg, 2004). Play provides valuable opportunities to explore and to undertake activities than can be surprisingly sophisticated from a mathematical point of view (Ginsburg, 2006), especially in block play (Hirsch, 1996). Play is essential for children's intellectual development generally and for mathematics learning in particular. But play is not enough. Children need experiences beyond the play to help them learn even more – especially how to communicate about their experiences and how to see them in explicit mathematical terms. Consequently, some degree of adult guidance is necessary.

The third component of EME is the *teachable moment*, a form of adult guidance that enjoys widespread acceptance in the preschool world. The teachable moment involves the teacher's careful observation of children's play in order to identify the spontaneously emerging situation that can be exploited to promote learning. The Creative Curriculum program (Dodge et al., 2002), which is extremely popular in the US, relies on use of the teachable moment.

No doubt, the teachable moment, accurately perceived and suitably addressed, can provide a superb learning experience for the child. But there are good reasons to believe that in practice the teachable moment is not an effective educational method or policy. First, most preschool teachers spend little time in the careful observation necessary to perceive such moments. Teachers tend to manage behavior during free play (Kontos, 1999) or to spend very little time with children during free play (Seo & Ginsburg, 2004); in practice, teachers do not even attempt to exploit teachable moments. Second, it is very hard to know what to do when such moments arise, especially in the unlikely event that a teacher is able to recognize the deep mathematical issues with which many children may engage. The teachable moment demands considerable and rapid creativity – a quality in short supply in all professions. It therefore seems grossly unfair to expect teachers to rely on the exploitation of teachable moments as the primary component of mathematics education. Third, extensive reliance on the teachable moment is an impractical educational policy. How can a teacher manage all the teachable moments (even if she were able to notice them) that might arise among the 15 or 20 or 25 children in a classroom during the course of a year? The task seems virtually impossible and would seem to be a less than ideal way of responding to young children's intellectual needs. In brief, exploiting the teachable moment is wonderful if it can be done, but usually teachers do not try to notice teachable moments, could not respond effectively to such moments even if noticed, and could not manage all those that could be noticed.

A fourth component involves *projects* (Katz & Chard, 1989). Projects are intended to engage children in extensive teacher initiated and guided explorations of complex topics related to the everyday world, like figuring out how to create a map of the classroom. A project of this type can involve consideration of measurement, space, perspective, representation, and a whole host of mathematical and other ideas (e.g., scientific) which have very practical application and appeal. They can help children learn that making sense of real-life problems can be stimulating and enjoyable.

Although projects can be enormously effective, they are not sufficient unto themselves:

> Teachers should ensure that the mathematics experiences woven throughout the curriculum follow logical sequences, allow depth and focus, and help children move forward in knowledge and skills. The curriculum should not become… a grab bag of any mathematics-related experiences that seem to relate to a theme or project. Rather, concepts should be developed in a coherent, planful manner (NAEYC/NCTM, 2002, p. 10).

Some kind of 'intentional curriculum' (Klein & Knitzer, 2006) is therefore necessary. Direct, intentional literacy instruction is particularly important in supporting achievement gains for low-SES children (Hamre & Pianta, 2005); the same is likely to be true for EME.

A mathematics *curriculum*, the fifth component, involves a sequence of planned activities designed to help children progress through the learning of key mathematical ideas throughout the year. The *Big Math for Little Kids* curriculum (Ginsburg et al., 2003), which provides the illustrative material for this paper, engages children first in learning key concepts of number, then shape, pattern, measurement, operations on number, and then space. Activities are offered for each day of the school year. Within each of the larger topics, the activities are arranged in order of difficulty, as indicated by research on the developmental trajectories of children's mathematics learning. Thus, in the case of number concepts, children first begin to learn number words, then encounter concepts of cardinal number, representation, and next ordinal number, in that rough order. Later activities revisit earlier concepts, for example, as when shape activities involve analysis of shapes into numbers of sides, and practice in several activities (like counting) is provided throughout the year. Research on the curriculum's effectiveness is currently underway.

In brief, EME involves a hierarchy of components. Adults provide the first two but do not intervene directly in them: a rich environment and the opportunity to play. But adults do take a more direct role in the next three components, the teachable moment, the project approach, and especially the curriculum. Consequently, the success of these components depends on the quality of teaching.

WHAT IS GOOD EARLY MATHEMATICS TEACHING?

Quality teaching in preschool resembles good teaching in the early elementary grades. The best preschool programs are those in which children are systematically, regularly, and frequently engaged in a mix of teacher-led and child-initiated activities that enhance the development of knowledge and skills (Barnett & Belfield, 2006). Also, teachers in quality classrooms show familiarity with children's academic needs, are sensitive toward individual children, and modify lessons and activities to fit the emotional and the academic needs of their students (Rimm-Kaufman et al., 2005). They also tend to promote children's learning through scaffolding and support and offer appropriate questioning and feedback (Rimm-Kaufman et al., 2005). Good teachers also prepare carefully, understand the mathematics they teach (Ma, 1999), motivate their students with games and interesting activities, employ useful materials and manipulatives and exploit their potentials for teaching ideas (Williams & Kamii, 1986), possess the pedagogical content knowledge necessary for implementing lessons effectively (Shulman, 2000), encourage language (Klibanoff et al., 2006) and metacognition (Bodrova & Leong, 1996), and blend formative assessment with teaching (Bransford et al., 1998). Good teachers also assign children to appropriate size groups – whole class, small group, and individual – depending on the nature of the activity.

Although early mathematics teaching has seldom been studied, perhaps because it is seldom done, quality teaching of young children is likely to have many of the characteristics identified in the context of elementary education.

TEACHERS' CONCEPTIONS ABOUT EME

Given that ECE has not until recently emphasized the systematic teaching of mathematics, many teachers, administrators, and policymakers have not had to think about what it means to teach mathematical content. Perhaps this explains why many EC teachers believe that focusing on social and emotional development is most appropriate for young children and that academic subjects, such as mathematics, are less important (Ackerman & Barnett, 2005; Graham et al., 1997; Kowalski et al., 2001; Lee & Ginsburg, 2007; Wesley & Buysse, 2003). Many early childhood educators think that it is developmentally inappropriate to teach children numbers and alphabet, to engage them in direct instruction, or to require them to participate in an activity. Play and self-directed activities are emphasized as the overarching principles of ECE. Many early childhood practitioners believe that teachers should intervene as little as possible and allow children to explore and play without adult guidance or support (Bowman, 2001). This view may have resulted in part from overly enthusiastic acceptance of the early NAEYC position paper (Bredekamp & Copple, 1986).

But other beliefs not necessarily related to the issue of DAP also play a role in teachers' conceptions and attitudes toward early mathematics teaching. For example, we have observed many pre-k teachers and administrators to believe that their role is simply to 'prepare' children to learn math but not to really teach math. They believe that 'real' learning begins in elementary school. Beliefs like these have a strong influence on EME.

Teachers' content knowledge also plays a role in their beliefs. Early elementary teachers who seem to understand the mathematics they teach tend to have more optimistic expectations of their students' knowledge of mathematics than do teachers who are not comfortable teaching mathematics (White et al., 2004). And it appears that many early childhood teachers are quite uncomfortable teaching early mathematics.

Socioeconomic status of teacher and child also plays a role in teacher beliefs. Pre-k teachers of low-income children are more likely to place a high priority on academic learning and working toward math and literacy goals whereas teachers of middle-SES children are more likely to value social development (Lee & Ginsburg, 2007). Many early childhood teachers, especially those from middle-SES backgrounds, have been trained *not* to teach content in explicit ways, but rather to focus on the social–emotional functioning of the children (Kowalski et al., 2001).

Teachers' beliefs about teaching practices are also influenced by their experiences working with children and their families (Williams, 1996). In this context, it does not seem surprising that the teachers of low-SES children favor structured and deliberate mathematics instruction (Lee & Ginsburg, 2007). 'Like it or not, their parents insist on this and so do many politicians' (Ginsburg & Ertle, 2008, p. 3). Children from low-income families begin kindergarten a year to a year and a half behind their middle-class peers so there is more pressure on low-SES teachers to transform their students' education and improve their knowledge (Stipek, 2006).

In summary, many early childhood teachers believe that teaching mathematics is developmentally inappropriate for various reasons. This is an important obstacle to overcome in implementing effective EME.

HOW GOOD IS EARLY MATHEMATICS TEACHING? ARE TEACHERS READY FOR IT?

Although we have some ideas about what EME should entail in terms of content and components, little is known about how mathematics is actually being taught in preschool classrooms. The small amount of available research suggests that current preschool mathematics teaching is not at the level needed.

Childcare teachers teach mathematics in minimal, unconnected, and sporadic ways (Graham et al., 1997). Preschool classrooms generally provide moderately high levels of emotional support but fairly low levels of instructional support, especially with regard to concept development and feedback (La Paro et al., 2004). In fact, Pianta and La Paro (2003) characterize EC environments as being 'socially positive but instructionally passive' (p. 28). We have already shown that preschool teachers seldom acknowledge, let alone build on, mathematical 'teachable moments' that come up during their interactions with children (Kontos, 1999; Seo & Ginsburg, 2004).

In addition, mathematics may be taught differently in classrooms of low-SES children than that of higher-SES children. For example, teachers serving economically disadvantaged students often devote less time and emphasis to higher-level thinking skills important in learning mathematics than do teachers serving more advantaged students (Copley and Padron, 1998).

Given that early mathematics teaching does not appear to meet the current recommendations, though, we must examine whether teachers are actually ready and able to meet the recommendations. In other words, do they have the necessary knowledge, skills, and resources with which to teach mathematics?

The answer to this question is also deeply entangled with SES. For example, in addition to the SES role in prioritization of content versus social–emotional foci, teachers of low- and middle-SES children differ in terms of their educational backgrounds and experiences (Lee & Ginsburg, 2007). Teachers of low-SES children tend to have less teaching experience and lower levels of education than teachers of middle-SES children. Therefore, although teachers of low-income children tend to place greater importance on teaching math, ironically they tend to lack the training and experience that might help them to teach it. Also, classrooms for low-SES children are generally of poorer quality than those for middle-SES children (Pianta et al., 2005), suggesting inadequate resources with which to teach early mathematics.

Research on the teaching of mathematics at the elementary level may also provide insight into preschool teachers' readiness to teach mathematics. Despite requisite schooling and credentialing, elementary teachers often do not have the deep knowledge necessary for teaching mathematics (Ma, 1999). Given that the ECE credentialing requirements are even lower than those for elementary school teachers, and given prior lack of attention to mathematics education in ECE, it seems likely that EC teachers would be less prepared than elementary teachers to teach mathematics.

Further, Copley and Padron (1998) found that although EC teachers generally like teaching reading and other language-oriented skills, they find math and/or science to be difficult subjects, ones they feel unable to teach. They are likely disinclined to give it the time and attention it needs. We have encountered this phenomenon in the teachers with whom we have worked. One teacher, in fact, felt so intimidated by the prospect of teaching mathematics that she turned the task over to her assistant teacher for much of the first year of our work together. And this occurred despite the fact that she attended our professional development workshops to develop her mathematical understanding and readiness to teach. This comes in sharp contrast to her later testimonial – after a year's experience with the program and her gradual increase in understanding and confidence – of how much she loved teaching math, how much her students loved math, and how math had become a part of each day in her pre-k classroom. This provides a promising indication that, with appropriate professional development, preschool teachers' beliefs and practices regarding mathematics teaching can change as their understanding and confidence is increased.

THE STATUS OF EME PROFESSIONAL DEVELOPMENT

Just as with later schooling, successful preschool programs offer ongoing professional development (Bowman et al., 2001; Klein & Knitzer, 2006; Pianta, et. al., 2005). Despite this, little is being done to better prepare preschool teachers to teach mathematics. Most EC teacher preparation programs require just one course in mathematics education, and, more often than not, such courses do not even focus on early childhood (Ginsburg et al., 2006; Sarama & DiBiase, 2004). Further, few early childhood professional development programs focus on mathematics at all (Copley & Padron, 1998; Martinez-Beck & Zaslow, 2006). Instead, most professional development programs aim to give general characterizations of developmentally appropriate curricula, to help build pre-literacy skills, to share classroom management techniques, and to improve children's social and emotional development (Copley and Padron, 1998).

The Good Start Grow Smart Early Childhood Initiative of the No Child Left Behind Act of 2001 also neglected mathematics professional development. Although the initiative states the importance of teaching and assessing 'numeracy' skills, it only provides Head Start teachers with opportunities to receive professional development aimed at improving early literacy. Therefore, despite the current demands for implementing and improving EME, little support is being provided to ensure its success.

Regardless of the lack of support for developing and providing professional development in EME, efforts have been made to define the requirements of effective mathematics professional development, primarily at the elementary level. Various academics, educators, and policymakers have created or assembled standards and guiding principles for effective professional development in mathematics (Lee, 2001; Loucks-Horsley et al., 1996; NAEYC/NCTM, 2002; NCTM, 1991). For example, NCTM (1991) defined a set of six standards for the professional development of teachers of mathematics. These standards include experiencing good mathematics teaching, knowing mathematics and school mathematics, knowing students as learners of mathematics, knowing mathematical pedagogy, developing as a teacher of mathematics, and the teacher's role in professional development. The joint NAEYC/NCTM (2002) position statement further attempted to clarify the characteristics of effective EME professional development. It states that in-service professional development has the most impact on teacher learning if it includes opportunities for teachers to network or form study groups, sustained and focused opportunities for learning, collective participation of staff who work in similar settings, content focused both on what and on how to teach, active learning techniques, and opportunity for professional development to be seen as a part of a coherent program of teacher learning.

One might believe that effective teacher training will simply result from school districts, government agencies, and policymakers using such standards or guidelines to create and implement professional development programs. However, this may be wishful thinking. After attending 13 professional development sessions and relating the workshops' content to eight common and measurable standards, Hill (2004) noticed that some of the workshops that met many of the standards lacked substance. They only briefly examined the mathematics content and student learning. Other workshops that met fewer standards actually delved more deeply into the math content and student learning. She concluded that a professional development program's adherence to the standards does not ensure workshop quality. Moreover, the current standards lack the necessary substance to help teachers, school districts, or policymakers to create, identify, or implement effective professional development.

We agree. Effective workshops need to offer more substance than the various Standards seem to propose. Preparing teachers and their supervisors for EME requires helping them to understand the necessary mathematics, children's learning and thinking, and pedagogical principles, all in the context of *specific* curriculum activities. It is to this topic that we turn next.

AN EXAMPLE: BIG MATH FOR LITTLE KIDS

It is within this interesting and challenging context that the *Big Math for Little Kids* (BMLK) curriculum and professional development program was introduced to a group of teachers from the New York City Administration for Children's Services Division of Child Care and Head Start (ACS DCCHS) centers. When the program first began, many of the teachers admitted to suffering from 'math phobia.' But they had also learned from academic test results that their children's mathematical competencies were lagging, and they passionately wanted to improve their chances for later school success (Cordero, 2004). At the same time, despite their desire to embrace a math program that would benefit their children, they questioned whether such a program was developmentally appropriate. They questioned whether their 4-year-old children were capable of learning the mathematics covered in the curriculum.

Our work with these teachers resulted in many surprises. As expected, we encountered resistance, but we also encountered enthusiasm, a willingness to learn, great learning potential, and a deep desire to help their children succeed in school. We witnessed amazing changes in attitudes, beliefs, and behaviors. In fact, it has been our experience that teachers who complete the BMLK professional development program become strong advocates for introducing content-oriented mathematics into the ECE. But before describing the program of professional development, we provide background on BMLK.

BIG MATH FOR LITTLE KIDS – AN OVERVIEW

BMLK is a pre-k and kindergarten curriculum developed with funding from the National Science Foundation (Ginsburg et al., 2003). It was developed to provide children with a developmentally appropriate and research-based curriculum that would help prepare them for elementary school. It was also developed with the premise that although mathematics learning in early childhood is different from what it is during later years, it still can engage children in deep thought.

BMLK provides teachers with many different opportunities to help their children learn 'Big Math' concepts. First, the curriculum offers teachers a sequenced, extensive, and in-depth coverage of various mathematical concepts. Second, the curriculum provides teachers direct ways to connect literacy, language, and mathematics. Finally, the curriculum presents opportunities for math learning to directly connect from the classroom to the home.

The BMLK curriculum covers six units: number, shape, patterns and logic, measurement, number operations, and space. Each of these math concepts is introduced in the pre-k curriculum and further developed in the kindergarten curriculum. In the *number* unit children learn to say the counting sequence, to use a number to tell how many (cardinality) and to use ordinal numbers to identify positions in a line (ordinality). In the *shape* unit children learn the names and important attributes of two- and three-dimensional shapes as well as the concept of symmetry. The *patterns and logic* unit gives children experience with patterns involving sound, color, shape, letters, and numbers. Children also learn to reason logically through the use of clues. In the *measurement* unit children develop basic measurement principles as they investigate length, weight, capacity, temperature, time, and money. The number *operations* unit extends children's understanding of number by introducing addition, subtraction, multiplication, and division concepts through manipulatives, stories, and games. In the *spatial relations* unit children learn to identify positions in space, navigate through space, and represent space using maps.

Teachers are meant to teach BMLK lessons throughout the year on a daily basis for ~15–30 minutes. Lessons involve playing games, reading storybooks, and engaging in activities with children. They include many manipulatives and other 'hands on' materials for children to explore and manipulate, and many opportunities to interact with the other children in the classroom. The curriculum provides explicit learning goals and outcomes, and suggestions for different ways that teachers can assess their children's mathematical understanding.

The curriculum also aids in deepening children's mathematical concepts by providing connections between language, literacy, and mathematics. Every activity has a list of mathematical terms that teachers should use and introduce to children, and each unit's storybook helps to link literacy and mathematics by allowing children to explore mathematical concepts with characters in the story.

The program further attempts to foster language development by encouraging children to explain, justify, and communicate their mathematical ideas. Teachers have reported that this is one of their favorite parts of the curriculum (Cordero, 2004). As one teacher stated 'What's so surprising is that kids use these words now... it's part of their everyday vocabulary.' Comments like these have led us to believe that BMLK is not just a mathematics curriculum but also a literacy curriculum 'in disguise.'

PROFESSIONAL DEVELOPMENT WORKSHOPS
FOR BMLK

Our workshops – developed and piloted over a 3-year period – begin in the summer with a one-day intensive introduction and include both teachers and administrators. This meeting is important for several reasons. First and foremost, it describes the overall structure of the program, allowing participants to become acquainted with the scope of the program and the expectations involved as they mentally prepare for the shifts in thinking that will be required. Secondly, some actual activities from each unit are covered, giving participants an idea of the kind of learning and teaching involved. This is particularly important in allowing both teachers and administrators to see how intentional mathematics teaching can be developmentally appropriate and enjoyable at the same time. Finally, it gives the participants an introduction to us, the people involved with creating and implementing the workshops, helping to create a community with a mutual interest in the improvement of mathematics education for young children.

The eight workshops that follow the summer introduction are all conducted in a similar structure. They begin with a short conversation about the previous month's workshop, to find out how the teachers fared with the curriculum thus far. These conversations offer a kind of 'warm-up' for the conversations intended for the rest of the workshop and help to establish the kind of atmosphere we hope to engender. In our experience, we find that treating these workshops less as lectures, and more as 'conversations among colleagues,' helps to make the experience more worthwhile and memorable for everyone involved. Not only do the teachers get a sense of self-importance from these interactions (which is so rare for most inner-city preschool teachers), but also we, the researchers, get a sense of their understanding of the content. In addition, this stylistic choice reflects the BMLK curriculum itself; workshop leaders, in a sense, model for the teachers the kind of respect, group-learning, and open-ended questions with which we hope that they will engage their own students.

Following this 'debriefing,' teachers are presented with a 'challenge question.' Originally initiated as a simple form of evaluation of the teachers' knowledge, each challenge question presents a mathematical scenario with various student responses, which teachers are asked to evaluate. The responses are designed to elicit many possible interpretations and provide insight into teachers' knowledge of the mathematics, children's understanding of the mathematics, and the assessment and teaching of the mathematics. Surprisingly, the first challenge question left a great impression on the workshop attendees. Given their embrace of this unintended learning experience, we received such strong positive feedback from the teachers that we decided to include similar 'challenge questions' followed by discussion as a regular part of the workshop structure.

Next we turn to the content of the current unit. Although each workshop is unique, each begins with a look at what young children already know and understand about the math topics being presented. This is accomplished with examination of video clips of children in naturalistic play and exercises conducted to exemplify these ideas. For example, to demonstrate how difficult it is to memorize the counting numbers from 1 to 20 in English, we ask the workshop attendees to attempt to learn these counting words in a language such as Tagalog, from the Philippines. They fail. This kind of exercise offers insight into the nature of the challenge preschoolers face when they learn counting.

After considering what kind of knowledge the children might already have in the topic under consideration, we look at the mathematical content of the unit. This is where goals for the unit are covered, and we discuss the mathematical ideas involved. While most who are unfamiliar with preschool math might assume that this part of the workshop is unnecessary because the mathematical content is trivial, the discussion often produces profound revelations for the teachers, many of whom have never considered the complexity of what is being taught. For example, many of the workshop attendees have never before considered that a square is actually a special type of rectangle. Content knowledge like this is discussed and debated. In fact, some of these conversations have even forced us, the researchers, to debate and investigate some mathematical quandaries that arise. For example, we found it very difficult to define clearly what a pattern is. Try it.

After an examination of the content, we discuss key unit activities (not all). They are addressed in a variety of ways: through role playing, discussions about various aspects of the activity, and examining video clip examples. Throughout these activities, we discuss issues of pedagogy, methods of assessment, grouping of children, and construction of materials. This allows teachers to get a realistic sense of the key activities, so that they leave with the confidence to return to their classrooms and teach them.

WHAT WE HAVE LEARNED ABOUT PROFESSIONAL DEVELOPMENT

We constructed our workshops by following guidelines and principles of good professional development seen in the field. But in the process of developing and implementing our workshops, we also discovered several additional guiding principles that we feel are key to successful professional development (Morgenlander & Manlapig, 2006).

Principle 1: Teachers are professionals and should be treated as such. In our workshop environment, we try to show professional respect for teachers and their knowledge. By purposefully setting up time for teachers to have conversations with one another regarding how to connect ideas from the presentation and actual classroom practice, we step back as experts and allow the teachers' expertise to come to play.

Principle 2: Teachers may have a fear of math. Many of the teachers attending these workshops have confessed to a fear of teaching math prior to participating in these workshops. It is important to consider such fear when we design our workshops. Our hope is that the workshops give teachers a comfort zone by showing examples on video, by explaining and discussing math concepts, and by having them try out math activities in a peer-group setting. We believe that all this will help them overcome math phobias.

Principle 3: Teacher incentives help. Although the teachers who have attended these workshops have all chosen to be there – they want to learn how to teach mathematics to their preschoolers – we recognize that the time to attend competes with all of the other demands on their time. As such, we want to make attendance as worthwhile as possible by offering incentives. We offer breakfast, 'on-time prize' for those who arrive on time, and 'take-away' items that are useful for teaching the mathematics content of the unit. Offering these incentives serves to boost attendance and bolster relationships between workshop presenters and teachers, both of which are important to the success of a long-term professional development program.

Principle 4: Allowing time for thoughtful discussions is important. Teachers often remark that one of the most helpful portions of each workshop is the discussion they have with other teachers. Our goal is to provide an environment where conversations about mathematics, children's thinking, and the curriculum can occur. These discussions are helpful for working out connections between the workshop topics and the realities of the classroom. In addition, discussions can also serve to encourage teachers who are hesitant to implement change.

Principle 5: Thoughtful discussions result from constant facilitation. Although discussion time is important, it also requires facilitation, which presents many challenges and unknowns into each workshop. On one hand, teachers often have great advice, insight, and knowledge to offer both the workshop presenter and other teachers. On the other hand, some teachers may want to discuss topics that can detract from the primary goals of the workshops. It is the responsibility of the workshop leader to set up and direct the conversation so that deep and meaningful conversation related to the workshop's goals occurs.

Principle 6. The use of video is crucial. Many workshops involve activities with hands-on manipulatives so that mathematics can be made concrete and 'real.' But videos offer other benefits. They can illustrate lessons in classrooms. They can show examples of children's behavior and thinking. They can be played and replayed, argued, and interpreted. They are in effect another kind of 'manipulative' that can be used to promote understanding of teaching, lessons, and children.

Principle 7. Each workshop should cover the mathematics, the child, and the activities to be taught. We have found that our practice of covering each of these topics, and relating them to each other, provides a practical perspective on teaching. Teachers need to understand the mathematics to be taught, but often do not. They need to understand how the child thinks about specific mathematical ideas, but they often do not go beyond vague (and we think virtually useless) platitudes about constructivism or cognitive development, for example that children are 'concrete.' And they need to learn how knowledge of the mathematics and understanding of the children need to be embedded in the teaching of lessons.

Principle 8. Theoretically grounded specificity is the key. Some workshops we have seen are mere collections of activities. They can be useful if teachers understand how and why to use them. But these 'low-level' workshops seldom explore these matters in any depth; they lack a conceptual framework for understanding the activities to be undertaken. Other, 'high-level' workshops traffic in abstract principles like constructivism or DAP. These principles can be useful if teachers understand how they relate to the teaching of specific activities. Yet the high-level workshops seem disconnected to a significant degree from the nitty-gritty of classroom practice.

We believe that teachers benefit most from a kind of theoretically grounded specificity. When covering the children, the mathematics, and the activities, the workshops need to be theoretically grounded, not intellectually vacuous, and at the same time not mindlessly empirical. For example, in introducing early addition, workshops need to help teachers understand that:

- Children often begin addition by combining two sets, counting them, and learning that order of objects counted and nature of objects counted is irrelevant to the result. In this case, both strategies and ideas are important features of children's behavior. It is inaccurate to say that children's thinking is mainly concrete.
- Addition of whole numbers can be considered to be a process of joining and enumerating elements of separate sets, in any order, regardless of the identity of the elements comprising the sets. These are the ideas and strategies to be learned, and in fact children often try to learn them on their own. Our teaching will be more effective to the extent that it recognizes what needs to be learned and what the children are trying to do.
- A particular activity, as figuring out how many objects are in two cups altogether, tries to capitalize on children's tendency to combine sets and on the mathematical concept that addition can be interpreted as the union of sets. The teacher needs to learn that it would be desirable in the activity to employ different items within each cup, so that children can learn that identity of the items is irrelevant. The teacher needs to learn that children should be encouraged to count the items in many different orders. The teacher needs to learn that systematic counting is to be encouraged, not discouraged in favor of helping the children to memorize the results. And the teacher needs to learn that children – who at this age are abstract thinkers – should not be discouraged from counting 'in their heads,' so long as they have ways to check the results.

All this is what we mean by theoretically grounded specificity. It is a way to give teachers useful practitioner knowledge.

ASSESSING THE SUCCESS OF OUR WORKSHOPS

In the first few years of doing workshops, we gave teachers written surveys at the end of the workshops to evaluate that day's discussion, as well as at the beginning of the next workshop to elicit any reactions the workshop attendees may have had after letting the last workshop 'sink in.' It became clear that all this paperwork revealed very little; most of the responses were flattery, and very little was learned.

It was not until the end of each year, when we held an end-of-the year celebration/debriefing workshop that interesting findings became apparent. Teachers really opened up in these sessions, given that we were primarily there to listen to their reflections on the year of undertaking this new curriculum. Some of these sessions have been videotaped and all analyzed (Cordero, 2004). Here are salient results.

First, we have learned that the workshops help teachers overcome their fears of teaching math. Many teachers recalled feeling apprehension or fear of mathematics at the beginning of the year. By the end of the year, though, the situation had changed. According to one teacher:

> I had a real math phobia and if it hadn't been for BMLK, I wouldn't know how to begin, where to start teaching my kids math. Now I feel that I'm much more confident and I'm much better at implementing math.

Secondly, teachers usually began the year with a concern about how to fit the curriculum into their already busy schedules. By the end of the year, teachers (and their students) were enjoying it so much that they had no problem finding the necessary time.

This finding is related to another one – teachers really enjoy teaching the activities by the end of the year. In part, this is because they see that their children are enjoying them too. While we always stressed during workshops that teachers need to have fun while teaching, this is sometimes easier said than done, especially if the teacher comes to the workshops with a negative disposition toward teaching math. But the fears of teaching math tend to dissipate, and what replaces them is a real joy.

Finally, teachers reported that by the end of the year, their students both look smarter and feel smarter. This is a vital point, given that the curriculum is intended to increase the confidence and abilities of some of our nations' highest-risk students. One teacher told us:

> They want to be smart, they want to know these things and at the end of a lesson, they all get it and are happy about that. That's the best thing about it; it makes their day because they know they are smart!

Stories like these indicate that not only does the curriculum work well, but so do our workshops for the teachers. We are very proud that our teachers can return to us with such positive results.

As the workshops progressed throughout the year and teachers were encouraged to share, discuss, and reflect on their BMLK-related experiences at the sessions, they grew more enthusiastic about the program. They noted that the activities progress from simple to complex and that these lend themselves to individualization; they also observed that new math ideas build on previous ones and that important mathematical ideas are revisited again and again within different mathematical contexts. The value and significance of a 'sequenced and coherent' math curriculum slowly became obvious. One teacher expressed her appreciation that the curriculum provided her with a sequence of activities that she did not have to try to develop on her own.

Teachers seemed most convinced by what they observed in the classroom. Their animated discussions were replete with stories about how much their children are enjoying the activities and how quickly they are learning new math skills, ideas, and language. These teachers became convinced of the value of the program and are its strongest advocates.

NEEDED SUPPORT FOR AN EME PROGRAM

Our BMLK professional development efforts at a publicly funded early care and education agency in New York City have proven to be both challenging and encouraging, and we anticipate that many more challenges lie ahead as the various education sectors attempt to close the achievement gap between disadvantaged and advantaged children. Our experience with BMLK also indicates that although essential, teacher training is not the only factor in play if city and state early care and education agencies intend to make a positive, system-wide, and sustainable impact on low-income children's math achievement. We need to obtain support for five constituencies that contribute to sustainable change.

TOP-LEVEL ADMINISTRATION

Top-level administrative officials in city and state early care and education agencies need to have a clear understanding of the ECE field, the significance of new research in education, and the vision, ability, commitment, and courage to make the necessary institutional changes that will support a plan for quality improvement. Not only will agency heads need to find ways of obtaining additional funds and resources, but they may also have to develop an infrastructure that may require a reorganization of their agency. This is much easier said than done. Resistance to change is a ubiquitous force, and top-level city and state officials are not immune to it.

SUPERVISORY STAFF

Supervisory staff in local or regional offices also play a critical role in enabling systemwide, sustainable change in ECE. These supervisors are usually expert teachers who have been in the system for a long time. Their major responsibility consists of providing support and technical assistance to early childhood programs based on agency policies that often have not been updated to reflect recent changes in the field. For example in New York City, regional supervisors provide technical assistance to childcare centers based on outdated program assessment tools. It is not uncommon for teachers to complain that regional supervisors are critical of some of the BMLK activities. Consultants penalize teachers for implementing activities that are considered too 'teacher-directed' in lieu of the more play-oriented, child-initiated approaches recommended by the out-dated program assessment protocol. The same holds true for using activities that involve written material that might superficially seem to resemble worksheets (in that writing is involved!), irrespective of their educational value or intention. And teachers are very much aware of these contradictions. As long as local or regional supervisors are not trained in the relevant mathematics program, it is likely that they will subvert it.

PROGRAM SUPERVISORS

Program supervisors such as directors of centers and education directors also play a critical role in supporting their teachers' professional development in an EME program and in ensuring the success of the program and the benefits for the children. Often, program supervisors are very eager to have their teachers trained in new approaches and evidence-based curricula, but they do not undergo the training themselves. Hence, they are not in the position to supervise, guide, or support their teachers' classroom practices. Furthermore, trained teachers will probably discontinue using BMLK over time if they do not feel guided and supported by a knowledgeable program supervisor. It has been our experience that when capable directors and teachers work in teams during the professional development phase, they report continued implementation of BMLK.

PARENTS

One of the most common concerns that low-income parents voice to preschool program directors and teachers is that they would much rather their children learn to read, write, and do mathematics than play. And although directors and teachers spend much time and energy trying to convince parents of the contrary, the latter are not easily dissuaded. And they have good reason to hold their ground; they know that their children are likely to fail in the schools as currently constituted and suspect that preschools do not offer adequate preparation.

Interestingly, teachers implementing BMLK report that parents very quickly respond with enthusiasm to the program. One program director recently reported that a group of parents decided not to transfer their children to another school at the end of the year when they found out that the children would continue with the BMLK program the following year. As this anecdote suggests, given the opportunity, low-income parents will place their children in high-quality early childhood programs. Parents vehemently want early childhood programs to prepare their children for school. Their voice and support in the pursuit of quality education cannot be underestimated.

CONCLUSION

Early math education is new and challenging. It involves deep mathematics and many different components, ranging from free play to an organized curriculum. Teaching it is not easy and in fact may be similar to teaching mathematics at the elementary level. But we have some idea of how to help; we need to provide teachers with theoretically grounded and specific professional development opportunities. We need to help various constituencies to understand the need for EME and how to support it. The major question is not whether children can learn mathematics. It is whether we can help teachers to teach it. The unresolved issue is whether the political system will support the effort to provide all young children with effective early education.

REFERENCES

Ackerman, D. J. & Barnett, S. (2005). *Prepared for Kindergarten: What Does 'Readiness' Mean?* (Preschool Policy Brief). New Brunswick, NJ: Rutgers University, National Institute for Early Education Research.

Aubrey, C. (1997). Children's early learning of number in school and out. In Thompson, I. (Ed.), *Teaching and Learning Early Number* (pp. 20–30). London: Open University Press.

Balfanz, R. (1999). Why do we teach young children so little mathematics? Some historical considerations. In Copley, J. V. (Ed.), *Mathematics in the Early Years* (pp. 3–10). Reston, VA: National Council of Teachers of Mathematics.

Barnett, W. S. & Belfield, C. R. (2006). Early childhood development and social mobility. *The Future of Children, 16*(2), 73–98.

Bodrova, E. & Leong, D. (1996). *Tools of the Mind: A Vygotskian Approach to Early Childhood Education.* Englewood Cliffs, NJ: Merrill.

Bowman, B. (2001). Facing the future. In *NAEYC at 75: Reflections on the Past, Challenges for the Future.* Washington, DC: NAEYC.

Bowman, B. T., Donovan, M. S., & Burns, M. S. (Eds.). (2001). *Eager to Learn: Educating Our Preschoolers.* Washington, DC: National Academy Press.

Brandon, R. N. & Martinez-Beck, I. (2006). Estimating the size and characteristics of the United States early care and education workforce. In Zaslow, M. & Martinez-Beck, I. (Eds.), *Critical Issues in Early Childhood Professional Development* (pp. 49–76). Baltimore, MD: Paul H. Brooks Publishing.

Bransford, J. D., Brown, A. L., & Cocking, R. R. (Eds.). (1998). *How People Learn: Brain, Mind, Experience, and School.* Washington, DC: National Academy Press.

Bredekamp, S. & Copple, C. (Eds.). (1986). *Developmentally Appropriate Practice in Early Childhood Programs Serving Children from Birth Through Age 8.* Washington, DC: NAEYC.

Brush, L. R. (1978). Preschool children's knowledge of addition and subtraction. *Journal for Research in Mathematics Education, 9*, 44–54.

Copley, J. V. & Padron, Y. (1998). Preparing teachers of young learners: Professional development of early childhood teachers in mathematics and science. Washington, DC: Forum on Early Childhood Science, Mathematics, and Technology Education.

Copple, C. & Bredekamp, S. (2006). *Basics of Developmentally Appropriate Practice: An Introduction to Teachers of Children 3 to 6.* Washington, DC: NAEYC.

Cordero, M. I. (2004). *Big Math for Little Kids Professional Development Series: An End-of-the-Year Report.* Unpublished manuscript.

Dodge, D. T., Colker, L., & Heroman, C. (2002). *The Creative Curriculum for Preschool* (4th edn). Washington, DC: Teaching Strategies, Inc.

Dowker, A. (2001). Numeracy recovery: A pilot scheme for early intervention with young children with numeracy difficulties. *Support for Learning, 16*(1), 6–10.

Duncan, G. J., Dowsett, C. J., Claessens, A., Magnuson, K., Huston, A. C., Klebanov, P., Pagani, L., Feinstein, L., Engel, M., Brooks-Gunn, J., Sexton, H., Duckworth, K., & Japel, C. (2007). School readiness and later achievement. *Developmental Psychology, 43*(6), 1428–1446.

Gelman, R. & Gallistel, C. R. (1986). *The Child's Understanding of Number.* Cambridge, MA: Harvard University Press.

Ginsburg, H. P. (2006). Mathematical play and playful mathematics: A guide for early education. In Singer, D., Golinkoff, R. M., & Hirsh-Pasek, K. (Eds.), *Play = Learning: How Play Motivates and Enhances Children's Cognitive and Social-Emotional Growth* (pp. 145–165). New York, NY: Oxford University Press.

Ginsburg, H. P., Cannon, J., Eisenband, J. G., & Pappas, S. (2006). Mathematical thinking and learning. In McCartney, K. & Phillips, D. (Eds.), *Handbook of Early Child Development* (pp. 208–229). Oxford, England: Blackwell.

Ginsburg, H. P. & Ertle, B. (2008). Knowing the mathematics in early childhood mathematics. In Saracho, O. N. & Spodek, B. (Eds.), *Contemporary Perspectives on Mathematics in Early Childhood Education.* Information Age Publishing.

Ginsburg, H. P., Greenes, C., & Balfanz, R. (2003). *Big Math for Little Kids.* Parsippany, NJ: Dale Seymour Publications.

Graham, T. A., Nash, C., & Paul, K. (1997). Young children's exposure to mathematics: The child care context. *Early Childhood Education Journal, 25*(1), 31–38.

Griffin, S. (2000). *Number Worlds: Preschool Level.* Durham, NH: Number Worlds Alliance, Inc.

Groen, G. & Resnick, L. B. (1977). Can preschool children invent addition algorithms? *Journal of Educational Psychology, 69*, 645–652.

Hamre, B. K. & Pianta, R. C. (2005). Can instructional and emotional support in the first-grade classroom make a difference for children at risk of school failure? *Child Development, 76*(5), 949–967.

Harms, T., Clifford, R. M., & Cryer, D. (1998). *Early Childhood Environment Rating Scale-Revised.* New York: Teachers College Press.

Hill, H. (2004). Professional development standards and practices in elementary school mathematics. *The Elementary School Journal, 104*(3), 215–231.

Hirsch, E. S. (1996). *The Block Book* (3rd edn). Washington, DC: National Association for the Education of Young Children.

Katz, L. G. & Chard, S. C. (1989). *Engaging Children's Minds: The Project Approach.* Norwood, NJ: Ablex.

Kaufmann, L., Handl, P., & Thöny, B. (2003). Evaluation of a numeracy intervention program focusing on basic numerical knowledge and conceptual knowledge: A pilot study. *Journal of Learning Disabilities, 36*(6), 564–573.

Klein, L. & Knitzer, J. (2006). *Effective Preschool Curricula and Teaching Strategies* (Pathways to Early School Success, Issue Brief No. 2). New York: Columbia University, National Center for Children in Poverty.

Klein, A., Starkey, P., & Ramirez, A. (2002). *Pre-K Mathematics Curriculum.* Glendale, IL: Scott Foresman.

Klibanoff, R. S., Levine, S. C., Huttenlocher, J., Vasilyeva, M., & Hedges, L. V. (2006). Preschool children's mathematical knowledge: The effect of teacher "math talk." *Developmental Psychology, 42*(1), 59–69.

Kontos, S. (1999). Preschool teachers' talk, roles, and activity settings during free play. *Early Childhood Research Quarterly, 14*(3), 363–382.

Kowalski, K., Pretti-Frontczak, K., & Johnson, L. (2001). Preschool teachers' beliefs concerning the importance of various developmental skills and abilities. *Journal of Research in Childhood Education, 16*, 5–14.

La Paro, K. M., Pianta, R. C., & Stuhlman, M. (2004). The classroom assessment scoring system: Findings from the prekindergarten year. *The Elementary School Journal, 104*(5), 409–426.

Lee, H. (2001). *Enriching the Professional Development of Mathematics Teachers*. ERIC Digest. ERIC Clearinghouse for Science, Mathematics, and Environmental Education: Columbus, OH (ERIC Reproduction Services N. ED 465 495).

Lee, J. & Ginsburg, H. (2007). Preschool teachers' beliefs about appropriate early literacy and mathematics education for low- and middle-SES children. *Early Education and Development, 18*(1), 111–143.

Loucks-Horsley, S., Styles, K., & Hewson, P. (1996). *Principles of Effective Professional Development for Mathematics and Science Education: A Synthesis of Standards*. NISE Brief (Vol.1). Madison, WI: National Institute for Science Education.

Ma, L. (1999). *Knowing and Teaching Elementary Mathematics*. Mahwah, NJ: Lawrence Erlbaum Associates, Publishers.

Martinez-Beck, I. & Zaslow, M. (2006). The context for critical issues in early childhood professional development. In Zaslow, M. & Martinez-Beck, I. (Eds.), *Critical Issues in Early Childhood Professional Development* (pp. 1–15). Baltimore, MD: Brookes Publishing Company.

Miller, K. F. & Parades, D. R. (1996). On the shoulders of giants: Cultural tools and mathematical development. In Sternberg, R. J. & Ben-Zeev, T. (Eds.), *The Nature of Mathematical Thinking* (pp. 83–117). Mahwah, NJ: Lawrence Erlbaum Associates, Publishers.

Morgenlander, M. & Manlapig, L. (2006, April). *Big Math for Little Kids Workshops: Background and Content*. Paper presented at the annual meeting of the American Educational Research Association, San Francisco, CA.

National Association for the Education of Young Children and National Council of Teachers of Mathematics (2002). *Early childhood mathematics: Promoting Good Beginnings. A Joint Position Statement of NAEYC and NCTM*. Washington, DC: NAEYC and NCTM.

National Council of Teachers of Mathematics (1991). *Professional standards for teaching mathematics*. Reston, VA: NCTM.

National Council of Teachers of Mathematics. (2000). *Principles and standards for school mathematics*. Reston, VA: NCTM.

No Child Left Behind (NCLB) Act of 2001, PL 107–110, 20 U.S.C.

Piaget, J. & Inhelder, B. (1969). *The Psychology of the Child* (H. Weaver, Trans.). New York: Basic Books, Inc.

Pianta, R. C., Howes, C., Burchinal, M., Bryant, D., Clifford, D., Early, D., & Barbarin, O. (2005). Features of pre-kindergarten programs, classrooms, and teachers: Do they predict observed classroom quality and child-teacher interactions? *Applied Developmental Science, 9*(3) 144–159.

Pianta, R. C. & La Paro, K. (2003). Improving early school success. *Educational Leadership, 60*(7), 24–29.

Reynolds, A. J. (1995). One year of preschool intervention or two: Does it matter? *Early Childhood Research Quarterly, 10*(1), 1–31.

Rimm-Kaufman, S. E., La Paro, K. M., Downer, J. T., & Pianta, R. C. (2005). The contribution of classroom setting and quality of instruction to children's behavior in kindergarten classrooms. *The Elementary School Journal, 105*(4), 377–394.

Sarama, J. & Clements, D. H. (2004). Building blocks for early childhood mathematics. *Early Childhood Research Quarterly, 19*(1), 181–189.

Sarama, J. & DiBiase, A. M. (2004). The professional development challenge in preschool mathematics. In Clements, D. H. & Sarama, J. (Eds.), *Engaging Young Children in Mathematics: Standards for Early Childhood Mathematics Education* (pp. 415–446). Mahwah, NJ: Lawrence Erlbaum Associates.

Seo, K.-H. & Ginsburg, H. P. (2004). What is developmentally appropriate in early childhood mathematics education? Lessons from new research. In Clements, D. H., Sarama, J., & DiBiase, A.-M. (Eds.), *Engaging Young Children in Mathematics: Standards for Early Childhood Mathematics Education* (pp. 91–104). Hillsdale, NJ: Erlbaum.

Shulman, L. S. (2000). Teacher development: Roles of domain expertise and pedagogical knowledge. *Journal of Applied Developmental Psychology, 21*(1), 129–135.

Sophian, C. (2004). Mathematics for the future: Developing a head start curriculum to support mathematics learning. *Early Childhood Research Quarterly, 19*(1) 59–81.

Stipek, D. (2006). Accountability comes to preschool: Can we make it work for young children? *Phi Delta Kappan, 87,* 740–745.

Van de Rijt, B. & Van Luit, J. (1998). Effectiveness of the additional early mathematics program for teaching children early mathematics. *Instructional Science, 26,* 337–358.

Wesley, P. W. & Buysse, V. (2003). Making meaning of school readiness in schools and communities. *Early Childhood Research Quarterly, 18*(3), 351–375.

White, C. S., Deal, D., & Deniz, C. B. (2004). Teachers' knowledge, beliefs, and practices and mathematical and analogical reasoning. In English, L. D. (Ed.), *Mathematical and Analogical Reasoning of Young Learners* (pp. 127–151). Mahwah, NJ: Lawrence Erlbaum Associates.

Williams, C. K. & Kamii, C. (1986). How do children learn by handling objects? *Young Children, 42*(2), 23–26.

Williams, L. R. (1996). Does practice lead theory? Teachers' constructs about teaching: Bottom-up perspectives. In Chafel, J. & Reifel, S. (Eds.), *Advances in Early Education and Day Care: Theory and Practice in Early Childhood Teaching* (Vol. 8, pp. 153–184). Greenwich, CT: JAI.

Young-Loveridge, J. (2004). Effects on early numeracy of a program using number books and games. *Early Childhood Research Quarterly, 19,* 82–98.

5

PROGRESSION IN NUMERACY AGES 5–11

RESULTS FROM THE LEVERHULME LONGITUDINAL STUDY

MARGARET BROWN[1], MIKE ASKEW[1],
JEREMY HODGEN[1], VALERIE RHODES[1],
ALISON MILLETT[1], HAZEL DENVIR[1], AND
DYLAN WILLIAM[2]

[1]*Professor of Mathematics, King's College London, University of London,
The Strand, London WC2R 2LS, UK*
[2]*Institute of Education, University of London, London WC1H 0AL, UK*

BACKGROUND AND AIMS

This chapter reports on aspects of the work of the Leverhulme Numeracy Research Programme, a 5-year study funded in the UK during 1997–2002 by the Leverhulme Trust. Following disappointing English performances in numeracy in international surveys, the purpose of the Leverhulme Programme was:

- *to take forward understanding of the nature and causes of low achievement in numeracy and provide insight into effective strategies for remedying the situation.*

The Programme is unique in encompassing a large-scale longitudinal survey and five distinct projects linked into it which each take the form of mainly qualitative case studies relating to a particular factor which affects the teaching and learning of numeracy in primary schools. This chapter focuses on only one aspect of the Leverhulme Programme, that of progression in learning.

85

It draws on longitudinal data from the large-scale survey and one of the case-study projects. The objectives of the relevant parts of the Programme were:

- *to inform knowledge about the progression in pupils' learning of numeracy throughout the primary school years;*
- *to obtain a clear and detailed longitudinal picture of the numeracy development of a range of pupils taught in a varied set of schools and to examine this in the light of their classroom experiences, to ascertain what works, what goes wrong, and why.*

The specific objective of this chapter is:

- *to report on a progression model in relation to both items and children;*
- *to relate test data for some case-study children on repeated occasions to classroom observation and interview data.*

During the Leverhulme Programme a systemic initiative was implemented in all English primary schools, the National Numeracy Strategy. The key curriculum feature was an increased emphasis on number and on calculation, especially mental calculation, but there were also significant changes in planning and pedagogy (National Numeracy Strategy, 1999). The National Numeracy Strategy will be referred to on occasion in order to explain some of the differences between comparable data gathered before and after its introduction in 1999/2000.

The meaning of numeracy which is preferred by the research team is that relating to social practices (Baker & Street, 1993), but for the purpose of this study the definition was taken pragmatically to be that of the National Numeracy Strategy, which regards numeracy as a 'proficiency' which requires a combination of understanding, skills, and confidence and includes the motivation to solve contextual problems (National Numeracy Strategy, 1999, p. 4). In the related documents it becomes clear that in the Strategy the emphasis is on decontextualized calculations, with a minor inclusion of traditional word problems.

The perspective of learning adopted is broadly Vygotskian social constructivist and highlights the classroom negotiation of meaning (e.g., Cobb & Bauersfeld, 1995).

METHODS AND DATA SOURCES

SAMPLE

The data which informs the chapter derives from a longitudinal survey with over 2,000 children in each of two different age cohorts.

Only a small subsample of 188, from 10 different secondary schools, was followed into year 7 since this extension required tracking children from primary into secondary schools.

TABLE 5.1   The Cohorts in the Study and Their Progression Through School

Year group	Year 1	Year 2	Year 3	Year 4	Year 5	Year 6	Year 7
Age (years)	5/6	6/7	7/8	8/9	9/10	10/11	11/12
Cohort 1	1998/1999	1999/2000	2000/2001	2001/2002			
Cohort 2				1997/1998	1998/1999	1999/2000	2000/2001

Table 5.1 shows that year 4 data is available from both cohorts, the older cohort in 1997/1998 and the younger cohort in 2001/2002. This data allows some evaluation of the effect of the National Numeracy Strategy which was implemented in 1999/2000, mid-way between these dates.

The pupils in the survey include all children in the two age cohorts in 40 different primary schools, 10 in each of four varied local education authorities (LEAs) in different regions of England. By the fifth year of the study 36 of the 40 schools were still participating.

The 10 schools were selected by quota sampling using LEA data and the perceptions of local advisors to ensure a range according to five variables (size, religious affiliation if any, socio-economic status (SES) of intake, attainment in national mathematics tests and value added). Thus the sample contains every type of school from small rural church schools to large inner city multi-ethnic schools. Although the sample is therefore technically neither random nor proportionately representative, the spread of schools and LEAs is such that the results are unlikely to deviate substantially from those of the whole English population in those cohorts (indeed the mean score on national tests at age 11 was within 1% of the national mean).

Although for each cohort there are over 2,000 children who at some time were members and are on the assessment data base, the numbers who completed any specific test vary between 1,500 and 1,700. This sample is generally used to calculate the facility of items in each test administration. However in the case of the year 4 data in order to compare results from the two different cohorts, one tested in 1997/1998 and one in 2001/2002, we have included only children from the 35 schools where the tests were fully completed at the start and end of year 4 for both cohorts, and within that group only children who were present at the testing at the start and end of the year. This reduces the sample size to 1,291 and 1,332, respectively for year 4. (This restriction of the year 4 sample to obtain comparability has changed the item facilities from those which would be obtained using the full groups of children tested, but never by more than 3%.)

TEST DESIGN

Children were tested towards the beginning and end of each school year, within a designated 2 weeks towards the end of October and the beginning of June. The same test was used at the start and end of the year, and was orally administered by teachers from a provided script with pupils answering in specially designed booklets. (This was partly to avoid problems for children whose reading was poor, and partly to control the time available for each item.) For some test items (questions) teachers were asked to display a poster for a fixed number of seconds. The number of items in the test varied from 41 in year 1 to 75 in year 4 and 81 in year 6. (The test used for year 7 was identical to that used in year 6.)

Tests were marked centrally by college students onto forms which were scanned into the computer. All questions were marked simply as correct, wrong or omitted, using a marking schedule. Various checks were made on the reliability of this process.

The sequence of tests, one for each year group, was derived from instruments developed from earlier research by members of the team (Askew et al., 1997; Denvir & Brown, 1986; Hart, 1981).

The items had in most cases first been designed for one-on-one diagnostic interviews and based on reviews of related research; Denvir and Bibby (2002) have updated in a format usable by teachers a diagnostic interview for low attaining primary pupils from which many of the items were drawn. These items were later adapted for whole class settings, and were thus extensively trialed in both formats. A small number of items, all fully trialed, were added at various stages so as to extend the age range and to provide a better match with the changing curricula in schools. The form of the tests used in this research was also trialed and adjusted where necessary before being finalized.

The reliabilities (using Cronbach's alpha) were found to be very high (of the order of 0.95). Denvir and Brown (1987) had earlier compared pupils' performance on interviews and class tests using many of the items, and found in general a reasonable agreement, although children tended to perform better in interview since the presence of the interviewer encouraged them to persevere and to monitor answers more carefully.

Items were designed to assess mainly conceptual understanding and cognitively based skills, including mental calculation; some recall items (e.g., multiplication facts) were included but the time allowed was sufficient to enable some children to derive these. The emphasis was on mental rather than written processes, although children were able to write in their booklets whenever they wanted to. They include contextual as well as purely numerical items. Most items were quickly answered by short open written responses but a small number were in multiple choice format. Areas assessed were *understanding of the number system*, *methods of computation*, and s*olving numerical problems*. All items were matched against the national curriculum level descriptions and the National Numeracy Framework in order to check the coverage both in the total bank and on each test.

The series of tests were designed to contain a large number of common items from one year to the next (including three items which were assessed in every year from year 1 to year 7). This was to enable individual children's progress to be assessed from year to year. Table 5.2 shows the distribution of the number of tests on which items were included, for the total number of 159 items which were used on one or more of the tests.

Many of the items used only for 1 year group were those used for year 1, where it was important to ensure that there were enough relatively easy items. Sometimes an item was used only in one test to improve the distribution of the item facilities in the test. In order to be able to monitor progress for children at all levels of attainment, it was necessary to attempt to have a uniform distribution of item facilities within each test (i.e., as many items with a facility in the range 0–10% as in the ranges 40–50% or 90–100%). Table 5.3 shows the distribution of the facilities of the 85 items in the year 5 tests as an example.

TABLE 5.2 Proportion of the Total Bank of 159 Items Which Were Tested in More Than One Year-Group

Items tested in 7 years	Items tested in 6 years	Items tested in 5 years	Items tested in 4 years	Items tested in 3 years	Items tested in 2 years	Items tested in 1 years
3	10	19	16	49	34	28
(2%)	(6%)	(12%)	(10%)	(31%)	(21%)	(18%)

TABLE 5.3 Distribution of Facilities (Percentage Correct) of the 85 Test Items in the Two 1998/1999 Administrations of the Year 5 Test

Item facility (%)	0–9%	10–19%	20–29%	30–39%	40–49%
Frequency of items in October	9	11	12	11	9
Frequency of items in June	5	5	10	8	8
Average frequency (October and June)	7	8	11	10	9

Item facility (%)	50–59%	60–69%	70–79%	80–89%	90–100%
Frequency of items in October	10	7	6	4	6
Frequency of items in June	11	13	9	8	8
Average frequency (October and June)	11	10	8	6	7

In a perfect distribution there would be 8.5 items (10% of the total 85 items) in each part of the range. This was not completely achievable, partly because facilities were not completely predictable even though tests had been trialed on smaller samples. But more importantly there was a problem since each test was taken twice (and the year 6 test three times), with higher facilities on the later occasions, so that a perfect uniform distribution on each occasion was impossible. In practice, as demonstrated in Table 5.3, although the tests are identical, more items predictably fall into the harder end of the range (0–30% success) in the October testing, and more into the easier end (70–100%) in the June testing. The combined mean of the October and June distribution is not biased towards either end and is more uniform, but with slightly more items in the center of the range than at the extremes.

These roughly uniform distributions of item difficulty also meant that approximately equal numerical gains could be made by children at different attainment levels between the October and June testing. The only exceptions to this were pupils who had either almost all items correct in October or who still had hardly any correct in June; but these ceiling and floor effects affected very few children (not more than 3%). Empirical checking confirmed that mean gains were indeed roughly uniform for children of different attainments.

Many items were linked with others assessing similar concepts/skills but often with varying difficulties. For example for each year group one set of items contained number lines; children were asked both to write the numbers represented by intermediate points indicated by arrows, and to mark on the line the points representing specific numbers. The number lines became more complex with older age groups.

In order to examine the overall progression of the cohort and of individual children a means had to be found of equating results of the same children over different tests taken in different years. An adaptation of the Rasch procedure was used, drawing on item response theory (Hambleton et al., 1991). First an index of difficulty was calculated for each item which indicated the estimated age at which 50% of the cohort could succeed on it. (This could not be done for some items which occurred only in a few tests or for those at the extremes of difficulty, i.e., those on which either more than 50% of the youngest children were successful or fewer than 50% of the oldest children were successful.) Then a sample of at least 100 pupils was taken for each test, with oversampling at the extremes to ensure full coverage. For each sampled pupil, a 'mathematical age' was then estimated at each test administration using a maximum likelihood method, drawing on the data of the difficulties of items on which they were successful and those for which they were not. This was then plotted against their test score. Since the plots obtained were reasonably linear, regression was then used to derive a linear relation between score and 'mathematical age' for each test. This allowed a conversion between test score on any test and 'mathematical age.' It thus enabled all children in each cohort to be assigned a 'mathematical age' for each sitting of the test. However because of irregularities in the progression curves over the summer periods (to be discussed in the next section), this method, although believed to be the best available, produced results with some misleading features; the results therefore need to be interpreted with caution.

CASE-STUDY METHODS

Children were chosen for longitudinal case study from the 40 schools in the larger sample. Five schools were first selected which were deemed to have interesting features, relating to variety in their teaching methods, their results and the SES of their intakes. The five schools came from the three LEAs within easy traveling distance of London. One class from each cohort was selected from each of these schools, and within the class initially nine pupils were selected by the teacher so that three were of above average attainment, three of average and three of below average attainment. After a year, 2 of the 3 children from each attainment range were selected to be part of the final sample. So far as possible the selection from each class was balanced for gender and ethnicity. This gave a total of 30 children, 6 from each of 5 classes, in each of the two cohorts. In some cases the initial assignment of attainment level changed during the study, and some children left the schools before the end of the study.

A pair of researchers was allocated to each school and each year observed between them five consecutive lessons in the first term and five in the third term for each of the two cohorts. The case-study children were informally interviewed about their activity during these lessons and their written work was copied and collected. The test scripts for these children have been carefully analyzed and compared with their classroom performances, providing a unique source of data comparing performances in different contexts.

Each child had a formal extended interview, at the end of year 3 for cohort 1 and at the end of year 6 for cohort 2. This included discussion of their progress, their observations on their teaching in each year and information on the mathematics they used or did at home and their home circumstances. Each child was asked to talk through a set of test items which had been judged from the results on a recent test to be near their threshold. Finally each teacher has been formally interviewed about the children and their progress, including any home or other factors which might affect it.

In the spring term each year, as with all remaining 40 schools, each school was visited on at least one occasion by a different member of the research team. This was to observe the teaching in each class which contained members of either of the two cohorts, interview the teachers, the mathematics co-ordinator (curriculum leader) and the head teacher.

RESULTS AND DISCUSSION

1. Many items have a model of progression across years which follow a broadly similar model to a section of an idealized item characteristic curve, but with some key differences.

We examined the progression trajectory for each of the 159 test items by plotting the item facilities (percentage of pupils correct) across the different test administrations, at the beginning (October) and the end (June) of each school year. Most of these trajectories followed a broadly similar shape, but with some key differences to be discussed in the next sections. Generally they rose slowly from 0% to 10% or 20%, then more quickly, at a rate of 10%–20% per year, then gradually more slowly again, plateauing out towards 100%. To illustrate this, facilities (success rates) are given in Table 5.4 and in Figure 5.1 for one of the three items included in the tests for all 6 years.

In this item, denoted '1 < 200,' children, having been asked to first write down in a box provided in their answer booklet the number 200, were then asked to write, next to it, the number which was one less than 200.

Here and elsewhere, unless the year 4 results are being compared directly between the two cohorts, year 4 results are the average of the results of the two cohorts tested in 1997/1998 and 2001/2002, respectively. (Year 7 results are only shown where essential since they were on a much smaller sample of 188 pupils and hence are not very reliable; the general trend will be discussed briefly later.)

The data illustrated in Figure 5.1 suggest that a few months under 5 years would be a reasonable estimate for the number of years between the age at which 5% of the population can succeed on an item and the age when 95% can succeed. However the other item tested across this time has a trajectory where

TABLE 5.4   Facilities (Percentage Correct) of '1 < 200' item from Years 1 to 6 ($n > 1300$)

	Year 1		Year 2		Year 3	
Item description	October	June	October	June	October	June
Write 1 less than two hundred	2	11	19	52	59	77

	Year 4		Year 5		Year 6	
Item description	October	June	October	June	October	June
Write 1 less than two hundred	79	81	87	94	95	97

the facility rises from 6% to 92% in 5 years and 7 months between the start of year 1 and the end of year 6 (see Table 5.6), suggesting that in this case the delay is nearer 6 years. But these estimates may only be valid for items where children in years 1–3 have a reasonable chance of success. For more difficult items, estimates of this gap suggest something more like 6–8 years, which support the conjecture in the Cockcroft report (DES/WO, 1982) of a '7 year gap.' The Rasch data, which were calculated to assign mathematical ages to each child, illustrated later in Figure 5.4, interestingly suggest that in year 6 the gap between children at the 5th and 95th percentile is of the order of 7 years of mathematical age.

Figure 5.1 in fact slightly distorts the shapes of the item profile since although the facilities for successive test administrations are shown at equal horizontal intervals, there was actually about 7.5 months between the tests at the start (October) and end (June) of each academic year (e.g., between 1O and 1J) and only 4.5 months between the June test at the end of the year and the October test at the start of the following year (e.g., between 1J and 2O). This distortion affects the gradient; where these are positive, the curves will tend to become smoother, although not completely smooth for reasons explained below.

Using the appropriate utility on *Datadesk* software, we showed that these trajectories appeared to be close to the shape of a segment of a logistic curve. Logistic curves are used in item response theory as they provide models for

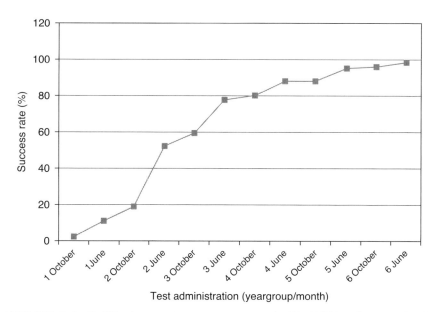

FIGURE 5.1 Facilities (success rates as percentage correct) of '1 < 200' item from years 1 to 6.

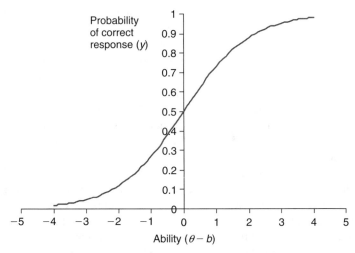

FIGURE 5.2   Idealized single parameter item characteristic curve for an item of difficulty *b*.

item characteristic curves. An item characteristic is the graph of the probabilities of pupils being successful on an item (usually expressed as a percentage of the sample successful) against the relative attainment level of the pupils (usually measured by total score on the test). For example, Figure 5.2 shows the single parameter logistic curve modeling an item characteristic curve:

$$y = \frac{e^{(\theta-b)}}{1 + e^{(\theta-b)}}$$

where θ is a measure of ability and b the difficulty of the item (Hambleton et al., 1991). As already noted above, the difficulty of an item was calculated as the estimated age at which 50% of the cohort could succeed on it.

The implication of noting that an item characteristic curve would be an acceptable model for our progression data is that attainment and age can be regarded as interchangeable variables along the horizontal axis; this means that a lower attaining pupil behaves mathematically like an average pupil at a younger age. (This assumption actually underpins the English national test reporting system, where, for example, a level 3, which is broadly criterion referenced, is above the national norm at age 7, on the national norm for age 9, below the national norm at age 11 and well below it at age 14.)

The empirical results in our data depart from such a logistic curve in three different ways, which will be described in the next three sections:

(a) Dips in facility sometimes occur between the end of one school year and the start of the next

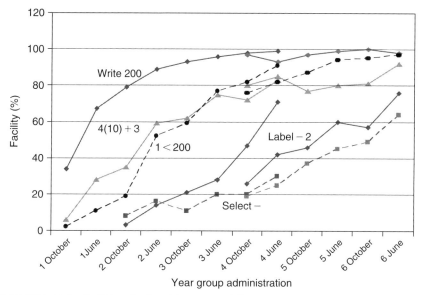

FIGURE 5.3 Facilities of selected items over different test administrations, for each cohort ($n > 1,290$).

The trajectories for many items show one or more drops in facility over time (some examples can be seen in Figure 5.3 and Table 5.6). These all occur between a June testing and the following October and suggest that facility is sometimes but not consistently lost during the 6-week summer break. This is in spite of the fact that the October tests occur after 5/6 weeks of teaching in the new school year. In fact such 'summer dips' occur with all types of item, as will be seen in later sections. Table 5.5 below shows that the average rate of improvement over the summer break from June to October is positive but much less than that during October to June even when the different lengths of the intermediate periods are allowed for. (It should be noted that in Table 5.5 the mean facility differences between October and the following June are calculated on the full set of items in the test for that year, whereas those for June and the following October are calculated only over those items which are common to the two tests for contiguous year groups.)

In Table 5.5 the year 7 results are shown as falling by 2%. (This is also the case when the difference is calculated over only the pupils present in both testings.) Although the year 7 sample is small it was chosen to be broadly representative and there is thus no reason to doubt that the decrease is of the correct order of magnitude. In fact it is fairly similar and in the same direction as other data across the transfer from primary to secondary schools (e.g., Hargreaves & Galton, 2002). Ofsted (2002a), using national test data, suggests

TABLE 5.5   Mean Increase in Facility on Common Items Since the Previous Test (cohort 2 data in Italic) (* Year 7 Data Based on Small Sample Only)

From	To	Increase
Year 1 October	Year 1 June	+20%
Year 1 June	Year 2 October	+5%
Year 2 October	Year 2 June	+20%
Year 2 June	Year 3 October	+2%
Year 3 October	Year 3 June	+13%
Year 3 June	Year 4 October	+2%
Year 4 October	Year 4 June	+10%
Year 4 October	*Year 4 June*	*+10%*
Year 4 June	*Year 5 October*	*+5%*
Year 5 October	*Year 5 June*	*+11%*
Year 5 June	*Year 6 October*	*+4%*
Year 6 October	*Year 6 June*	*+11%*
Year 6 June	*Year 7 June*	*−2%**

the dip is nearer to 10%, but this may be because of inflated test scores after focused coaching.

(b) Children appear to learn more quickly in the early years of primary school

A second way in which the curves differ from idealized item characteristic (logistic) curves is the tendency for larger mean annual increases in facility in the younger age groups. In fact as can be seen from Table 5.5, over those items common to successive years, the annual increments in facility between years 1 and 2, or between years 2 and 3, are nearly 70% greater than those between years 4 and 5, or years 5 and 6.

It is not clear why this happens. One possible explanation is that as the mathematical ideas become more complex, more children take longer to learn them. A second possible cause is that many children may have had the potential to learn these concepts and skills at a younger age and thus make especially fast progress in years 1 and 2 when they are first exposed to numeracy ideas at school. It is of course also possible that there is some neurological reason for the more rapid development in younger pupils.

(c) School curricula affect item profiles; in particular the introduction of the National Numeracy Strategy is likely to have caused changes in facility where the data crosses from the younger cohort to the older one

So far in this section we have averaged the results for the two cohorts where they overlap in year 4. Cohort 2 was tested in year 4 in 1997/1998, 2 years before the National Numeracy Strategy was implemented, and cohort 1 was tested in year 4 in 2001/2002, 2 years after the implementation. However there were differences, in the case of some items quite large ones, which can be attributed to the Strategy. Curriculum effects will thus be discussed in the next section.

2. While there is clear evidence from some items that curriculum affects progression, a major and expensive process of systemic curriculum change has produced only very minor overall effects in attainment.

Results are given in Table 5.6 and in Figure 5.3 for the three items included in the tests for all 6 years and for two of the items which were tested in 5 consecutive years, selected because of special features described later. (The data for the item '1 < 200' has already been displayed in Figure 5.1 and Table 5.4, but here the two sets of year 4 results for the two different cohorts are disaggregated.)

In Figure 5.3 the facilities for each item in the two cohorts are shown by the same icons. The descriptions of the items are somewhat cryptic in Table 5.6 and especially in Figure 5.3, but will be elaborated when the items are discussed.

While some features already alluded to can again be seen, for example the occasional summer dip and high gradients for some items between years 1 and 3 in comparison to between years 4 and 6, some new points emerge from these data relating to the curriculum:

(a) In some cases item profiles have very different gradients although in ranges where facility values are similar, sometimes leading to the profiles crossing over

We will illustrate this first by examining the two items described as '4(10) + 3' (shown on Figure 5.3 by triangular icons) and '1 < 200' (shown by circle icons and dotted lines).

In the first item the teacher first showed the children a picture of a bag of apples and told them that it contained 10 apples. The teacher then told a story about a girl being given some apples and showed a picture of 4 bags of apples and three loose apples; the children were asked to write down how many apples the child received. In the item '1 < 200,' as previously described, children were asked to first write down in a box the number 'two hundred' and on the next space to write down the number that is one less than two hundred.

It is clear from Table 5.6 and Figure 5.3 that the '4(10) + 3' item starts off as the easier of the two items, with higher facilities in years 1 and 2 and the beginning of year 3. However during year 3 the relative position changes, and the item '1 < 200' has higher facilities from then until the end of year 4 for the younger cohort (cohort 1). For cohort 2, however, the switch in difficulty between the two items does not take place until the start of year 5. This suggests that there

TABLE 5.6 Progression in Facilities (Percentage Correct) for Selected Items Which Span Several Year Groups (Older Cohort in italics) ($n > 1290$)

Item description	Year 1		Year 2		Year 3		Year 4		Year 5		Year 6	
	October	June	October	June	October	June	October	June	October	June	October	June
Write 200	34	67	79	89	93	96	98 *97*	99 *93*	97	99	*100*	98
Bags of 10 apples 4 bags and 3 are ?	6	28	35	59	62	75	72 *80*	83 *85*	77	80	*81*	92
Write 1 less than two hundred	2	11	19	52	59	77	82 *76*	91 *82*	87	94	*95*	97
Label −2 on number line			3	14	21	28	47 *26*	71 *42*	46	60	*57*	76
Select operation in problem (−)			8	16	11	20	20 *19*	30 *25*	37	45	*49*	64

is no fixed ordering in terms of difficulty between these items. It seems possible that the item with the higher numbers is more difficult for younger children perhaps because they have less experience of such numbers; according to the National Numeracy Strategy (1999) this should happen in the year 2 curriculum. Once this experience is consolidated, the fact that the structure is simpler for '1 < 200' (counting back 1 rather than composing tens and units), may render it the easier of the two items. It would therefore be possible to argue for an inherent ordering by facility only once the necessary knowledge and experience have been gained.

It is not difficult to explain in curriculum terms why the crossover occurs later for the older pupils for whom the National Numeracy Strategy started in year 6, than for the younger pupils who encountered it first in year 2. In the early years the Strategy emphasizes oral counting, forwards and backwards, at the cost of place value understanding which underlies the '4(10) + 3' item. The early stress on place value work is now postponed as written methods are introduced later than was traditionally the case.

A crossover also apparently occurs between 'Select −' (an item with a word problem where children are told the number of miles for the whole car journey and the number of miles already covered and asked to select the 'sum' (expression) which they would need to perform to work out the number of miles still to drive) and 'Label −2' (a number line item showing marks from −10 to +10, with 0 and 10 labeled, on which children are asked to label the point which represents −2). However since the former is unusually a multiple choice item with a probability of 12.5% of obtaining the correct answer by guessing, it seems likely that the initially higher facility of the 'Select −' item is due to this chance factor and that when this is allowed for it is actually more difficult for all age groups.

There are also some large step changes in facility of around 40% per year, which is unusual even in the early years where the mean gain is about 20%. These large increases are particularly marked for the items designated 'Write 200,' '1 < 200' and 'Label −2.' For the '1 < 200' item as already discussed this seems likely to be due to curriculum factors; this also seems likely to be the case for 'Write 200' and 'Label −2,' both of which depend strongly on knowledge of conventions of how to represent numbers rather than on reasoning ability. They are hence likely to increase in facility strongly at the time when the conventions are introduced in the classroom. There is a contrast between such patterns and the item which requires children to select the correct operation for a word problem ('Select −'), where even allowing for a guessing correction of up to 12.5%, there is a very slow increase with no clear large jumps. This may characterize items where the demand is more in terms of understanding than taught conventions or procedures, and for which there is little direct teaching in the current curriculum.

(b) Although the mean difference in item facility in year 4 before and after the implementation of the National Numeracy Strategy is only small, there is

considerable diversity in the magnitudes of the changes over the set of items, corresponding broadly to related curriculum changes

Table 5.7 shows the changes between 1997/1998 and 2001/2002 in mean item facility in relation to the year 4 items, for both October and June testings. These are fairly consistent and indicate mean increases of just over 3% points over the period of implementation of the National Numeracy Strategy, differences which are small but in statistical terms highly significant ($p < 0.01$). At the time of testing in 2001/2002 the cohort 1 children had been following the National Numeracy Strategy for 3 years. (In our visits to the 35 schools included in the year 4 comparison we were able to observe that all schools and teachers were conscientiously implementing the Strategy, as indicated also by the official evaluation by Earl et al., 2002 and Ofsted, 2002b).

The mean changes in facility between October and June testings of 9.8% and 10.1% points in 1997/1998 and 2001/2002, respectively, indicated in Table 5.7, suggest that pupils learned more but not significantly more over the course of the school year after the Strategy had been implemented. This also enables the 3% point rise in facility values to be interpreted as the equivalent of just over 2 months' learning. The effect size is also low at 0.17/0.18, respectively, depending whether calculated in October or June.

These effects are in a numeracy test which closely reflects the National Strategy emphases on mental calculation strategies, and not in a mathematics test sampling from the full curriculum. Given that the new emphasis on numeracy is at the expense of other parts of mathematics, such as geometry and data handling, there is a question as to whether an overall assessment of mathematics would have shown any significant change at all. It should be noted that the Government, and following their lead other commentators, have repeatedly stated that the National Numeracy Strategy has been a great success; yet if changes for other year groups are of a similar size to those seen here for year 4, whether such a small change in numeracy attainment is worth the expenditure of more than £100 million must be open to doubt.

However the Leverhulme year 4 data does demonstrate large increases in facility for some items. The largest change is in the item referred to in Table 5.6

TABLE 5.7 Comparison of Mean Facility (Percentage Correct) for Year 4 Items Between Cohort 2 in 1997/1998 and Cohort 1 in 2001/2002 ($n > 1,290$)

	October testing	June testing
1997/1998	51.8	61.6
2001/2002	54.7	64.8
Rise	3.0	3.2
Equivalent	2.2 months	2.4 months
Effect size	0.17	0.18

and Figure 5.3 above as 'Label -2,' which at first appears strange since knowledge of negative numbers is not a priority of the Strategy. However the fact that one of the two items with the second largest increase (19% and 14% points, respectively in October and June testings) is also a number line item in which students are asked to identify the mark at 267, strongly suggests that it is greater familiarity with the number line representation, particularly emphasized by the Strategy, which accounts for the change. Other items with especially significant increases include those dealing with counting and recording of large numbers, (some of these are similar to the 'Write 200' and '1 < 200' items described earlier, but with larger numbers) and use of the inverse relation between addition and subtraction (deriving the answer to $143 - 86$ quickly given that $86 + 57 = 143$). All these ideas do indeed figure strongly in the Numeracy Strategy curriculum, which would seem to account for the difference between the cohorts.

Similarly in those items receiving less emphasis, such as word problem solving, the facilities have not increased significantly and in some cases have decreased (see the items '4(10) + 3' and 'Select $-$' in Figure 5.3 and Table 5.6).

The introduction of new representations, for example number lines, horizontal recording, seems to have had significant effects, whereas expected changes in some basic skills, for example knowledge of multiplication facts, have not emerged.

The overall summary of changes to items in specific areas of the curriculum is shown in Table 5.8.

Of course these results refer only to year 4, and may be different by the end of year 6.

Such discontinuities in item profiles which are clearly attributable to changes in the curriculum seem however to be quite short term; it is not clear whether there are any longer term effects of the curriculum change.

The relatively large differences between performance on some individual items between the year 4 cohorts, combined with the relatively small overall

TABLE 5.8   Changes In Mean Year 4 Facilities for Groups of Items in Different Areas of the Numeracy Curriculum Between June 1998 and June 2002

Group	Number of items	1998	2002	Difference
Number system	31	63	69	$+6$
Addition/subtraction	18	60	65	$+4$
Multiplication/division	9	72	68	-1
Fractions/decimals/ratio	13	41	42	$+1$
Solving real life problems	10	40	39	-1

change, suggests that it is the curriculum changes in the National Numeracy Strategy rather than the teaching methods which have had an effect on the results.

3. Progression in learning for many individual children is not smooth and may include periods of stasis until new ideas are fully grasped

A study of the progress of individual children shows that some children at all ability levels appear to make steady progress over time and thus remain at roughly the same percentile with respect to the rest of the sample. Others vary considerably in their rates of progress, for example after a plateau they can make large jumps.

In this section examples will be given of three case-study pupils, Debbie, Joseph and Damien, whose progress is not steady; results from classroom observations and interview data will help to validate this data and indicate some factors which may explain these variations.

(a) Debbie

Debbie, in the older cohort (cohort 2) at Pinedene school, is a child whose test results oscillate considerably around the median, with no obvious long term trend. In Figure 5.4, Debbie's mathematical age at each test administration is plotted against the distribution of mathematical ages for cohort 2 and the mean age of Debbie's class.

Debbie's score started at about the median in year 4, moving up to about the 65th percentile at the end of the year but her performance dropped gradually through year 5 until it reached about the 35th percentile at the start of year 6. By the end of year 6 and again at the end of year 7 she was back at about the 60th percentile. Examining her test performance for reasons for her failure to progress in year 5, we noted that she made no progress on any items in the areas of place value and decimals between the end of year 4 and the start of year 6. However there was considerable improvement at the end of year 6. This improvement was maintained in year 7, although the year 7 data is not shown on Figure 5.4. However Debbie's test performance was generally consistent, both within tests and between them.

Debbie was quiet in class but quite independent and determined. In year 4 we saw her working confidently with a partner, on one occasion to develop a good understanding of equivalent fractions in the context of pictures of multi-paned windows. But in year 5 it was clear in class as well as on our test papers that more abstract equivalent fractions (e.g., changing tenths into hundredths), place value and decimals were all problematic for her. Debbie volunteered to us in class in year 5 that she did not understand these ideas and always got wrong answers in class tests. The teaching we observed on fractions in that year was not addressing her problems, and we observed that both she and other members of the class became frustrated. When we interviewed Debbie at the end of year 6, she felt that she had learned a lot in year 4 but had found the teacher and the

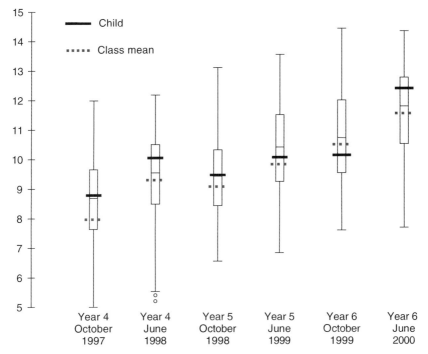

FIGURE 5.4 Debbie's progression in terms of mathematical age, in relation to the whole distribution and the mean for her class.

work in year 5 difficult to understand. She felt, and we observed both in class and on our tests, that she had recovered in year 6 with a more supportive and more relaxed teacher who tried hard to assist the children in understanding the basis of the mathematics. (However his reassuring approach was perhaps not challenging enough for all children, as the class as a whole dropped during the year in relation to the rest of the sample.)

Thus Debbie's performance, and her perceptions of the quality of the teaching and of her reaction to it, correspond to our classroom observation data. This, and the fact that the changes in her performance are similar to, but more extreme than, the changes in the class performance over these years suggests that in her case the quality of teaching is a key factor and that Debbie was particularly sensitive to it. (Some case-study children in that class did not follow the trend of class performance.) Debbie was keen to understand the basis of what she was doing, and once she had obtained a correct answer to a test item did not regress. She seemed to need teachers who could help her achieve this understanding, since she did not get much help at home, being the eldest of three girls with a single mother. (The fact that her parents split up in year 5 seem likely to have contributed to the problems that year.)

(b) Joseph

Joseph, at St. Luke's School and like Debbie in the older cohort, had a very different profile. This is shown in Figure 5.5. (He was absent for the test in June 1998.)

Joseph's relative position in the whole cohort gradually declined from near the 80th percentile at the start of year 4 to about the 60th at the end of year 6 and year 7. When we examined his tests his performance seemed very inconsistent; unlike Debbie he quite often got questions wrong that he had answered correctly on earlier occasions, and within the same paper he made quite basic errors in place value while in more difficult areas like equivalent fractions he appeared to show quite sophisticated understanding. After a year in a high set at secondary school, Joseph's performance in the test deteriorated, both on fractions and on place value questions.

Classroom observations of Joseph suggest that he tried to remember standard algorithms, rather than trusting to informal methods based on understanding, but he often became confused and had little basic knowledge of place value to fall back on when his memory was insufficient. Nor did he seem to have any belief that mathematics made sense, as he showed very little metacognitive inclination

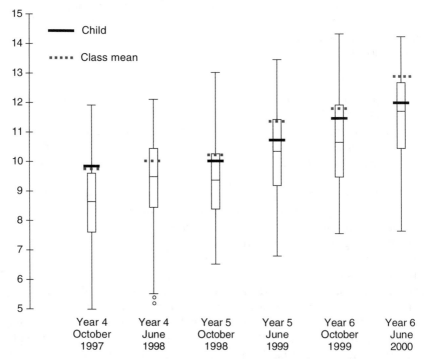

FIGURE 5.5 Joseph's progression in terms of mathematical age, in relation to the whole distribution and the mean for his class.

to monitor and check his answers. He also appeared to be unwilling to make any cognitive effort and seemed to lack commitment to improving his own learning. These factors appear to explain his inconsistent results on specific items, with his success depending on whether he happened randomly to remember appropriate knowledge.

Yet Joseph was the only child of caring and well-educated parents, who had made sure that he attended a prestigious Catholic primary school (mean attainment for his class was the highest in the sample and in the top quartile for the whole pupil population). From here he gained entry to an even more prestigious Catholic London secondary school. His parents were sufficiently concerned about his mathematics to have arranged for a private tutor in year 3 (although Joseph said he did not find this useful so asked to discontinue it). The primary school were keen to move children on fast and, prior to the introduction of the Numeracy Strategy, used textbooks intended for children a year older, starting from reception (age 4–5). One possible explanation of Joseph's results are that he was a victim of a procedural approach in both primary and secondary schools; his uncertain grasp of fundamental ideas had not been tackled by either his teacher or his private tutor. His own lethargy and disinclination to engage with mathematics, about which all his teachers complained, has also prevented him from sorting this out for himself. However he was not apparently lacking intelligence. He was generally characterized by teachers as 'lazy' but this did not seem to do justice to his complex perceptions and beliefs.

(c) Damien

Damien was in the younger cohort at Pinedene School. His progress is shown in Figure 5.6.

Damien was a direct contrast to Joseph. He was absent for the test at the start of year 1, but at the end of year 1 his test score was low, at about the 20th percentile. His performance improved dramatically by the start of year 2, reaching the median, and continued to improve dramatically until it reached the 70th percentile by the end of year 3. Unfortunately he left the school at the end of year 3 to attend a private school some distance away so we lost contact with him in year 4. Damien's performance both between and within tests was, like Debbie's, much more consistent than that of Joseph.

Some of Damien's dramatic improvements can also be attributed to his teachers. In year 1 when his score was very low the whole class did very badly (the mean being below the 30th percentile for the pupil population, although later they rose to above the 60th percentile). The teacher was in her first year of teaching and subsequently left the profession. She found classroom organization difficult (which may mean that test results at the end of year 1 are unreliable) and the teaching we observed was undemanding and sometimes the objectives were unclear. However Damien's later progress was not only due to improved teaching as his scores rose considerably faster than those for the rest of the class. He was diagnosed as dyslexic which explained why his reading and writing were

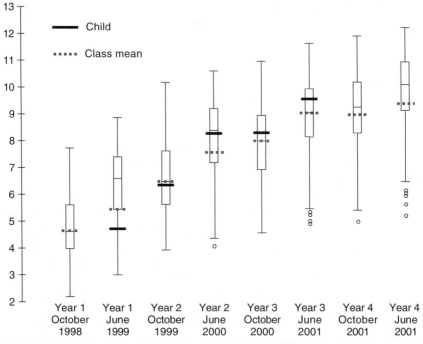

FIGURE 5.6   Damien's progression in terms of mathematical age, in relation to the whole distribution and the mean for his class.

poor, but he was very enthusiastic about mathematics and determined to do well. He spent a lot of time in his bedroom playing computer games involving numbers, and enjoyed discussing mathematics with a high attaining boy in his class. In an interview at the end of year 3 he showed a very mature appreciation of his abilities and a determination to do well in maths. However the school had always regarded him as naughty; sometimes his poor behavior in class seemed to reflect his frustration that his language problems were impeding his progress.

CONCLUSIONS

These results confirm that the generally smooth patterns of progression in the facility of items across the whole population contain much variation at the level of the individual child. While some children stayed at roughly the same percentile over the course of 4 years, others shifted position radically, either moving up, moving down or oscillating.

The progress of individual children appeared to depend on many factors, relating to the child's ability, personality and inclinations, the home circumstances, and on whether the teaching addressed their needs, especially in relation to mathematical ideas which commonly cause problems. For different children the balance of importance of these factors is different, and is likely to change over time for any particular child. In spite of general trends, it therefore seems to be impossible to predict the future progress of any specific child from their earlier test results.

Although there are a number of key longitudinal *intervention* studies (e.g., Maher & Martino, 1996; Steffe & Cobb, 1988), there is a dearth of longitudinal studies of children's progress in learning mathematics in ordinary classrooms either on a large scale or as case studies.

The Leverhulme Programme filled this gap across the curriculum range of numeracy in the primary school and provided both a generic model of progression, and information about how and why both individual test items and individual children depart from the generic model. Such information is important as an evidence base for researchers, curriculum developers and teachers, allowing both a more precise picture of median attainment and of the attainment spread across each year group, and how this changes from one age group to the next.

It also provided insight for each of these user groups into the idiosyncratic trajectories of individual students, and some factors which may contribute to these differences in progress.

Finally, the results highlighted the complex yet weak relationships between teaching and learning, and in particular that a major attempt at systemic change has had at most a small effect on attainment in most areas of numeracy.

REFERENCES

Askew, M., Brown, M., Rhodes, V., Wiliam, D. & Johnson, D. (1997). *Effective Teachers of Numeracy*. London: King's College London, for the Teacher Training Agency.

Baker, D. A. & Street, B. (1993). Literacy and numeracy. *International Encyclopaedia of Education* (pp. 3453–3459). Oxford: Pergamon.

Cobb, P. & Bauersfeld, H. (1995) *The Emergence of Mathematical Meaning*. Hillsdale, NJ: Lawrence Erlbaum Associates.

Denvir, H. & Bibby, T. (2002) *Diagnostic Interviews in Number Sense*. London: BEAM Publications.

Denvir, B. & Brown, M. (1986) Understanding of number concepts in low attaining 7–9 year olds: Parts 1 and 2. *Educational Studies in Mathematics, 17*, 15–36 and 143–164.

Denvir, B. & Brown, M. (1987). The feasibility of class-administered diagnostic assessment in primary mathematics. *Educational Research, 29*(2), 95–107.

Department of Education and Science/Welsh Office (DES/WO); Committee of Inquiry into the Teaching of Mathematics in Schools (1982). *Mathematics Counts (The Cockcroft Report)*. London: HMSO.

Earl, L., Levin, B., Leithwood, K., Fullan, M., Watson, N., et al. (2002). *Watching and Learning 3: OISE/UT Evaluation of the Implementation of the National Literacy and Numeracy Strategies, Third and Final Report*. Toronto: OISE/UT.

Hambleton, R. K., Swaminathan, H. & Rogers, H. J. (1991). *Fundamentals of Item Response Theory*. Newbury Park, CA: Sage.

Hargreaves, L. & Galton, M. (2002). *Transfer from the Primary School: 20 Years On.* London: Routledge.

Hart, K. (Ed.) (1981). *Children's Understanding of Mathematics: 11–16.* London: John Murray.

Maher, C. A. & Martino, A. M. (1996). The development of the idea of mathematical proof: a 5-year case-study. *Journal for Research in Mathematics Education, 27*(2), 194–214.

National Numeracy Strategy (1999). *Framework for Teaching Mathematics from Reception to Year 6.* London: Department for Education and Employment.

Office for Standards in Education (Ofsted) (2002a). *Key Stage 3 Strategy: Pilot Year.* London: Ofsted.

Office for Standards in Education (Ofsted) (2002b). *The National Numeracy Strategy: the first three years 1999–2002.* London: Ofsted.

Steffe, L. & Cobb, P. (1988). *Construction of Arithmetical Meanings and Strategies.* New York: Springer-Verlag.

6

AN ANALYSIS OF CHILDREN'S NUMERICAL DIFFICULTIES WITH THE AID OF A DYSCALCULIA TEST BATTERY AND A PRESENTATION OF REMEDIAL APPROACHES TO FACILITATE ASPECTS OF NUMERICAL DEVELOPMENT

CHRISTINE LAWSON

CAMHS, IoM/Independent, UK

INTRODUCTION

When considering various cultures, human body parts have been used as aids to counting in the development of some number systems. Also, the significance of fingers has been highlighted particularly in the context of early numerical development from a neuropsychological perspective by Butterworth (1999). A variety of functions have been associated with the fusiform gyrus which is a structure located in the superior temporal region of the brain. Recognition of Arabic numerals presented visually involves the fusiform gyrus, particularly the left as highlighted by Ramachandran and Hubbard (2005) with reference to Pesenti et al. (2000) and Rickard et al. (2000). In relation to neuroimaging research findings McCandliss et al. (2003) have suggested that the process of abstract visual word form perception is associated with a cortical area located within the left fusiform gyrus. Also, they note with reference to Haxby et al. (2000) that evidence has suggested there is activation in this area resulting from object and face recognition. Further discussions concerning the notion of a visual word form area and related issues have been given by Cohen and Dehaene (2004) and Price and Devlin (2003, 2004). For developmental perspectives in relation to facial perception and the fusiform gyrus reference could be made to Passarotti et al. (2003), Gathers et al. (2004), Aylward et al. (2005) and Scherf et al. (2007).

Facial features are some aspects of the body that have been noted in relation to number systems and they have been considered particularly by certain investigators in connection with numerical disabilities. Badian (1983) considered that a deficit in visual attention to exact detail as suggested in young children's human figure drawings might provide information concerning later numerical abilities. In Badian's discussion concerning those who might be described as dyscalculic, the omission of the nose was noted and sometimes the inclusion of an incorrect number of fingers.

Also, findings from research by Lawson (2000c, 2001a) with first-year junior-aged children suggested that directing their attention to specific arithmetical details and associated numerical concepts or, alternatively, particular omissions and poorly depicted aspects concerning their drawings of people enhanced their development and performances in both areas. Additionally, in another study by Lawson (2001b), first-year junior-aged pupils practised a task involving subitizing which concerns the fast apprehension of small numerosities. The numerosities were associated with dots for some presentations and for others with schematic facial features. The results suggested a facilitative effect in relation to the inclusion of details in their human figure drawings as well as more realistic depictions.

The findings presented by Noël (2005) indicated that in first-grade children finger gnosia was a good predictor of numerical skills. Also, this occurred for left–right orientation. Finger gnosia predicted performance equally on numerical tasks whether or not they depended particularly on finger representation or on magnitude representation. Also, Rusconi et al. (2005) found that in adults repetitive transcranial magnetic stimulation (rTMS) over the left angular gyrus disrupted finger gnosis and number magnitude processing. 'In a more recent study by Gracia-Bafalluy and Noël (2008) with first grade children, it was suggested that finger differentiation training improved performances in finger gnosis, subitizing, counting representations of raised fingers and ordinality involving Arabic digit processing. In the finger gnosis assessment the children were required to differentiate their fingers when touched and without visual cues. The specific task had been used by Noël (2005). Also, as part of the finger gnosis assessment the children were involved in a 'Draw a Man' and a 'Draw a Hand' task. On the latter, participants in the finger differentiation training group demonstrated enhanced performances in comparison with those in the control group who had received story comprehension training, after individuals in each group had received their specific interventions. The possibility was considered of improvements in internal representations concerning the fingers and hands but with no change for those involving the whole body.'

Additionally, Sato et al. (2007) used TMS to investigate changes in excitability relating to hand muscles of right-handed adult participants during their involvement with a visual, odd or even parity judgment task. It concerned the Arabic numerals from 1 to 9, with the exclusion of 5 and there was not a requirement for counting. No modulation was indicated for the left-hand muscles, but an increase in amplitude concerning the motor-evoked potentials was demonstrated for the right-hand muscles. The increase was apparent only for the smaller numbers from 1 to 4 as opposed to the larger numbers from 6 to 9. Hence a neural association was suggested between hand/finger and numerical representations. Also, in a study by Andres et al. (2007) right-handed adult female participants were involved with a counting task requiring the use of numbers or letters of the alphabet to enumerate items. Changes in corticospinal activity (CS) were assessed via TMS. The results indicated an increase in CS excitability relating to hand muscles when the participants were performing the task using numbers or letters. The increase in CS excitability was identical when the activity involved small arrays of dots from 1 to 4 as opposed to large arrays comprising 9 to 12 dots. No changes were apparent in relation to the arm and foot muscles. Hence, the involvement of hand motor circuits was considered for tasks requiring items to be placed correspondingly with the elements of any ordered series.

In research by Riggs et al. (2006), subitizing was investigated in relation to tactile perception via the simultaneous stimulation of the fingertips on both hands of adult participants. A discontinuity in accuracy was shown with near perfection for one to three fingers and severe impairment for four to six fingers. Also, there was a discontinuity in the naming-times slope for one to six fingers. Hence it was concluded that subitizing was apparent in tactile perception within this context. In a different context but still involving touch, the results of research by Gallace et al. (2006) suggested that adults were able to discriminate to a certain extent between different numbers of tactile stimuli when multiple tactors were activated simultaneously across the surface of the body. However, the accuracy of tactile numerosity judgments decreased considerably with relatively modest increases in the number of activated tactors. The participants indicated the ability to estimate differences in the number of tactors comprising the pattern presented on the body, but this was less so for the correct perception of information concerning the actual quantity. There was no indication of a discontinuity in the slope corresponding to the reaction time or the error data, so subitizing was not suggested by the results. Also, reference could be made to Gallace et al. (2007a) in relation to numerosity judgments concerning visual and tactile stimuli and for detailed discussions of cutaneous tactile stimulation within a multisensory context to Gallace and Spence (2008) and Gallace et al. (2007b).

In a functional magnetic resonance imaging (fMRI) study by Thompson et al. (2004), adult participants viewed videos of a hand with small numbers being represented by finger movements or faces where lip movements presented the same numerical information. Control stimuli comprised the same hand half opening and closing or the same mouth opening and closing for each comparable test item. Activation relating to lip reading of numbers was apparent in the left posterior superior temporal sulcus (STS). Identification of numbers conveyed by the fingers was indicated by preferential activation in the left inferior parietal region (IPR). Also, activation in relation to numbers via the presentation of finger stimuli was shown in the right IPR. This response was not specific to the number representation via finger stimuli, and there was a small area of common activation in the right IPR associated with the identification of numbers in the finger and lip numerical presentations. In relation to their findings the authors referred to an fMRI study by Eger et al. (2003). Adult participants were asked to respond to target items within each category of numerals, letters and colors presented in the visual and the auditory modalities. Specifically, this nonarithmetical processing of numerals in comparison with letters and colors activated a bilateral region in the horizontal intraparietal sulcus for the visual and auditory modal presentations. Thompson et al. (2004) noted that this supramodal number region as termed by Eger and colleagues was proximal to the intraparietal regions activated by fingers representing numerical information in their study.

As indicated below concerning the presentation here, the fingers were used particularly in relation to the tactile aspects of the remedial technique as the participants felt the shape of each solid Arabic numeral. Also, they might use fingers overtly or covertly for counting when necessary although the extent to which they were used varied as different strategies and direct recall became available increasingly during the development of their numerical abilities. Apart from moving their lips as they said the number words, they watched my lips move sometimes during the interactions and including the times when I spoke the number words. Also, there were no restrictions on the movement of the hands except for the specific application as described for the multisensory technique for learning the multiplication tables. The importance of the hands not only in relation to their use for the representation of the attentional and declarative aspects of cognitive activities but in terms of providing support within a dynamic context for the procedural aspects of these activities has been discussed in some detail by Carlson et al. (2007). Specifically they considered the use of the hands in elementary arithmetic tasks and emphasized the importance of studying the embodiment of cognition. For a specific discussion concerning the embodied mind and mathematics, reference could be made to Lakoff and Núñez (2000).

The angular gyrus which has been highlighted above is situated within the inferior parietal lobule and is located at the junctions of the temporal, parietal and occipital lobes. Generally this region has been considered to be involved in the multisensory convergence of information from touch, hearing and vision to facilitate the construction of higher-level abstractions (Ramachandran and Hubbard, 2005). It would appear that at birth we are predisposed to manage multisensory input in an environment which provides information mainly of a multimodal nature. Also, multisensory processing and integration have been of particular interest in association with theories and interventions concerning some specific conditions such as those within the autism spectrum (Iarocci and McDonald, 2006). In relation to numerical development some studies, for example, Kobayashi et al. (2005) and Jordan and Brannon (2006) have suggested that infants are able to relate sets with small numerosities when they are presented in different sensory modalities. Consequently, it would seem reasonable to consider teaching/learning approaches that emphasize multisensory stimulation with the aim that compensatory mechanisms might be facilitated for those individuals who might experience difficulties in certain areas.

The first two children discussed here had been selected originally because they had experienced difficulties in learning the multiplication tables. Before their involvement in a remedial program to help them overcome these specific problems and to promote more mature numerical development, they were assessed in terms of their levels of cognitive and psychosocial functioning as well as their attainments in literacy and numeracy. The third child given in this presentation had problems also in learning the multiplication tables so it was appropriate to involve him in a similar remedial program. However, because of social and communication difficulties he participated also in other assessments and interventions some of which had been designed specifically by the present author.

As part of the assessment, items were developed in relation to the Dyscalculia Test Battery described by Macaruso et al. (1992) and there were some specific additional tasks too. Their battery was based on the cognitive model of number processing and calculation suggested by McCloskey et al. (1985) and supported by evidence of specific deficiencies in adults with acquired dyscalculia. In this model a number processing section comprised distinct components for comprehension and production, lexical and syntactical elements and separate Arabic and verbal number processes. Another aspect involved knowledge relating to number facts including the meaning of signs and knowledge of tables. Also, an area concerned procedural knowledge including the necessary algorithms for carrying out exercises involving the four arithmetical operations.

Difficulties might be experienced by individuals described as dyscalculic in any of the spheres concerning numerical processing, knowledge of number facts and procedural knowledge. Temple (1989, 1991, 1994a, b, 1997a, b) discussed the main characteristics of some young people who might be described as dyscalculic within a developmental cognitive neuropsychological context and with some considerations support was given for the model proposed by McCloskey and his colleagues. Reference could be made to Campbell and Epp (2005) who have reviewed studies and considered challenges in relation to aspects of the model and possible modifications. Additionally, Kaufmann and Nuerk (2005) have highlighted issues concerning the use of adult numerical cognitive models in relation to children and adolescents, and their discussion has included aspects relating to the model by McCloskey and his colleagues.

Also, a recent discussion concerning dyscalculia including developmental and acquired considerations associated with various hypotheses as well as implications for educational aspects and interventions has been presented by Wilson and Dehaene (2007). They highlight the significance of the angular gyrus and a suggested impairment involving this region and associated with difficulties in the learning and retrieval of arithmetical facts, especially relating to multiplication. Additionally, reference could be made to the various discussions concerning mathematical learning difficulties and disabilities in the book edited by Berch and Mazzocco (2007). Specifically, Simon and Rivera (2007) emphasize caution concerning the findings of neuroanatomical correlates relating to numerical cognition in neuroimaging studies involving adults and interpretations concerning children and adolescents as differences in neural activity might be found in young people with typical and atypical presentations at various stages in their development. Also, there are a limited number of published neuroimaging investigations concerning numerical development involving children and adolescents.

In an fMRI study by Kawashima et al. (2004), young people of both sexes, aged 9–14 years and adults, men and women aged 40–49 years were involved in mental calculation tasks concerning addition, subtraction and multiplication with single-digit operands. Brain activation was demonstrated in the prefrontal, intraparietal, occipital and occipito-temporal cortices for both groups of participants and in relation to when they performed each of the arithmetic operations. The young people who took part in my research were involved with learning items from the multiplication tables, and some of these had single-digit operands whereas others involved two-digits. Also, although the number of items that they could retrieve directly increased with training, if they were unable to recall an answer immediately they might recall another item and use mental addition or subtraction to obtain the correct answer. Additionally, because of their difficulties and the nature of the training they experienced the multiplication items in a variety of modalities. In the study highlighted above the items were presented on a computer screen, and the participants were instructed to perform the tasks mentally and not to vocalize or move parts of their bodies.

Generally, I have noted the results of some studies with children, adolescents and adults which seemed of interest and relevance to the discussion presented here. Overall, assumptions have not been made in relation to these findings and the location of neural activation in the young people who have participated in my projects. Also, I implemented items which I had developed in relation to a particular dyscalculia test battery as the resulting assessment tool was expected to be helpful in highlighting specific numerical difficulties experienced by the young participants in my studies.

In relation to some of the terms and ideas used by myself and in various studies, reference could be made to Shalev (2007) for a discussion of aspects concerning developmental dyscalculia in the context of definitions, assessments and prevalence. Shalev and Gross-Tsur (1993) considered a marked impairment of arithmetical skills combined with a lack of response to educational interventions as the criteria for developmental dyscalculia in the children involved with their investigation. Specific arithmetical impairments had been noticed by staff or parents concerned with the young people described here, and they had not responded to remedial interventions or only to a limited extent. The case reports presented here give analyses of the difficulties experienced by three boys. The findings are related to other investigations concerning children's numerical development, case studies of young people with developmental dyscalculia and research involving individuals or groups of adults with acquired dyscalculia.

Mainly, information obtained from the Dyscalculia Test Battery Assessment is presented here but a few points will be noted in relation to some specific numerical tasks which were administered to the children as part of the whole assessment. The first two cases, namely Child A. and Child M., were involved with their assessments and remedial programs some time ago, whereas Child L. was seen more recently and he participated in other sessions concerned with different aspects of his development because of his disposition as indicated below. Consequently, some different tests or more revised versions of some assessments were used for Child L. as opposed to the other two boys. Detailed presentations of the programs for Child A. have been given by Lawson (1995b, 2000b) and for Child M. by Lawson (2000b) with summaries by Lawson (2001a). Also, certain aspects relating to these two children reported here were presented initially by Lawson (2002). A comprehensive presentation concerning the assessments and interventions for Child L. has been given by Lawson (2005).

Initially, a detailed description of the Dyscalculia Test Battery is given as well as the remedial technique used to help children who experienced difficulty with certain types of addition problems. Also, a Multisensory Remedial Approach for Learning the Multiplication Tables developed by the present author is described here. This technique involved the visual, auditory, tactile and kinesthetic modalities and is similar in certain respects to that described for reading and spelling by Bryant and Bradley (1985). Also, the modified procedure for learning the operation names, words and symbols is given in this presentation.

As discussed by Fogassi and Gallese (2004), multisensory integration is a pervasive characteristic of cortical regions concerned with motor planning and control. Cortical premotor regions possess sensory features and posterior parietal regions that have been considered association areas possess motor features. Parietal regions which are connected with frontal regions jointly comprise cortical networks for the processing and integration of multisensory data for the execution of action and the representation of the environment in which the action occurs. The multisensory technique that I developed involved a motor component and this aspect is a feature of other approaches described below.

Specifically, my approach shares some similarities as well as differences with TouchMath (Bullock, 2002) which has been highlighted by Naglieri and Pickering (2003). This is a multisensory method for learning computation with applications in relation to all four arithmetical processes. Also, my approach has certain aspects in common with the ARROW technique (Lane & Chinn, 1986; Lane, 1992) and cited by Chinn and Ashcroft (1998). ARROW, which is an acronym for Aural-Read-Respond-Oral-Written is a multisensory teaching/learning approach. The learner's own voice is replayed on tape and connected with skills in writing, listening and speech in a set of processes concerning spelling, comprehension and reading books. Lane and Chinn (1986) and Chinn and Ashcroft (1998) describe the technique in relation specifically to learning the multiplication tables.

The author would like to emphasize that the relatively simple techniques concerning addition and multiplication discussed here were accompanied always by instructional support aimed at integrating and promoting the development of numerical concepts and knowledge of arithmetical procedures with the acquisition of number facts. The iterative nature of factual, procedural and conceptual knowledge concerning numbers has been emphasized in a developmental context by Baroody (2003) and highlighted in relation to the rehabilitation of acquired calculation and numerical processing disorders by Lochy et al. (2005). Also, Zamarian et al. (2007) have emphasized the influence of inter-relationships concerning the different aspects of numerical knowledge in promoting the development of meaningful and efficient processing in this area. In relation to my participants, often the children offered comments and ideas spontaneously which indicated the nature of their understanding and these could be developed further. For those who were less forthcoming, they could be prompted to question and think about various aspects concerning the items that had been problematic.

Also, although I refer to Arabic numerals I do acknowledge consideration in relation to the Indian numerical symbolic notation as highlighted, for example, by Ifrah (1998). Additionally, McCloskey et al. (1985) refer to Arabic and verbal numbers. The distinction between numbers and their symbolic representation via the use of the term 'numerals' has been highlighted by McCloskey (1992) in relation specifically to Arabic numerals for numbers represented symbolically in digit form as well as spoken and written verbal numerals for numbers represented as words. Hence, I have used the term 'numerals' in connection with the dyscalculia model which I have described here. However, in line with everyday usage of the term 'number' I might have used this terminology when making a request to a child, for example, to find a number when referring to solid plastic numerals in Arabic form for the Tactile Recognition and Naming of Numerals task. Also when I refer to number(s) in the discussion, the exact representation and any conceptual associations should be clear from the context.

A DYSCALCULIA TEST BATTERY

NUMERAL PROCESSING TASKS

Magnitude Comparison

Arabic Magnitude Comparison. Two Arabic numerals were presented to the child who on request pointed to the larger or smaller number. The test items included units, tens, hundreds and thousands. There were 10 comparisons for the units with the numbers ranging from 0 to 9 and 10 comparisons each for the tens in the range 10–19 and in the range 20–99. For the hundreds and the thousands there were five comparisons each that were selected respectively within the ranges 9,999. The items were chosen so that a broad selection was offered and included odd and even numbers and those involving zeros. Also, they were written and presented on white cards.

Spoken Verbal Magnitude Comparison. Two verbal numerals were presented in spoken form and the child indicated which was larger. On a piece of white card, two squares had been drawn one above the other. The assessor pointed to the top square while reading the first number and to the bottom square when reading the second number. When asked to respond to the larger or smaller number the child responded by pointing to the appropriate square. The test items were the same as those used for the Arabic Magnitude Comparison tasks.

Written Verbal Magnitude Comparison. Two written verbal numerals were presented to the child and he/she pointed to the larger or smaller number as requested. The test items were the same as those used for the Arabic Magnitude Comparison Tasks except that they were in written verbal form.

Transcoding Tasks

On these tasks the child was asked to perform six possible conversions among Arabic, spoken verbal and written verbal numerals. All of the test items used were the same as for the magnitude comparison tasks.

Transcoding Arabic Numerals to Spoken Verbal Numerals. Arabic numerals were presented visually and the child read each numeral aloud.

Transcoding Spoken Verbal Numerals to Written Verbal Numerals. Verbal numerals were dictated and the child wrote each numeral in verbal form.

Transcoding Spoken Verbal Numerals to Arabic Numerals. Verbal numerals were dictated and the child wrote each numeral in Arabic form.

Transcoding Arabic Numerals to Written Verbal Numerals. Arabic numerals were presented visually and the child wrote each numeral in verbal form.

Transcoding Written Verbal Numerals to Spoken Verbal Numerals. Written verbal numerals were presented and the child read each numeral aloud.

Transcoding Written Verbal Numerals to Arabic Numerals. Written verbal numerals were presented and the child wrote each numeral in Arabic form.

Additional Item: Tactile Recognition and Naming of Numerals. Solid plastic Arabic numerals from 0 to 9 were placed under a cloth and the child was asked to find individual numbers at random and to name them one at a time while they were under the cover. Also, the child was asked to retrieve named numbers that were chosen individually at random from under the cloth.

CALCULATION TASKS

Operation Symbol and Word Comprehension

Operation Symbol Comprehension. This task comprised items probing comprehension of the operation symbols for addition, subtraction, multiplication and division. For each item an operation name was presented visually and aurally. Arithmetic problems with identical operands but different operation symbols were presented visually. The child's task was to point to the problem corresponding to the specified operation. The test items included units, tens and hundreds. There were four items involving two numbers each in the units for assessing comprehension of the four arithmetical operations. Also, there were four items involving two numbers each, with a number in the 10–40 range and a number in the 1–9 range and another group of four items each involving two numbers where one number was in the range 100–400 and the other number was in the range 10–60.

Operation Word Comprehension. In this task, items were used which probed comprehension of the spoken operation words 'plus', 'minus', 'times' and 'divided by'. An operation name was presented visually and aurally for each item. Then an arithmetic problem was dictated and the child indicated whether or not the problem corresponded to the operation name. A yes/no procedure was used for the response. The test items were selected from the Operation Symbol Comprehension tasks.

Written Arithmetic Tasks

These tasks were used to investigate the retrieval of arithmetic facts and execution of the calculation procedures for addition, subtraction, multiplication and division. For Child A. and Child M. three arithmetic tests were administered, specifically the first 25 questions of the Graded Arithmetic–Mathematics Test (Junior) by Vernon and Miller (1976), the Basic Number Diagnostic Test by Gillham (1980) and the British Ability Scales (BAS)-Basic Number Skills by Elliot et al. (1983). Child L. was administered both sections of the Weschler Objective Numerical Dimension (WOND)-Mathematical Reasoning (MR) and Numerical Operations (NO) (Rust, 1996). For the MR section, the questions are seen visually by the child and they are read to the participant. Some items require a written answer but for many questions an oral response is required by the individual and a few items require the child to point in response to a question. On the NO section the answers to all of the questions have to be written.

Additional Item: Specific Rectangular and Non-Rectangular Addition Exercises. The children were administered certain types of rectangular and non-rectangular addition questions, groups (A, B) and (A1, B1) which I had prepared myself and the necessary teaching involving groups (A2, B2) and re-assessment with groups (C1, D1) as required if they experienced difficulty with these exercises. The non-rectangular addition problems had been high-lighted by Friend (1979) and confirmed by Lawson (1986, 1989) as being a source of particular difficulty for some children, and these studies had noted three specific types of errors. Examples of items in the different groups and particular errors are shown below. The terms rectangular and non-rectangular referred to the digital arrangement in the addends. The non-rectangular questions contained a single-digit in the far left column and there was no carry to be added into this column. I presented the children with rectangular exercises that matched the non-rectangular questions in terms of the number of columns and rows and no carrying was required in the calculations. The difficulties concerning the non-rectangular problems had been considered in relation to conceptual issues concerning the join of a single set and the sum of a single number. The questions could be completed accurately after instruction with a simple technique involving a zero being placed in the space in the far left column and a discussion to clarify the associated conceptual basis for the procedures (Lawson, 1990, 1995a, 2000a, 2001a).

Examples of the rectangular and non-rectangular addition exercises given in each of the groups:

$$
\begin{array}{llll}
\text{A} & \begin{array}{cc} 4 & 3 \\ +\ 2 & 1 \end{array} & \text{B} & \begin{array}{ccc} 3 & 1 & 2 \\ +\ 4 & 3 & 4 \end{array} \\[2em]
\text{A1} & \begin{array}{cc} 6 & 3 \\ + & 2 \end{array} & \text{B1} & \begin{array}{ccc} 5 & 6 & 1 \\ + & 3 & 1 \end{array} \\[2em]
\text{A2} & \begin{array}{cc} 6 & 3 \\ +\ 0 & 2 \end{array} & \text{B2} & \begin{array}{ccc} 5 & 6 & 1 \\ +\ 0 & 3 & 1 \end{array} \\[2em]
\text{C1} & \begin{array}{cc} 3 & 1 \\ + & 6 \end{array} & \text{D1} & \begin{array}{ccc} 4 & 3 & 2 \\ + & 5 & 3 \end{array}
\end{array}
$$

Examples of the specific types of errors on the non-rectangular addition exercises:

Type 1: A number is added from another column e.g.

$$
\begin{array}{cc} 6 & 3 \\ +\ & 2 \\ \hline 8 & 5 \end{array} \qquad \begin{array}{ccc} 5 & 6 & 1 \\ +\ & 3 & 1 \\ \hline 8 & 9 & 2 \end{array}
$$

Type 2: The single digit is added into the column on the right e.g.

$$
\begin{array}{cc} 6 & 3 \\ +\ & 2 \\ \hline & 1 & 1 \end{array} \qquad \begin{array}{ccc} 5 & 6 & 1 \\ +\ & 3 & 1 \\ \hline 1 & 4 & 2 \end{array}
$$

Type 3: The odd digit is ignored e.g.

$$
\begin{array}{r}
6\ 3 \\
+\quad 2 \\
\hline
5
\end{array}
\qquad
\begin{array}{r}
5\ 6\ 1 \\
+\quad 3\ 1 \\
\hline
9\ 2
\end{array}
$$

Oral Arithmetic Tasks

These tasks probed arithmetic fact retrieval and involved the four calculation procedures. Each problem was presented aurally and the child said the answer aloud. Five questions were presented with each item involving two numbers in the range 0–9 for the arithmetic operations addition, subtraction, multiplication and division. Also, Child A. and Child M. were administered the Arithmetic subtest of the Weschler Intelligence Scale for Children–Revised UK (WISC-R UK), Weschler (1976). Child L. was administered the Arithmetic subtest of the Weschler Intelligence Scale for Children–Third Edition UK (WISC-III UK). For both versions of the Arithmetic subtest, the children were administered aurally presented word problems requiring oral responses.

Additional Item: Recitation of Multiplication Tables. The child was asked to recite any of the multiplication tables or any items that he/she was able to recall.

It should be noted that division items were included in the calculation section here whereas they were not specified in the dyscalculia test battery described by Macaruso et al. (1992).

A MULTISENSORY REMEDIAL APPROACH FOR LEARNING THE MULTIPLICATION TABLES

As indicated earlier the teaching approach used to help the children learn the multiplication tables involved a multisensory method with an emphasis on four different sensory modalities. Prior to the remedial sessions, cards had been prepared on which there were written numerals in verbal and Arabic form. Also, there were cards for the four arithmetic operations and expression for equality in verbal and symbolic form. Plastic characters were available that represented Arabic numerals and the four arithmetic symbols and there was one for equality. For some multiplication items the children displayed the word and symbol cards and solid characters in an appropriate order. As they placed the items, they said the names of the numerals and arithmetic operations out aloud and similarly they acknowledged equality. The cards could be used as aids for those with limited literary skills or until the child became more proficient at accessing items, but they were not implemented for every exercise. For all multiplication exercises the children wrote the number words and the arithmetic operation words and they named them aloud as they wrote the items. Then they wrote out the numerals in Arabic form and the arithmetic operation symbols and again they said the names out aloud as they wrote the items. Also, the children placed solid plastic characters under the written Arabic numerals and operation symbols or on a board if the characters were magnetic for each multiplication item and they said the names out aloud. Then they felt and named these solid characters with their eyes closed and with them open. When they repeated the procedure for other table entries they removed only the cards if used and the solid characters that were not needed to form the new items. If a child showed confusion particularly with arithmetic operation names, words and symbols a similar procedure was carried out using the same operands in each case but with different operations.

Example of the items and procedure used for learning the multiplication tables:

three	times	four	equals	twelve(written)
3	×	4	=	12(written)
3	×	4	=	12(solid characters)

Example of the items and procedure used for learning the operation names, words and symbols:

Multiplication:	ten	times	five	equals	fifty(written)
	10	×	5	=	50(written)
	10	×	5	=	50(solid characters)

Addition:	ten	plus	five	equals	fifteen(written)
	10	+	5	=	15(written)
	10	+	5	=	15(solid characters)

Subtraction:	ten	minus	five	equals	five(written)
	10	−	5	=	5(written)
	10	−	5	=	5(solid characters)

Division:	ten	divided by	five	equals	two(written)
	10	÷	5	=	2(written)
	10	÷	5	=	2(solid characters)

CHILD A.

Initially when A. participated in the project he was aged 11 years 1 month and he was in the last year of his primary education. He was expecting to move on to secondary school for the next academic year and some of the comments made here relate to discussions that I had with A. during his first year at secondary level. He had attended mainstream schools throughout his school life and he had not received any form of specialist educational support. As indicated earlier, A. was involved with a variety of assessments but mainly information is presented concerning the Dyscalculia Test Battery. However a few points involving specific numerical tasks are mentioned in relation to this. On the

WISC-R (UK), Weschler (1976) his performance was not strong on the Arithmetic subtest which involves aurally presented word problems with various arithmetical operations that have to be solved mentally by the child and require an oral response. Also, he showed particular difficulty on Digit Span and this was reflected by his limited performance both on the Forward and on the Backward Digit Span tasks. Hence, it was suggested that A. might have some difficulties concerning the storage of numerical data and the manipulation of stored numerical information as discussed by Hoard et al. (1999) in relation particularly to performances on Backward Digit Span within the context of working memory.

DYSCALCULIA TEST BATTERY ASSESSMENT

NUMERAL PROCESSING TASKS

Magnitude Comparison

Arabic Magnitude Comparison. All items were completed correctly.
Spoken Verbal Magnitude Comparison. All items were completed correctly.
Written Verbal Magnitude Comparison. All items were completed correctly.

Transcoding Tasks

Transcoding Arabic Numerals to Spoken Verbal Numerals. A. was required to read aloud each Arabic numeral presented in a visual format. This was a reading task of a similar type to that used by Power and Dal Martello (1997) with Italian children aged 7 years. Various errors were made by these children who were much younger than A. whereas he was correct on all items.

Transcoding Spoken Verbal Numerals to Written Verbal Numerals. All items were completed correctly.

Transcoding Spoken Verbal Numerals to Arabic Numerals. A. made one error when he wrote 9,804 in response to the spoken numeral 'nine thousand and thirty-four' (9,034). The dictation task used here was of a similar form to that used by Power and Dal Martello (1990) with Italian children aged 6–8 years. Generally in the area of numeral processing, the lexical processing component is concerned with the processing of individual number words and digits whereas syntactic processing concerns the relationships among the elements that comprise a numeral. Hence, as highlighted by Power and Dal Martello (1990) in relation to a dictation task, a response for example to the spoken verbal numeral 'three hundred and sixty-five' might involve a lexical error as apparent in 364 as opposed to the correct answer 365. A syntactical error might involve an incorrect number of zeros as in responses such as 3,065 or 30,065 as opposed to the correct answer 365.

Following Power et al. (1978), the investigators gave a theoretical formulation of these errors in which it was proposed that in the production of an Arabic numeral like 365, the numerals 300 and 65 need to be combined via a string operation which they termed 'over-writing'. Children who had not yet acquired competence with this operation tended to rely on concatenation. Generally, they found that syntactical errors were much more frequent than lexical errors and when considering the types of syntactical errors the insertion of zeros was predominant as opposed to the incorrect ordering of digits, such as 563 or 653 instead of the correct response of 365, in the example given above. Also, the insertion of zeros was not apparent for numbers less than hundred. The error made by A. in response to a spoken verbal numeral, when he wrote 9,804 instead of 9,034, appeared to have both syntactical and lexical components as there seemed to be a reversal of two digits and then a digit was written incorrectly. Temple (1989, 1997a, b) described an 11-year-old child who produced incorrect digits when he was required to read Arabic numerals or write Arabic numerals that had been dictated but he demonstrated accurate syntactic processing. More errors were made in relation to reading number words in comparison with Arabic numerals but they were of a similar type. As indicated above and below respectively, A. did not make any errors when reading Arabic numerals or number words.

Transcoding Arabic Numerals to Written Verbal Numerals. A. made two errors when transcoding visually presented Arabic numerals to written verbal numerals with the written verbal response of 'twelve thousand and seventy-eight' being given instead of 'one thousand two hundred and seventy-eight' or 'twelve hundred and seventy-eight' and 'five thousand and sixty-three' being written instead of 'five thousand six hundred and three'. In the first incorrect response written by A., he appeared to have transcoded erroneously the first part of the numeral from 'twelve hundred' to 'twelve thousand' so he made a 'Stack' error by retaining the 12th position within the stack but the information relative to the stack itself was altered, that is from the hundreds to the thousands. In the second case the information regarding the position within the stack, that is, the sixth position was preserved but the information relative to the stack itself was altered, that is from the hundreds to the tens. In a study by Seron and Deloche (1983) using a similar task, patients with Broca's or Wernicke's aphasia made both 'Stack' and 'Stack Position' errors with both groups making more stack than stack position errors. A stack position error occurs where there is erroneous information processing in relation to the position in the stack but with preservation of stack information. Also, both of these error types were found with a similar task in an investigation by Seron and Deloche (1984) involving a mixed group of adult aphasics.

Transcoding Written Verbal Numerals to Spoken Verbal Numerals. All items were completed correctly.

Transcoding Written Verbal Numerals to Arabic Numerals. A. was incorrect on one test item as he wrote 417 instead of 475 when presented with it in written verbal form as 'four hundred and seventy-five'. In this reading task A. appeared to have read incorrectly seventy as seventeen and then omitted the five, so two types of error were made apparently by him. A. made these errors in a task where he had to read number words and then write them in Arabic notation which is a task described by Deloche and Seron (1982a) involving adult aphasics in which the first type of error made by A. would have been termed a 'Stack' error and the second error type would have been categorized by the term 'Partial Processing of the Numeral'. In relation to the stack concept in neuropsycholinguistics, a stack is a file which contains elements in a serial order such as the names for numbers or for the days of the week (Deloche and Seron, 1984). As indicated earlier when considering numerical processing, a stack error occurs when the stack of a lexical element of a numeral is incorrectly coded but there is preservation of information in relation to its position in the stack. For partial processing one of the elements is not processed and this might occur at the beginning, the middle or at the end of the presented item.

Additional Item: Tactile Recognition and Naming of Numerals. A. performed well on the task concerning the tactile recognition and naming of numerals as he responded quickly and correctly to all items on his first attempts.

CALCULATION TASKS

Operation Symbol and Word Comprehension

Operation Symbol Comprehension. All items were completed correctly.

Operation Word Comprehension. A. showed confusion on several items. On the problems involving only units A. said that 'Divided by' and 'Plus' corresponded to the operation name 'Subtraction'. 'Times' did not but when given 'Minus' he was sure that this was the correct operation word. On the problems involving tens and units A. said that 'Times' corresponded and 'Minus' did not correspond to the operation name 'Subtraction'. Also, 'Divided by' corresponded but 'Times' did not correspond to the operation name 'Multiplication'.

Written Arithmetic Tasks

A. made errors on basic subtraction questions and when presented with those that involved borrowing he added the numbers. Also, he responded to some multiplication questions as problems in addition. He could give correct answers only to the very simple multiplication and division questions.

Additional Item: Specific Rectangular and Non-Rectangular Addition Exercises. A. completed accurately the specific rectangular and non-rectangular addition exercises designed by the present author and he indicated an understanding of the associated concepts.

Oral Arithmetic Tasks

A. was correct on the addition and subtraction questions used as oral arithmetic tasks. He corrected himself quickly after giving two erroneous answers to multiplication exercises. A. was unable to complete any division problems presented orally. Also, as indicated above A. had experienced some difficulties on the Arithmetic subtest of the WISC-R (UK) which involves an oral presentation and response although more verbal interpretation is involved than on the simple arithmetic tasks mentioned in this section.

Additional Item: Recitation of Multiplication Tables. A. showed very marked difficulties in relation to remembering the multiplication tables. In an attempt to recite them he tended to work out each answer by counting on from the previous response. Hence he was able to reply correctly on some items. Although he used this method frequently he was able to respond accurately sometimes using direct recall when smaller numbers were involved, for example, $2 \times 3 = 6$. Also, he was able to retrieve directly most of the items from the 10 and 11 times tables. Some of the inaccurate responses that A. made in the multiplication tables were termed 'Bond' errors and 'Shift' errors by Temple (1991, 1997b). 'Bond' errors occur when an individual retrieves an answer which indicates that the correct table is being accessed for one of the numbers in the computation but the selection is incorrect, for example, $6 \times 3 = 15(18)$. Hence, there was the consideration of table entries being stored in an interconnected fashion and bond errors being categorized as semantic (Temple, 1997b). 'Shift' errors are described when erroneous responses are not alternative table values and they contain a single digit that is incorrect, for example, $9 \times 3 = 37(27)$. The second digit is correct and the answer does not occur in the 9 or the 3 times tables. Also, A. made 'Perseverative' errors as described by Temple and Marriott (1998). These are inaccurate responses that have occurred previously in relation to other problems.

CHILD M.

M. was aged 10 years 6 months when he participated initially in the project and he was in a mainstream setting which had been the case for all of his primary education. Also, he had not received specialist educational support in any form before or during his school years. As indicated above, M. was involved with various assessments but mainly information is discussed here concerning the Dyscalculia Test Battery. However, a few aspects involving specific numerical tasks are mentioned in relation to this. On the WISC-R (UK) he did not perform well on the Arithmetic subtest. On Digit Span he showed some facility on the Forward Digit Span task which is a relatively simple short-term memory test. This is in contrast to his particularly weak performance on Backward Digit Span which as highlighted earlier is a more complex task. In fact he could repeat correctly only two numbers backwards for both trials on the first item in this section. Hence, his difficulties might be considered in terms of problems associated with aspects of working memory involving the manipulation of stored numerical data.

DYSCALCULIA TEST BATTERY ASSESSMENT

NUMERAL PROCESSING TASKS

Magnitude Comparison

Arabic Magnitude Comparison. All items were completed correctly.
Spoken Verbal Magnitude Comparison. All items were completed correctly.
Written Verbal Magnitude Comparison. All items were completed correctly.

Transcoding Tasks

Transcoding Arabic Numerals to Spoken Verbal Numerals. M. was correct on all items. As noted earlier, this test was similar to the reading task used in the study described by Power and Dal Martello (1997) involving 7-year-old Italian children.

Transcoding Spoken Verbal Numerals to Written Verbal Numerals. M. made one error when he gave a written verbal response of 'one thousand two hundred and thirty-eight' instead of 'one thousand two hundred and seventy-eight' which was the correct response. This lexical error was termed a 'Substitution' error by Noël and Seron (1995) in relation to a neuropsychological investigation of an adult with a suggested diagnosis subsequently of Alzheimer's disease. M. was able to correct himself on a second attempt.

Transcoding Spoken Verbal Numerals to Arabic Numerals. M. gave several erroneous answers when he was required to write Arabic numerals in response to spoken verbal numerals in a dictation task similar to that described in the study highlighted earlier by Power and Dal Martello (1990) involving 6–8-year-old Italian children. M.'s errors varied in type and in relation to the ease with which he was able to correct them himself. He made two syntactical errors where extra zeros were inserted, namely 10,016 instead of 116 but he was able to correct himself on a second attempt and in another case when he wrote 30,264 instead of 3,264. However, for this item he was incorrect more dramatically on a second attempt when he wrote an erroneous answer as 3,000 200 64 but 2 weeks later he was able to correct himself. Both of his responses are examples of a child resorting to concatenation as opposed to applying the operation termed 'over-writing' by Power and Dal Martello (1990).

In a study by Seron and Fayol (1994), a similar task was presented to 7-year-old children from France and Wallonia, a region of Belgium. Some similar errors were made by these children and the investigators applied the terms 'Full Literal Transcoding' errors to those such as 10,016 instead of 116 and 'Partial Literal Transcoding' errors to those such as 30,264 instead of 3,264 in relation to M.'s errors mentioned above. It is interesting to note here also, that on a second attempt M. made a full literal transcoding error when he wrote 3,000 200 64 instead of 3,264. Also, M. made another syntactical error but of a different type in which he reversed the order of two digits in a four-digit number, when he wrote 5,063 instead of 5,603 and in fact, he made the same error on a second attempt but 2 weeks later he corrected himself.

M. made one lexical error when he wrote 7,822 instead of 7,802 but he gave the correct answer on a second attempt. In the discussion concerning child A. reference was made to a case study described by Temple (1989, 1997a, b) concerning an 11-year-old boy. An impairment in lexical processing was demonstrated which resulted in the incorrect selection of digits when he was required to read Arabic numerals or to write Arabic numerals to dictation whereas there was accurate syntactic processing. Also, he made more errors when reading numeral words than when reading Arabic numerals but the errors were of a similar form.

As noted above, M. did make one lexical error when writing Arabic numerals to dictation but he was accurate on items in the tasks where he was required to read Arabic numerals or number words. All of the errors made by M. in the dictation task where he had to respond by writing Arabic numerals occurred toward the end of a session and he was incorrect on a second attempt for two of the test items which were corrected by him in a further session 2 weeks later. Hence, there is an indication perhaps of the amount of effort that some children have to make in order to develop their numerical skills.

Various error types that were demonstrated by M. and others have been highlighted in neuropsychological data from adult patients as discussed, for example, by Deloche and Seron (1982a, b, 1987), Seron and Deloche (1983, 1984) and McCloskey and Caramazza (1987). Specifically in this context is an interesting case study reported by Cipolotti et al. (1994) of an adult neurological patient with a non-fluent aphasia and right arm weakness after his stroke involving the left parietal lobe. When he was seen for a neuropsychological assessment there was almost complete recovery in terms of his motor impairment and aphasia. A neuropsychological deficit was demonstrated concerning a very weak performance on the Arithmetic subtest on the WAIS and on the Graded Difficulty Arithmetic Test (Jackson & Warrington, 1986). There was further investigation of his numerical processing and arithmetical skills and the results demonstrated unimpaired numeral reading and comprehension but a transient and selective syntactic impairment in numeral writing to dictated numerals. These errors were discussed in the context of a dissociation between the concatenation and the over-writing rules described in the theoretical formulation by Power and Dal Martello (1990) considered earlier. In line with the children in this study, the adult patient demonstrated syntactical errors involving too many zeros but whereas the children showed errors of this type for numbers above 100, the adult patient showed the errors for numerals with four or more digits on the first day and five or more digits on the second day.

Reference was made to research discussed by Seron et al. (1992) involving 7- and 8-year-old pupils on tasks where they had to read aloud Arabic numerals and to write Arabic numerals after dictation. The children became competent with the over-writing rules with three-digit numbers before they reached the same level of competence with four-digit numbers. Hence, it seemed that the adult man had difficulty with those numerals for which there would be a later application of the over-writing rules and for which there would be the requirement of more effort. Also, after he noticed his errors in writing Arabic numerals, he was able to write correctly all of the items. As indicated above, the boy M. who participated in my study inserted extra zeros in a three-digit number and a four-digit number. He was able to correct himself quite easily on the three-digit number where he had inserted two zeros in the hundred position. However, on the four-digit number he made an insertion of one zero in the thousand position on the first attempt and a combination of three and two zeros respectively for the thousand and hundred positions on the second attempt before giving a correct answer 2 weeks later. Hence, M. demonstrated a very persistent weakness which was reflected in his continued use of concatenation with this higher-order number but eventually with the necessary effort he was able to overcome his difficulty and he could apply appropriately, the over-writing rule.

Transcoding Arabic Numerals to Written Verbal Numerals. Some of M.'s errors are interesting in relation to a case study described by Cohen et al. (1994) of a 43-year-old right-handed man who was severely aphasic after a left hemispheric subdural hemorrhage. His performance on various word and non-word reading tasks indicated deep dyslexia. Specifically, he showed difficulties reading aloud non-words and unfamiliar Arabic numerals but there was a significant improvement in relation to real words and familiar Arabic numerals. In reading unfamiliar numerals the authors suggested that the man appeared to use his semantic route as he showed a tendency to decompose the unfamiliar numerals into meaningful sub-groups of familiar numerals. As an example, when presented with '726' the patient responded with 'seven, two, six'.

Some errors were made by M. concerning the transcoding of visually presented Arabic numerals to written verbal numerals. For 7,802 M. wrote 'seven thousand eight hundred zero two' and for 2,191 M. wrote 'two thousand one ninety-one'. As suggested by Cohen et al. (1994) in consideration of the type of responses given by the man described above, a complex non-familiar numeral was fractionated into more simple and basic numerals. M. demonstrated an apparently similar process but concerning the transcoding of visually presented Arabic numerals to written verbal numerals as opposed to the transcoding of visually presented Arabic numerals to spoken verbal numerals. The examples described here by Cohen et al. (1994) and by myself in relation to M. were similar also to those described by Power and Dal Martello (1997) as 'Fragmentation' errors. In a particular instance, a child read the Arabic numeral 495 and gave a spoken response of 'forty nine and five'.

Also, when transcoding visually presented Arabic numerals to written verbal numerals M. made a stack error as described by Seron and Deloche (1983) in relation to adults with Broca's or Wernicke's aphasia and noted by Seron and Deloche (1984) in a mixed group of adult aphasics, with both investigations involving the use of similar tasks. When M. was presented with 9,034 he responded with 'nine thousand three hundred and four' indicating the preservation of the third position within the stack but not in relation to the stack itself, with the hundreds replacing the tens in this example. As in the case of the erroneous responses mentioned earlier, these errors occurred toward the end of the assessment session and after a week he gave correct answers to the first two questions but made the same mistake again for 9,034 although he corrected himself on a further attempt during the same session. Hence, again the specific nature of some errors was emphasized and their persistence as well as the effort required to overcome the difficulties associated with their production.

Transcoding Written Verbal Numerals to Spoken Verbal Numerals. All items were completed correctly.

Transcoding Written Verbal Numerals to Arabic Numerals. M. made two errors which involved the insertion of extra zeros. Specifically, for 'three thousand two hundred and sixty-four' he wrote 32,064 and for 'two thousand three hundred and eleven' he wrote 23,011. In a study mentioned earlier by Deloche and Seron (1982a) with adult aphasic patients from France and Wallonia in Belgium and involving a similar task, these types of errors were noted and they were classified as 'Intra-item Perseveration' errors. Again, these errors had been made by M. toward the end of a session but when re-tested after a 4-week break he wrote in response respectively to these two numbers, 31,264 and 21,311. Hence, M. made two errors again where the length of the numeral was increased and this was due to the insertion of the digit '1', as described for example by Deloche and Seron (1982a). As indicated, he wrote respectively '12' instead of '2' and '13' instead of '3' but when he was questioned about his answers he was able to give correct responses.

Additional Item: Tactile Recognition and Naming of Numerals. M. made several errors when he was asked to find numbers at random and then to name them while they were covered by a cloth after which they were checked for correct identification. He found the task easier when specific numbers were requested and he made only one error in finding a 3 instead of a 5 but a correct number was found on a second attempt. Hence, M. experienced some difficulty involving the tactile modality mainly for number naming more than recognition. However, when he was assessed in a later session in relation to the tactile naming of numbers he was able to perform accurately on this task.

CALCULATION TASKS

Operation Symbol and Word Comprehension

Operation Symbol Comprehension. When the operation name 'Subtraction' was presented M. identified incorrectly the division symbol. When presented with the operation name 'Division' M. identified correctly the division symbol. Later when presented with the operation name 'Subtraction' he identified correctly the symbol for subtraction. These identifications occurred for items involving units, tens and hundreds.

Operation Word Comprehension. When presented with the operation name 'Subtraction' M. identified incorrectly 'Divided by'. When presented with the operation name 'Division' M. was correct in identifying 'Divided by'. These identifications occurred in relation to items involving units, tens and hundreds.

Written Arithmetic Tasks

M. managed some of the simpler exercises involving all four arithmetical operations but there were errors also on some of the very elementary questions. On one exercise he added the numbers when the required operation was subtraction. Also, he demonstrated difficulties with carrying on the more complicated addition exercises and he showed a lack of understanding in relation to borrowing for the more advanced subtraction problems.

Additional Item: Specific Rectangular and Non-Rectangular Addition Exercises. M. demonstrated a particular difficulty with the specific non-rectangular addition problems mentioned in the discussion on child A. He made errors of the first specific type shown by some other children in studies by Friend (1979) and Lawson (1986, 1989) as he added a number from another column on to the single digit in the far left column. M. did not appear to have understood conceptual issues concerning the join of a single set and the sum of a single number. However, he seemed to develop more understanding of these concepts and to answer related questions correctly after a relevant discussion and instruction with a simple technique presented in one teaching session and described by Lawson (1990, 1995a, 2000a, 2001a). When re-assessed he completed accurately all of the non-rectangular exercises.

Oral Arithmetic Tasks

M. made one error in each group of questions concerning addition, subtraction and multiplication but he was able to correct himself very quickly. He could not complete any of the division exercises presented in an oral form. Also, as indicated above his performance was not strong on the Arithmetic subtest of the WISC-R (UK) involving aurally presented word problems requiring oral responses.

Additional Item: Recitation of Multiplication Tables. M. demonstrated particular problems in remembering the multiplication tables. He was able to recall the answers sometimes when smaller numbers were involved and many items from the 2, 5 and 10 times tables. When M. attempted to recite the tables, if he could not retrieve an answer directly he tended to work out each item by counting on from the previous answer. He made some 'Bond', 'Shift' and 'Perseverative' errors that were noted earlier in the discussion concerning child A.

CHILD L.

Initially when L. participated in the program he was aged 8 years 5 months. He attended a mainstream primary school and prior to the interventions he had not received specialist support in any form. His presentation was characteristic of the autism spectrum, more precisely Asperger syndrome although he was making noticeable progress in coping with specific problematic aspects. Some relatively mild areas of concern were apparent in relation to particular tasks involving fine or gross motor skills associated respectively, with graphic and certain physical activities. Reference could be made to Dziuk et al. (2007) for a recent investigation and discussion involving basic motor coordination and dyspraxic aspects concerning impairments in the performance of skilled gestures in relation to individuals on the autism spectrum. Generally L. was doing well in terms of his academic work at school but he had experienced considerable difficulty in learning the multiplication tables.

As mentioned earlier, a more comprehensive discussion including the assessments and interventions concerning aspects of L.'s disposition including his social and communication difficulties as well as those relating to the multiplication tables had been given in a presentation by Lawson (2005). In relation to the considerable controversy concerning diagnostic criteria I am sympathetic to Wing (2005) who favors a multidimensional as opposed to categorical approach to the study of the autism spectrum. In line with this perspective I tried to clarify and facilitate development in L.'s weaker areas with the support of his relative strengths in other aspects.

Only L.'s problems associated with learning the multiplication tables and the assessment and intervention are highlighted here. However, a few points will be mentioned in relation to these aspects as for the other two children in this presentation. Also, as indicated earlier this boy participated in the program more recently so he was administered some different or updated versions of tests. In particular, he was assessed on the Arithmetic subtest of the WISC-III UK, Weschler (1992) and this was not specifically problematic for him. Also, L. was presented with the Recall of Digits, Forward and Backward subtests on the British Ability Scales II (BAS II), Elliot et al. (1996). The digits on these subtests are presented at a faster rate in comparison with similar tasks on the WISC-R. L. did not demonstrate difficulties particularly with either section so within this context it was not suggested that the storage and manipulation of numerical information was problematic.

DYSCALCULIA TEST BATTERY ASSESSMENT

NUMERAL PROCESSING TASKS

Magnitude Comparison

Arabic Magnitude Comparison. All items were completed correctly.
Spoken Verbal Magnitude Comparison. All items were completed correctly.
Written Verbal Magnitude Comparison. All items were completed correctly.

Transcoding Tasks

Transcoding Arabic Numerals to Spoken Verbal Numerals. All items were completed correctly.

Transcoding Spoken Verbal Numerals to Written Verbal Numerals. All items were completed correctly.

Transcoding Spoken Verbal Numerals to Arabic Numerals. All items were completed correctly.

Transcoding Arabic Numerals to Written Verbal Numerals. All items were completed correctly.

Transcoding Written Verbal Numerals to Spoken Verbal Numerals. All items were completed correctly.

Transcoding Written Verbal Numerals to Arabic Numerals. All items were completed correctly.

Additional Item: Tactile Recognition and Naming of Numerals. L. found both tactile tasks quite demanding and he responded slowly to each request. However, without any time constraints when he had to retrieve named numbers, he was incorrect on only one item. For the number '2' his response was '8' but he was correct on a second attempt. When he was asked to find individual numbers at random and to name them one at a time he was incorrect on three items. Specifically, he responded with '3' for a '2', '8' for a '3' and '6' for an '8' but he gave correct responses on second attempts in each case.

CALCULATION TASKS

Operation Symbol and Word Comprehension

Operation Symbol Comprehension. All items were completed correctly.
Operation Word Comprehension. All items were completed correctly.

Written Arithmetic Tasks

These tasks were used to investigate the retrieval of arithmetic facts and execution of the calculation procedures for addition, subtraction, multiplication and division. As indicated earlier a standardized arithmetic test, the WOND was administered with the NO section requiring written answers.

The test results showed that L. could manage some arithmetic questions involving addition and subtraction. However, he added instead of subtracting for some questions whether presented horizontally or vertically. Some of his errors indicated difficulties with carrying and borrowing. Also, he was correct on a very simple multiplication question but he could not attempt any division exercises. In relation to the multiplication exercises he made a 'Shift' error where one digit in the answer is incorrect and the erroneous response is not a table entry as noted earlier. On another question he added instead of multiplying.

Additional Item: Specific Rectangular and Non-Rectangular Addition Exercises. L. did not demonstrate any difficulties with the exercises in groups (A1, B1) so he was not administered any other questions.

Oral Arithmetic Tasks

These tasks probed arithmetic fact retrieval and involved the four calculation procedures. Each problem was presented aurally and the child said the answer aloud. Five questions were presented with each item involving two numbers in the range 0–9 for the arithmetic operations addition, subtraction, multiplication and division.

L. made one error when he responded $7 \div 7 = 56(49)$. However, soon he corrected himself and gave the answer 1. He noted that he had multiplied instead of divided but he had given an incorrect table entry which was an adjacent answer in the same table, that is, a mistake termed a 'Bond' error as indicated above.

Also, as mentioned earlier L. was administered the Arithmetic subtest on the WISC-III UK. He was presented aurally with questions that required only an oral response. He did not have to read any items. L. responded accurately until he could not give any more answers.

Additional Item: Recitation of Multiplication Tables. The child was asked to recite any of the multiplication tables or any items that he/she was able to recall. The results for the responses given by L. are presented below.

Table	Incorrect Items (Correct)	
2	$9 \times 2 = 19(18)$	Shift Error (Not a table entry, one digit incorrect)
3	$5 \times 3 = 16(15)$	Shift Error
	6,7,8,9	No Response
4	6,7,8,9	No Response
5	Correct responses on all items	
6	$3 \times 6 = 19(18)$	Shift Error
7	2,3,4,5,6,7,8,9,12	No Response
8	2,3,4,5,6,7,8,9,12	No Response
9	$8 \times 9 = 62(72)$	Shift Error
10	Correct responses on all items	
11	$10 \times 11 = 111(110)$	Shift Error
12	2,3,4,5,6,7,8,9,11,12	No Response

Recall of Items from the Multiplication Tables

As expected, when assessed initially L. showed some difficulties in relation to remembering the multiplication tables. If he had difficulty with recall he might work out an answer by counting on from the previous response. Hence he was able to reply correctly for some items. As shown above, for the initial assessment L. gave correct replies, no responses or incorrect answers involving 'Shift' errors. During the remedial sessions he made 'Bond', 'Shift' and 'Perseverative' errors.

GENERAL DISCUSSION AND CONCLUSION

The children presented here demonstrated some difficulties in all three areas concerning numerical processing and knowledge of number facts as well as procedures. In the studies discussed by Temple (1989, 1991, 1994a, b, 1997a, b), selective deficiencies were highlighted in relation to lexical number processing, number fact and procedural disorders. It was suggested that these different types of selective impairment in developmental dyscalculia indicated a modular organization of the developing arithmetical system. The perspective considered by Temple in relation to this system allowed for some communication between modules.

More recently Kaufmann (2002) described an adolescent young man who was 14 years of age initially when he participated in their investigation. His presentation included severe developmental dyscalculia and problems with literacy including reading and writing as well as marked difficulties with spelling. He had relatively preserved procedural skills and marked deficits concerning number fact retrieval with particularly problematic areas relating to multiplication and division. Also, he performed poorly on Forward and Backward Digit Span tasks. As indicated above in my presentation here, Child A. experienced difficulties on Forward and Backward Digit Span tasks and Child M. had problems specifically associated with Backward Digit Span. As noted earlier, the interpretations relating to their performances in this respect were considered in terms of impairments concerning working memory involving numerical information. In the Kaufmann (2002) study it was suggested that the memory deficit demonstrated by the young man was not just the result of poor numeric fact representations in long-term memory but there was a substantial contribution from a deficiency specifically of a numerical nature relating to working memory. In a later investigation concerning the same young man when he was 18 years of age, Kaufmann et al. (2004) emphasized the significance of working memory in the activation of information from long-term memory. Numerical fact retrieval difficulties were considered in relation to a combined access and storage deficiency.

As indicated earlier in the context of my own research, Child L. did not present with difficulties particularly concerning the Forward and Backward Digit Span subtests. Also as noted above, the presentation rate for digits on these subtests was faster than the rate on similar tasks used with the other two participants. Facilitation of working memory and its associations with long-term memory in relation to numerical development was promoted via the implementation of a specific multisensory technique within the context of a remedial approach involving the integration of factual, procedural and conceptual aspects of numerical knowledge.

In my research presented here, the children had been highlighted by their teachers or parents because they had demonstrated a particular difficulty in learning the multiplication tables. Other areas of numerical difficulty were clarified with the assistance of the dyscalculia test battery as well as some strengths. In the context of a flexible and interconnected system, it should be possible to use strengths in various areas to compensate for weaknesses elsewhere or to promote development in weaker areas and to facilitate the maturation of numerical concepts and skills. The importance of associations and commonalities as well as dissociations and differences in relation to specific syndromes has been highlighted in the neuroconstructivist approach (Karmiloff-Smith, 1998; Oliver et al., 2000) with increasingly specialized or modularized cortical pathways being produced by development. The teaching/learning approach suggested and implemented by the present author (Lawson, 1995b, 2000b, 2001a) was aimed at using the various strengths of the children to influence their developmental courses in a positive direction with the assistance of a specific multisensory technique.

As indicated above, this involved the visual, auditory, tactile and kinesthetic modalities in relation to items in the multiplication tables. Also, a slightly modified approach was applied to assist the apprehension of arithmetical operation symbols, words and names but with the operation items being changed in the process as opposed to the operands.

The discussion presented here concerned information that had been obtained from an assessment involving a dyscalculia test battery. The aim of the project was to analyze the children's numerical difficulties and to provide a remedial approach that would help them to learn the multiplication tables. Also, the facilitation of more mature development was expected in relation to number concepts and numerical skills through the establishment of flexible associations between specialized areas or modules as emphasized by Dehaene (1997). It is apparent from the results obtained that a detailed assessment with the aid of a dyscalculia test battery provided clear information concerning the numerical difficulties experienced by the participants. After taking part in the remedial sessions, the children could access any item from the multiplication tables, obtain the answers more quickly and retrieve them more often by direct recall. Also, they could use other approaches such as locating an item near the correct answer as a cue and then recall the required item or count up or down in various ways to reach the appropriate answer. Alternatively, they might use some arithmetical knowledge involving addition or subtraction, perhaps that associated with doubles or make use of commutativity as an aid to retrieving the correct answer. Also, the three children discussed here noticed specific patterns in the 5, 10 and 11 times tables and the use of this knowledge was encouraged during the sessions to assist the retrieval of other items.

In a particular study by Krueger (1986) it was indicated that adults could use odd–even rules efficiently, for example, if either multiplier is even the answer must be even, in a product verification task. This was an aspect that I emphasized when teaching the multiplication tables and the children were encouraged to use this information to help them check and correct answers that they had retrieved. As the sessions progressed, use of this knowledge was demonstrated very clearly to some extent as it was used overtly. Hence, in addition to some strategies mentioned already the use of another mature strategy demonstrated in adults had been developed and was being used appropriately by these children.

Sherin and Fuson (2005) categorize multiplication strategies in relation to what they term as the number-specific computational resources that are used in their execution. The count-all strategy which involves counting from '1' to the product is available to most individuals when they become involved with multiplication. Also, because of their experiences concerning addition the children have access to related strategies which these authors call additive calculations. When considering other categories, count-by strategies were discussed as pupils learn count-by sequences of numbers such as '4, 8, 12, 16, . . .'. Pattern-based strategies which might involve for example, 0's, 1's or 10's are learnt often alongside count-by sequences. The learned product strategy involves many number-specific resources, namely the multiplication triads. Also, hybrid strategies might be used which involve various combinations of those noted above. As indicated earlier, the young people involved with the approach discussed here used various strategies and combinations which could be categorized in this way. Also, they could recognize a variety of applications as well as implement appropriately their newly acquired understanding and skills in different situations.

As suggested by Thelen and Smith (1994) while acknowledging the multimodal nature of most of our experiences of objects and events, when considering perception and action in the real world, development might be concerned more with the selection than with the construction of the most relevant multimodal associations. The participants in my research discussed here had considerable difficulties in accessing items from the multiplication tables and initially construction of some numerical ideas was not easy. The aim of the teaching/learning approach used here was to help the children with the selection and integration of the most salient information from the stimuli which were presented simultaneously in various modalities. As they developed the ability to store and access sufficient quantities of information and to form meaningful associations, newly acquired knowledge could be used in the construction of further numerical concepts and ideas given different applications. Hence, their numerical and certain other aspects of their mathematical development were enhanced by the careful analysis using the dyscalculia test battery and the multisensory remedial intervention presented here.

Generally the young people demonstrated substantial improvements in relation to their abilities to access items from the multiplication tables and in the development of their number concepts and arithmetical skills. Boys were selected here but the same approaches to assessment and remediation could be offered to girls. Also, the difficulties demonstrated by the boys were related to the findings in other studies concerning younger children, individuals in a developmental neuropsychological context and adults with acquired neuropsychological disabilities. The successful remedial approach which was implemented after the assessment might be considered applicable to individuals with similar numerical difficulties but generally of a different disposition. In fact, L. was much younger and as indicated above his overall presentation was quite different when compared with the other two boys. Apart from the recall of more items and the development of many strategies for accessing items from the multiplication tables, these children were able to apply their knowledge in various contexts, hence demonstrating their enhanced numerical understanding and ability to generalize.

ACKNOWLEDGMENTS

My grateful thanks to the children and their families as well as school staff and other supportive individuals who contributed to the investigations presented here.

REFERENCES

Andres, M., Seron, X., & Olivier, E. (2007). Contribution of hand motor circuits to counting. *Journal of Cognitive Neuroscience*, *19*, 563–576.

Aylward, E. H., Park, J. E., Field, K. M., Parsons, A. C., Richards, T. L., Cramer, S. C., & Meltzoff, A. N. (2005). Brain activation during face perception: Evidence of a developmental change. *Journal of Cognitive Neuroscience*, *17*, 308–319.

Badian, N. A. (1983). Dyscalculia and non-verbal disorders of learning. In Mykelbust, H. R. (Ed.), *Progress in Learning Disabilities* (Vol. V). New York: Grune and Stratton.

Baroody, A. J. (2003). The development of adaptive expertise and flexibility: The integration of conceptual and procedural knowledge. In Baroody, A. J. & Dowker, A. (Eds.), *The Development of Arithmetic Concepts and Skills: Constructing Adaptive Expertise*. Mahwah, NJ: Lawrence Erlbaum Associates.

Berch, D. B. & Mazzocco, M. M. M. (Eds.) (2007). *Why is Math so Hard for Some Children? The Nature and Origins of Mathematical Learning Difficulties and Disabilities*. Baltimore, MD: Paul H. Brookes Publishing Co.

Bryant, P. & Bradley, L. (1985). *Children's Reading Problems*. Oxford: Blackwell.

Bullock, J. (2002). *TouchMath: The TouchPoint Approach for Teaching Basic Math Computation* (4th edn). Colorado Springs, CO: Innovative Learning Concepts.

Butterworth, B. (1999). *The Mathematical Brain*. London: Macmillan.

Campbell, J. I. D. & Epp, L. J. (1995). Architectures for arithmetic. In Campbell, J.I.D. (Ed.). *Handbook of Mathematical Cognition*. New York & Hove: Psychology Press.

Carlson, R. A., Avraamides, M. N., Cary, M., & Strasberg, S. (2007). What do the hands externalise in simple arithmetic. *Journal of Experimental Psychology: Learning, Memory and Cognition*, *33*, 747–756.

Chinn, S. J. & Ashcroft, J. R. (1998). *Mathematics for Dyslexics: A Teaching Handbook* (2nd edn). London: Whurr Publishers Ltd.

Cipolotti, L., Butterworth, B., & Warrington, E. K. (1994). From 'one thousand nine hundred and forty-five' to 1000, 945. *Neuropsychologia*, *32*, 503–509.

Cohen, L. & Dehaene, S. (2004). Specialisation within the ventral stream: The case for the visual word form area [Letter to the Editor]. *NeuroImage*, *22*, 466–476.

Cohen, L., Dehaene, S., & Verstichel. P. (1994). Number words and number nonwords: A case of deep dyslexia extending to Arabic numerals. *Brain*, *117*, 267–279.

Dehaene, S. (1997). *The Number Sense: How the Mind Creates Mathematics*. New York: Oxford University Press.

Deloche, G. & Seron, X. (1982a). From one to 1: An analysis of a transcoding process by means of neuropsychological data. *Cognition*, *12*, 119–149.

Deloche, G. & Seron, X. (1982b). From three to 3: A differential analysis of skills in transcoding quantities between patients with Broca's and Wernicke's Aphasia. *Brain*, *105*, 719–733.

Deloche, G. & Seron, X. (1984). Semantic errors reconsidered in the procedural light of stack concepts. *Brain and Language*, *21*, 59–71.

Deloche, G. & Seron, X. (1987). Numerical transcoding: A general production model. In Deloche, G. and Seron, X. (Eds.), *Mathematical Disabilities: A Cognitive Neuropsychological Perspective*. Hove: Lawrence Erlbaum Associates.

Dziuk, M. A., Gidley Larson, J. C., Apostu, A., Mahone, E. M., Denckla, M. B., & Mostofsky, S. H. (2007). Dyspraxia in autism: Association with motor, social, and communicative deficits. *Developmental Medicine and Child Neurology*, *49*, 734–739.

Eger, E., Sterzer, P., Russ, M. O., Giraud, A.-L., & Kleinschmidt, A. (2003). A supramodal number representation in human parietal cortex. *Neuron*, *37*, 719–725.

Elliot, C. D., Murray, D. J., & Pearson, L. S. (1983). *British Ability Scales*. Berks: NFER-NELSON.

Elliot, C. D., Smith, P., & McCulloch, K. (1996). *British Ability Scales II*. Berks: NFER-NELSON.

Fogassi, L. & Gallese, V. (2004). Action as a binding key to integration. In Calvert G., Spence C. & Stein B. E. (Eds.). *The Handbook of Multisensory Processes*. Cambridge, MA: MIT Press/ Bradford Books.

Friend, J. E. (1979). Column addition skills. *Journal of Children's Mathematical Behavior*, 2(2), 29–57.

Gallace, A. & Spence, C. (2008). The cognitive and neural correlates of 'tactile consciousness': A multisensory perspective. Consciousness and Cognition: An International Journal, *17*, 370–407.

Gallace, A., Tan, H. Z., & Spence, C. (2006). Numerosity judgments for tactile stimuli distributed over the body surface. *Perception, 35*, 247–266.

Gallace, A., Tan, H. Z., & Spence, C. (2007a). Multisensory numerosity judgments for visual and tactile stimuli. *Perception and Psychophysics, 69*, 487–501.

Gallace, A., Tan, H. Z., & Spence, C. (2007b). The body surface as a communication system: The state of the art after 50 years. *Presence, 16*, 655–676.

Gathers, A. D., Bhatt, R., Corbly, C. R., Farley, A. B., & Joseph, J. E. (2004). Developmental shifts in cortical loci for face and object recognition. *Neuroreport, 15*, 1549–1553.

Gillham, W. E. C. (1980). *Basic Number Diagnostic Test*. Kent, U K: Hodder and Stoughton.

Gracia-Bafalluy, M. and Noël, M.-P. (2008). Does Finger Training Increase Young Children's Numerical Performance. *Cortex, 4*, 368–375.

Haxby, J. V., Hoffman, E. A., & Gobbini, M. I. (2000). The distributed human neural system for face perception. *Trends in Cognitive Sciences, 4*, 223–233.

Hoard, M. K., Geary, D. C., & Hamson, C. O. (1999). Numerical and arithmetical cognition: Performance of low- and average-IQ children. *Mathematical Cognition, 5*, 65–91.

Iarocci, G. & McDonald, J. (2006). Sensory integration and the perceptual experience of persons with autism. *Journal of Autism and Developmental Disorders, 36*, 77–90.

Ifrah, G. (1998). *The Universal History of Numbers: From Prehistory to the Invention of the Computer* (Translated from the French by Bellos, D., Harding, E. F., Wood, S. & Monk, I.). London: The Harvill Press.

Jackson, M. & Warrington, E. K. (1986). Arithmetic skills in patients with unilateral cerebral lesions. *Cortex, 22*, 611–620.

Jordan, K. E. & Brannon, E. M. (2006). The multisensory representation of number in infancy. *Proceedings of the National Academy of Sciences of the USA, 103*, 3486–3489.

Karmiloff-Smith, A. (1998). Development itself is not the key to understanding developmental disorders. *Trends in Cognitive Sciences, 2*, 389–398.

Kaufmann, L. (2002). More evidence for the role of the central executive in retrieving arithmetic facts – A case study of severe developmental dyscalculia. *Journal of Clinical and Experimental Neuropsychology, 24*, 302–310.

Kaufmann, L. & Nuerk, H.-C. (2005). Numerical development: current issues and future perspectives. *Psychology Science, Special Issue: Brain and Number*, 47(1), 142–170.

Kaufmann, L., Lochy, A., Drexler, A., & Semenza, C. (2004). Deficient arithmetic fact retrieval – Storage or access problem? A case study. *Neuropsychologia, 42*, 482–496.

Kawashima, R., Taira, M. Okita, K., Inoue, K., Tajima, N., Yoshida, H., Saaki, T., Sugiura, M., Watanabe, J., & Fukuda, H. (2004). A functional MRI study of simple arithmetic-A comparison between children and adults. *Cognitive Brain Research, 18*, 225–231.

Kobayashi, T., Hiraki, K., & Hasegawa, T. (2005). Auditory-visual intermodal matching of small numerosities in 6-month-old infants. *Developmental Science, 8*, 409–419.

Krueger, L. E. (1986). Why 2 × 2 = 5 looks so wrong. On the odd-even rule in product verification. *Memory and Cognition, 12*, 141–149.

Lakoff, G. & Núñez, R. E. (2000). *Where Mathematics Comes From: How the Embodied Mind Brings Mathematics into Being*. New York: Basic Books, A Member of the Perseus Books Group.

Lane, C. (1992). Now listen hear. *Special Children, 54*, 12–14.

Lane, C. & Chinn, S. J. (1986). Learning by self-voice echo. *Academic Therapy, 21*, 477–481.

Lawson, C. (1986). Experiment to Investigate Column Addition Skills in Rectangular and Non-Rectangular Addition Problems in Primary Aged Children. Unpublished Dissertation for the Course in Educational Psychology. The Tavistock Clinic, London.

Lawson, C. (1989). An Investigation of Column Addition Skills in Rectangular and Non-Rectangular Addition Problems in Primary Aged Children. Presentation at the *British Psychological Society, Developmental Section Annual Conference*. University of Surrey, UK.

Lawson, C. (1990). Children's errors in non-rectangular addition problems. Presentation at *the British Psychological Society, Cognitive Psychology Section Annual Conference*. University of Leicester, UK.

Lawson, C. (1995a). Children's difficulties with non-rectangular addition exercises. Presentation at *the British Psychological Society Annual Conference and Division of Clinical Psychology Conference*. University of Warwick, UK.

Lawson, C. (1995b). Developmental dyscalculia: Assessment and remediation. Presentation at *the International Conference, Language and Mathematical Thinking: Current Issues in Developmental, Neuropsychological and Educational Research*. University College London, UK.

Lawson, C. (2000a). Theory, assessment and remediation of arithmetical disabilities 1: Column addition skills. Presentation at *the XXVII International Congress of Psychology*. Stockholm, Sweden. Abstract in Mathematics Education, *International Journal of Psychology*, 35(3/4), 213.

Lawson, C. (2000b). Theory, assessment and remediation of arithmetical disabilities 2: Multiplication skills. Presentation at *the XXVII International Congress of Psychology*. Stockholm, Sweden. Abstract in 'Learning disabilities; developmental disorders; mental retardation I', *International Journal of Psychology*, 35(3/4), 345.

Lawson, C. (2000c). Theory, assessment and remediation of arithmetical disabilities 3: Early indications. Presentation at *the XXVII International Congress of Psychology*. Stockholm, Sweden. Abstract in 'Learning disabilities; developmental disorders; mental retardation II', *International Journal of Psychology*, 35(3/4), 431.

Lawson, C. (2001a). Theory, assessment and remediation of arithmetical disabilities: Three Presentations at *the XXVII International Congress of Psychology*. Stockholm, Sweden, 23–28 July 2000. *The British Psychological Society Division of Educational and Child Psychology Newsletter*, 97, 31–34.

Lawson, C. (2001b). The apprehension of small numerosities, facial features and children's human figure drawings. Unpublished manuscript.

Lawson, C. (2002). An analysis of children's numerical difficulties with the aid of a dyscalculia test battery. Presentation as an Invited Speaker at *the Conference on Mathematical Difficulties: Psychology, Neuroscience and Interventions*. Department of Experimental Psychology, University of Oxford, UK.

Lawson, C. (2005). Successful remedial interventions for a child with an autism spectrum disorder and specific numerical difficulties. Presentation at *the XIIth European Conference on Developmental Psychology*. University of La Laguna, Tenerife, Canary Islands, Spain.

Lochy, A., Domahs, F., & Delazer, M. (2005). Rehabilitation of acquired calculation and number processing disorders. In Campbell, J. I. D. (Ed.), *Handbook of Mathematical Cognition*. New York & Hove: Psychology Press.

Macaruso, P. & Sokol, S. M. (1998). Cognitive neuropsychology and developmental dyscalculia. In Donlan, C. (Ed.), *The Development of Mathematical Skills*. Hove: Psychology Press.

Macaruso, P., Harley, W., & McCloskey, M. (1992) Assessment of acquired dyscalculia. In Margolin, D. I. (Ed.), *Cognitive Neuropsychology in Clinical Practice*. Oxford: Oxford University Press.

McCandliss, B. D., Cohen, L., & Dehaene, S. (2003). The visual word form area: Expertise for reading in the fusiform gyrus. *Trends in Cognitive Sciences*, 7, 293–299.

McCloskey, M. (1992). Cognitive mechanisms in numerical processing: Evidence from acquired dyscalculia. *Cognition*, 44, 107–157.

McCloskey, M. & Caramazza, A. (1987). Cognitive mechanisms in normal and impaired number processing. In Deloche, G. & Seron, X. (Eds.), Mathematical disabilities: A cognitive neuropsychological perspective. Hove: Lawrence Erlbaum Associates.

McCloskey, M., Caramazza, A., & Basili, A. G. (1985). Cognitive mechanisms in number processing and calculation: Evidence from dyscalculia. *Brain and Cognition, 4*, 171–196.

Naglieri, J. A. & Pickering, E. B. (2003). Helping children Learn: Intervention Handouts for use in School and at Home. Baltimore, MD: Paul H. Brookes Publishing co.

Noël, M.-P. (2005). Finger gnosia: A predictor of numerical abilities in children. *Child Neuropsychology, 11*, 413–430.

Noël, M-P. & Seron, X. (1995). Lexicalisation errors in writing Arabic numerals: A single case study. *Brain and Cognition, 29*, 151–179.

Oliver, A., Johnson, M. H., Karmiloff-Smith, A., & Pennington, B. (2000). Deviations in the emergence of representations: A neuroconstructivist framework for analysing developmental disorders. *Developmental Science, 3*, 1–40.

Passarotti, A. M., Paul, B. M., Bussiere, J. R., Buxton, R. B., Wong, E. C., & Stiles, J. (2003). The development of face and location processing: An fMRI study. *Developmental Science, 6*, 100–117.

Pesenti, M., Thioux, M., Xavier, S., & De Volder, A. (2000). Neuroanatomical substrates of Arabic number processing, numerical comparison and simple addition: A pet study. *Journal of Cognitive Neuroscience, 12*, 461–479.

Power, R. J. D. & Dal Martello, M. F. (1990). The dictation of Italian numerals. *Language and Cognitive Processes, 5*, 237–254.

Power, R. J. D. & Dal Martello, M. F. (1997). From 834 to eighty thirty four: The reading of Arabic numerals by seven-year-old children. *Mathematical Cognition, 3*, 63–85.

Power, R. J. D. & Longuet-Higgins, H. C. (1978). Learning to count: A computational model of language acquisition. *Proceedings of the Royal Society of London, B200*, 391–417.

Price, C. J. & Devlin, J. T. (2003). The myth of the visual word form area. *NeuroImage, 19*, 473–481.

Price, C. J. & Devlin, J. T. (2004). Reply to letter to the editor, *NeuroImage, 22*, 477–479.

Ramachandran, V. S. & Hubbard, E. M. (2005). The emergence of the human mind: Some clues from synesthesia. In Robertson, L. C. & Sagiv N. (Eds.), *Synesthesia: Perspectives from Cognitive Neuroscience*. New York: Oxford University Press.

Rickard, T. C., Romero, S. G., Basso, G., Wharton, C., Flitman, S., & Grafman, J. (2000). The calculating brain: An fMRI study. *Neuropsychologia, 38*, 325–335.

Riggs, K. J., Ferrand, L., Lancelin, D., Fryziel, L., Dumur, G., & Simpson, A. (2006). Subitizing in tactile perception. *Psychological Science, 17*, 271–272.

Rusconi, E., Walsh, V., & Butterworth, B. (2005). Dexterity with numbers: rTMS over left angular gyrus disrupts finger gnosis and number processing. *Neuropsychologia, 43*, 1609–1624.

Rust, J. (1996). *Wechsler Objective Numerical Dimensions*. London: Harcourt Assessment.

Sato, M., Cattanco, L., Rizzolatti, G., & Gallese, V. (2007). Numbers within our hands: Modulation of corticospinal excitability of hand muscles during numerical judgment. *Journal of Cognitive Neuroscience, 19*, 684–693.

Scherf, K. S., Behrmann, M., Humphreys, K., & Luna, B. (2007). Visual category-selectivity for faces, places and objects emerges along different developmental trajectories. *Developmental Science, 10*, F15–F30.

Seron, X. & Deloche, G. (1983). From 4 to four: A supplement to 'from three to 3'. *Brain, 106*, 735–744.

Seron, X. & Deloche, G. (1984). From 2 to two: An analysis of a transcoding process by means of neuropsychological evidence. *Journal of Psycholinguistic Research, 13*, 215–236.

Seron, X. & Fayol, M. (1994). Number transcoding in children: A functional analysis. *British Journal of Developmental Psychology, 12*, 281–300.

Seron, X., Deloche, G., & Noel, M. P. (1992). Number transcribing by children: Writing Arabic numbers under dictation. In Bideaud J., Meljac, C. & Fisher, J.-P. (Eds.), *Pathways to Number*. Hove: Lawrence Erlbaum Associates.

Shalev, R. S. (2007). Prevalence of developmental dyscalculia. In Berch, D. B. & Mazzocco, M. M. M. (Eds.), *Why is Math so Hard for Some Children? The Nature and Origins of Mathematical Learning Difficulties and Disabilities*. Baltimore, MD: Paul H. Brookes Publishing Co.

Shalev, R. S. & Gross-Tsur, V. (1993). Developmental dyscalculia and medical assessment. *Journal of Learning Disabilities*, *26*, 134–137.

Sherin, B. & Fuson, K. (2005). Multiplication strategies and the appropriation of computational resources. *Journal for Research in Mathematics Education*, *36*, 347–395.

Simon, T. J. & Rivera, S. M. (2007). Neuroanatomical approaches to the study of mathematical ability and disability. In Berch, D. B. & Mazzocco, M. M. M. (Eds.), *Why is Math so Hard for Some Children? The Nature and Origins of Mathematical Learning Difficulties and Disabilities*. Baltimore, MD: Paul H. Brookes Publishing Co.

Temple, C. (1989) Digit dyslexia: A category-specific disorder in developmental dyscalculia. *Cognitive Neuropsychology*, *6*, 93–116.

Temple, C. (1991). Procedural dyscalculia and number fact dyscalculia: Double dissociation in developmental dyscalculia. *Cognitive Neuropsychology*, *8*, 155–176.

Temple, C. (1994a). Developmental dyscalculias: Dissociations and parallels. *ANAE*, *6*(Suppl. No. 30), 1–5.

Temple, C. (1994b). The cognitive neuropsychology of the developmental dyscalculias. *Current psychology of cognition/Cahiers de Psychologie Cognitive*, *13*, 351–370.

Temple, C. (1997a). Cognitive neuropsychology and its application to children. *Journal of Child Psychology and Psychiatry*, *38*, 27–52.

Temple, C. (1997b). *Developmental Cognitive Neuropsychology*. Hove: Psychology Press.

Temple, C. & Marriott, A. J. (1998). Arithmetic ability and disability in Turner's syndrome: A cognitive neuropsychological analysis. *Developmental Neuropsychology*, *14*, 47–67.

Thelen, E. & Smith, L. B. (1994). A dynamic systems approach to the development of cognition and action. Cambridge, MA: MIT Press/Bradford Books.

Thompson, J. C., Abbott, D. F., Wheaton, K. J., Syngeniotis, A, & Puce, A. (2004). Digit representation is more than just hand waving. *Cognitive Brain Research*, *21*, 412–417.

Vernon, P. E. & Miller, K. M. (1976). *Graded Arithmetic-Mathematics Test (Junior)*. Kent, UK: Hodder and Stoughton.

Wechsler, D. (1976). *Wechsler Intelligence Scale for Children-Revised UK (WISC-R UK)*. Kent, UK: The Psychological Corporation.

Wechsler, D. (1992). *Wechsler Intelligence Scale for Children-Third Edition UK (WISC-III UK)*. London: The Psychological Corporation.

Wing, L. (2005). Reflections on opening Pandora's Box. *Journal of Autism and Developmental Disorders*, *35*, 197–203.

Wilson, A. J. & Dehaene, S. (2007). Number sense and developmental dyscalculia. In Coch, D. Dawson, G. & Fischer, K. W. (Eds.), *Human Behavior, Learning and the Developing Brain: Atypical Development*. New York: The Guildford Press.

Zamarian, L., López-Rolón, A., & Delazer, M. (2007). Neuropsychological case studies on arithmetic processing. In Berch, D. B. & Mazzocco, M. M. M. (Eds.), *Why is Math so Hard for Some Children? The Nature and Origins of Mathematical Learning Difficulties and Disabilities*. Baltimore, MD: Paul H. Brookes Publishing Co.

7

CHILDREN WITH AND WITHOUT MATHEMATICS DIFFICULTIES

ASPECTS OF LEARNER CHARACTERISTICS IN A DEVELOPMENTAL PERSPECTIVE

SNORRE A. OSTAD

*Department of Special Needs Education, University of Oslo,
PP1140 0317 Oslo, Norway*

The study was designed to investigate the extent and character of differences between children with (MD children) and without difficulties in mathematics (MN children) reflected in their strategy use for solving basic fact and word problems. Particular concern was with accuracy and speed of professing differences, especially in light of measures indicating the developmental maturity of children's strategy use. The sample included 32 MD children in grade 1, 33 MD children in grade 3, 36 MD children in grade 5 and a corresponding number of MN children in each of the grades. The children were observed systematically over a period of 2 years, that is, grade 1 children from the end of grade 1 to the end of grade 3, grade 3 children from the end of grade 3 to the end of grade 5, and grade 5 children from the end of grade 5 to the end of grade 7.

The study involved the close cooperation of 12 primary schools, that is, all primary schools in two Norwegian urban municipalities. The current presentation has the intention to give an overview of this study and discuss the main results in general view.

Several investigators have determined that mathematical learning problems are relatively common (e.g., Badian, 1983; Kosc, 1974). More specifically, a more recent published study (Ostad, 1998a) shows that the schools' support services had picked out about 10% of the children in some primary schools as needing remedial programs in mathematics when these children were in grade 2 (e.g., 8–9 year old children). Nevertheless, mathematical learning problems remain relatively neglected in the research literature. Only few empirical studies of the cognitive mechanisms potentially contributing to mathematical learning problems have been conducted, even though much has been learned about the acquisition of basic mathematical concepts and procedures in mathematically normal children (Dowker, 2005; Robinson et al., 2002). Success or failure in mathematics has often been defined by performance on standardised achievement tests. These tests, however, do not provide information about the mental processes that are likely contributing to the children's achievement. An alternative is to compare groups of children, who vary in achievement levels, on tasks for which a developmental progression of skills are differentiated. Simple basic fact problems[1] and simple arithmetic word problems are examples of such tasks. The studies described in the current presentation followed this approach suggesting that comparisons of developmental differences of MD and MN children of varying age levels might provide useful information about factors potentially contributing to mathematical learning problems.

It was suggested that the analysis of individual differences in strategy use might be useful for several general purposes, for example, getting acquainted with the problem-solving process to understand how children achieve scores in standardized tests. Thus, a substantial body of empirical work has been devoted to examining the acquisition and development of MN children's strategy use. These include a focus on strategies as a function of subject characteristics. A variety of earlier findings have shown that children's strategy use vary with age and ability, but also that a single child will often use different strategies on different occasions. Developmental studies of MN children have revealed that a normal course of development indicate an obvious progression over time from immature, inefficient counting strategies, through verbal counting, and finally to arithmetic fact retrieval as children move through primary school (Ashcraft, 1992; Carpenter & Moser, 1984; Siegler & Jenkins, 1989). Moreover, a growing body of research has provided valuable insight regarding the strategy use by MD children. As compared with that of their mathematically normal peers, these children are characterised by the use of developmentally immatureproblem-solving strategies. That is, these children often use strategies more commonly employed by younger MN children (Geary et al., 1987; Goldman et al., 1988).

Several earlier studies in this area had determined that, across development, performance of MN children as compared to their mathematically disabled peers has been shown to be generally more rapid and more accurate in producing answers for basic fact problems (e.g., Geary et al., 1987; Russell & Ginsburg, 1984; Svenson & Broquist, 1975). In summary, the MD children are characterised by a rather long solution time, and frequent computational and memory-related errors (Garnett & Fleischner, 1983; Geary & Burlingham-Dubree, 1989; Geary et al., 1991). However, research studies are mixed with regard to the question of speed of processing differences between MD and MN children (Geary, 1990; Geary & Brown, 1991).

In general, the majority of studies that have been conducted on cognitive mechanisms potentially contributing to mathematical difficulties have shown several methodological limitations. Probably because of the time and effort needed to study such mechanisms in a long-term perspective, few studies of developmental differences between MD and MN children have been carried out. For instance, most often the research on strategy use has focused on one single age level and on the youngest age groups in particular. Left unanswered, therefore, was whether the pattern of differences between MN and MD children could be found throughout the elementary school years. Perhaps even more significantly, most often the starting point for the constitution of MD groups (samples) had been the children's achievement on just one single mathematics test. It seems not enough consideration has been given to the fact that, for the youngest age groups, mathematical difficulties encountered during the above mentioned test may have a relatively short duration. Thus, it was possible that the researchers may have operated with heterogeneous samples, composed partly of children with temporary difficulties and partly of children with difficulties of a more permanent nature. Moreover, earlier studies of strategy use differences between MN and MD children have been dominated by chronometric procedures for the collection of data. Most commonly, the children have been instructed to solve simple addition basic fact problems using the strategy they themselves found most suitable for the case in hand, and also at the same time to respond as quickly as possible (e.g., Geary & Brown, 1991; Geary & Burlingham-Dubree, 1989; Geary et al., 1987; Goldman et al., 1988). There are, I suggest, reasons for anticipating that this emphasis on speed might influence the strategy use.

The present study was designed to address some of the above mentioned limitations: First, it reports assessment of developmental differences between MD and MN children in a longitudinal perspective over an extended period of time: that is, the age range of 7 to 13(14) years. This made it possible to obtain an overview of the development differences throughout the elementary school. Second, the children who were unsuccessful in mathematics for less than 2 years were excluded from the group designated MD children in this project.[2] Third, the samples of MD children were relatively large compared with the samples in earlier studies. Fourth, the strategy use research data were recorded without focusing on the time the children spent in solving the problem. Fifth, the study of strategy use differences between MD and MN children was carried out within a relatively broad frame of reference that included basic fact problems in addition, basic fact problems in subtraction, as well as arithmetic word problems.

Four separate laboratory investigations were performed to investigate the extent and character of developmental differences between MN and MD children reflected respectively in strategy use for solving addition problems (Ostad, 1997b), strategy use for solving subtraction problems (Ostad, 1999), strategy use for solving arithmetic word problems (Ostad, 1998a), and in accuracy and speed of processing for solving basic fact problems (Ostad, 2000).

RESULTS AND DISCUSSION

In general, across times of measurement the MN children showed an increased reliance on retrieval strategies, and a decreased reliance on backup strategies. This change was consistent with earlier research assessing the strategy use development of basic arithmetic skills (e.g., Ashcraft, 1992; Geary et al., 1991; Goldman et al., 1988; Siegler & Jenkins, 1989). Nevertheless, the course of development clearly shows that backup strategies play a dominant role in the problem-solving process through the primary school stage. These findings provide substantial support for arguments advanced by Siegler (1988) that children make use of a mixture of strategies, usually combining counting with direct retrieval.

In contrast, the MD children characteristically used backup strategies almost exclusively throughout the same period. Earlier studies have already shown that MD children most frequently use reconstructive counting strategies and not retrieval strategies (Fleischner et al., 1982; Geary & Brown, 1991; Russell & Ginsburg, 1984). The present study documents that this applies to MD children year after year throughout the primary school stage. The MD children's consistent use of backup strategies might reflect both fact retrieval problems and working memory problems (Garnett & Fleischner, 1983; Geary, 1990, 1993; Geary et al., 1992; Goldman et al., 1988). Since the data from this study showed that the typical MD children use backup strategies only during the whole phase of primary education, it would be a reasonable assumption that the exclusive use of backup strategies reflects a critical factor for normal development.

Among the MN children the characteristic course of development shows the use of new strategies, both backup and retrieval strategies. In a longitudinal perspective, a course of development was observed involving an age-determined shift in strategy use, not only away from backup to retrieval, but also within the framework of the backup strategies themselves, that is, away from the most primary counting strategies, so that other backup strategies, especially verbal counting, were used more frequently (Carpenter & Moser, 1984). It was suggested that the corresponding data for the MD children would reflect a developmental delay model, establishing that the difference between the two ability groups would converge early in the elementary school years (Geary, 1993; Goldman et al., 1988). Unexpectedly therefore, the typical MD children were characterised not only by little use of retrieval strategies but also by much more frequent use of the most primary backup strategies throughout the whole primary school stage.

These results seem to conflict with the arguments proposed by Geary (1993) that the development of the procedural and memory-retrieval skills of MD children are largely modular; that is, functionally distinct. Consistent with the developmental difference model (Goldman et al., 1988), the acquisition of strategy skills by MD children seemed to follow a sequence that is fundamentally different from that observed in normal achievers.

Earlier studies have shown that domain-specific knowledge, that is, substantial factual knowledge, is an important component in the effective strategy use (Ohlsson & Rees, 1991; Pressley et al., 1990). There is therefore reason to assume that the amount of domain-specific knowledge, that is, the amount of factual knowledge the child possesses about the various strategies and how and where to apply them, will be reflected in problem solving through the range of variation in the strategies used.

Most frequent, when MN children were asked to solve basic fact problems and arithmetic word problems, they normally used several different strategy variants for this purpose. Thus, a course of development was observed which showed a gradual but marked increase in the number of strategy variants used as the children became older. This result might indicate that these children have at their disposal a rich amount of domain-specific strategy knowledge, that is, substantial knowledge of various strategies and their areas of application. Consequently, the study confirms the results of earlier studies (Ashcraft, 1992; Carpenter & Moser, 1984; Geary & Burlingham-Dubree, 1989; Siegler & Shrager, 1984). The results further document that the number of different strategy variants used by the MN children increases as they move up through the primary school.

In the case of the MD child, however, the course of development showed far less frequent use of a large number of different strategies throughout the primary school. While a wealth of substantial strategy knowledge was typical of the MN children it seemed, on the other hand, that the MD children had *a lack of strategies*. As indicated above, the result of the present study gives argument to the suggestion that the MD children's insufficient domain-specific strategy knowledge in itself limits the choices available to them. Accordingly, I suggest the existence of important individual differences in the wealth of domain-specific strategy knowledge. More precisely, I argue that the amount of factual knowledge the child possesses about the various strategies, and how and where to apply them, might be reflected in problem solving through the range of variation in the strategies used. If this suggestion is valid, there are reasons to assume that the quantity of domain-specific strategy knowledge could be a critical factor for normal development.

When the research on the individual child's strategy use was repeated 2 years after the first time of measurement, the MN children, who had already used several different strategy variants 2 years before, continued to change their strategy use in the direction of new strategy variants. This result could reflect an increase in the quantity of domain-specific strategy knowledge they possess, but could also relate to *strategic flexibility* indicating that children have the ability to 'call forth' appropriate strategies by actively selecting and judging between the strategies at their disposal (Ashcraft, 1992; Geary & Burlingham-Dubree, 1989; Siegler & Jenkins, 1989; Siegler & Shrager, 1984). The MD children, on the other hand, did not change their strategy use to nearly the same degree. The typical MD child seemed to use the same strategy variant(s) again and again, year after year, right through the entire primary school, which implies that their pattern of development is characterised by *strategic rigidity*.

Thus, the results from the present study indicates that at an early stage, probably already in grade 1, the MD children seemed to adopt a characteristic pattern of development, featuring primary backup strategies, a minimum of strategies, and strategic rigidity. This pattern of development might provide substantial support for the suggestion that inefficient strategy use might be a consequence, in part, of persistent use of primary backup strategies (e.g., Goldman et al., 1988). Several years ago, Gestalt psychologists presented what may be a related phenomenon, that is, *functional fixedness* (Wertheimer, 1959). When a particular approach or procedure is practiced it can become fixed, making it difficult to think of the problem situation in another way.

Moreover, the study examined the differences between MN and MD children in regard to the pattern of development that unfolds when the children move up through primary school, as reflected in their level of performance, discrepancy between their performance on simple basic fact problems (the NF test) compared with simple word problems (the WP test), as well as in their use of task-specific strategies identified as material, verbal, and mental strategies.

In contrast to the MN children, the MD children's performance showed a course of development with a large and constant discrepancy, throughout the primary school period, between the levels of performance in the two tests. The level of performance for solving basic fact problems and arithmetic word problems as well as their characteristic strategy use seemed to have been almost permanently established by second grade (Ostad, 1998a).

According to the conceptual understanding hypothesis, strategies acquired in isolation from their conceptual basis tend to be error prone, and do not transfer easily to novel problems (Hiebert & Lefevre, 1986; Ohlsson & Rees, 1991). Thus, when the MD children's performance showed a course of development with a large and constant discrepancy, throughout the primary school period, between their level of performance for solving basic fact problems and arithmetic word problems it could be argued that these children do not have a good conceptual understanding of arithmetic. That is, they approach simple arithmetic in a rather rigid, algorithmic manner, as they do counting.

MD children produced significant more errors than the MN children on all the grade levels included in the study, and the younger produced more errors than the older ones. Furthermore, the results were also consistent with several other investigations showing that the MD children required more time to solve arithmetic problems than their normal peers (e.g., Garnett & Fleischner, 1983; Geary & Burlingham-Dubree, 1989; Geary et al., 1991). Thus, the results argue for Kirby and Becker's (1988) position that MD children are consistently slower than normal children at executing basic numerical operations. The mixed pattern of the results reported from earlier studies (e.g., Geary, 1990; Geary & Brown, 1991) and, which according to Geary probably reflects the likely heterogeneity of MD groups, was not observed in the present study. It should be noted, however, that the overall error rate for the MD children was relatively low. However, analysis of the data of the present study did not suggest significant relationship between accuracy and strategy use for solving basic fact problems. There is evidence that the relatively low error rate produced by the MD children is consistent with the effect reported by Siegler and Jenkins (1989) suggesting that 'back-up strategies can yield accurate performance on problems where retrieval cannot' (p. 28). On the other hand, when the analysis of the results indicated that speed of processing were significantly related to the developmental maturity of the children's strategy use throughout the elementary grades, this result argues against Kirby and Becker (1988) suggestion that MD children use the same type of strategies as MN children to solve arithmetic problems but are slower at executing basic operations. An alternative explanation would be that MD and MN children use a different mix of problem-solving strategies (Ostad, 1997a, b), which in turn leads to differences in overall solution times.

A number of earlier studies have, on the basis of different criteria, characterised MD children as a heterogeneous group. These children show different levels of intelligence, different language skills, etc. The results from the present study indicated that approximately half of the MD children, that is, about 5% of the children in the actual schools, also had language-based difficulties. However, this observed comorbidity was primarily found among children who represented the most prevalent cases of language-based difficulties (Ostad, 1998b). From this viewpoint, it would be a reasonable assumption that this observed heterogeneity within the group would be clearly reflected in the pattern of strategy development. Therefore, it may seem paradoxical that the present study documents surprisingly little variability in strategy use for solving both basic fact problems and arithmetic word problems. When the MD children (supposedly including children with different potentials for development) reach the end of grade 7, large deviations from the main pattern described above are a rare occurrence. Thus, the most striking feature of the pattern of strategy development, as is pictured in the results of this study, is the marked degree of similarity in the strategy use among the group of MD children as a whole. Perhaps even more significant, this pattern of development seems to have been almost permanently established early in primary school, probably at the end of first grade. The early and striking convergence (flatten) of the developmental curve is consistent with the developmental difference model (Goldman et al., 1988).

In summary, the pattern strategy use presented the typical MD child as being characteristic of (a) use of backup strategies only, (b) use of the most primary backup strategies, (c) small degree of variation in the use of strategy variants and, (d) limited degree of change in the use of strategies from year to year through the primary school. Perhaps even more significantly, this pattern of development seemed to have been almost permanently established at an early age level.

EDUCATIONAL IMPLICATIONS AND
RECOMMENDATIONS

In general, *weak recall of basic facts* is often cited as one of the most common characteristics seen in children with difficulties in mathematics (e.g., Geary, 1993, Grene, 1999; Ostad, 2000). Failure to acquire mastery of basic facts seems to create a 'cascade' of failure in mathematical learning, since fluent recall of basic addition, multiplication, division, and subtraction facts makes it easier to solve more complex problems in which these basic mathematical operations are embedded (Robinson et al., 2002). The results of the present study have shown that weak recall of basic facts appears fairly early in the children's mathematical development and thus can serve as an early warning sign to alert teachers to possible emergent difficulties.

According to Ginsburg (1997), the most reasonable explanation for the MD children's failure in mathematics is the conventional system of instruction. Several projects were initiated to address the need for better mathematics instruction. The importance of metacognition to mathematical problem solving is well acknowledged in the literature (Hiebert & Carpenter, 1992). Cognitive strategy instruction is a promising alternative to current approaches for teaching mathematics to students with learning difficulties (Montague, 1997).

Teachers should bear in mind the suggestion that children can be channeled into inappropriate development patterns, for which the teaching itself might be partly responsible. The consistency with which some MD children used backup strategies could indicate that these strategies may very well have been restrictively taught. One could, for example, expect strategy variability to be influenced by the extent to which an individual's school instruction had encouraged or discouraged such variability. If the above suggestion is valid, the characteristic pattern of development of the MD children might have been created by excessive emphasis on teaching methods that invite the use of primary counting procedures. This seems particularly relevant when teaching the youngest age groups (as in the schools included in the present study) is based to a large extent on ready-printed exercise books, often with concretes functioning as counting instruments; 'the main thing' the pupil has to do is to count the concretes and write in the answers (Ostad, 1992). MD children require more than ready-printed exercise books, concretes, or real-word practice in solving mathematical problems to become good problem solvers. By contrast, the results of the present study might suggest that remedy of mathematics difficulties should include instruction on task-specific strategies involved in efficiently solving of arithmetic word problems and arithmetic basic fact problems. To address the needs of the MD children, there is evidence that the instructional methods generally need to change focus, early in the elementary school years, *from how to learn more mathematics to how to learn mathematics by means of appropriate approaches*, that is, providing MD children with instruction to help them become good strategy users and move beyond rote application of basic skills.

The results of the present study suggest that good strategy users; (a) have available a knowledge base of task-specific strategies to perform a particular task or a particular problem type, (b) are flexible in the use of particular strategies in specific situations, and (c) are actively engaged in monitoring the course of the solution and in evaluating of success. The basic question then becomes how individual differences in strategy use relate to the acquisition of the performance on simple arithmetic word problems and simple basic fact problems. But do the MD children have sufficient knowledge of the different task-specific strategies available to them? It could well be that their knowledge in this respect is limited to backup strategies alone. The results of the study indicate a possible relation between children's difficulties and the absence of an adequate domain-specific knowledge base of task-specific strategies. However, to what degree early convergence (flatten) of the MD children's developmental curves can be counteracted by extended strategy instruction in the early age groups focused directly on the above noted points remains an open question. More valid classroom research is needed to find answer to this question.

In summary, the results of the present study presented the MD children by the use of developmentally immature strategies that is, characterized with the lack of movement through the typical chain of increasingly sophisticated strategies to achieve eventual retrieve upon request (Jordan & Montani, 1997). However, broad explanations such as 'developmental immature strategies' do not answer questions concerning the etiology of the children's difficulties. An important step further involves identification of the deficient cognitive processes that underlie the behavioral manifestations of the difficulties. Until now, there is not a research based agreed upon explanation for the difficulties in mathematics in terms of weaknesses in specific cognitive processes. Actually, to go beyond general explanations based on behavioral components of the difficulties we need to search for the processing weaknesses that have a relatively focused impact on children's thinking and learning ability. Adequate understanding of difficulties in mathematics requires that these cognitive processing weaknesses be addressed and explained.

REFERENCES

Ashcraft, M. H. (1992). Cognitive arithmetic. A review of data and theory. *Cognition, 44*, 75–106.

Badian, N. A. (1983). Dyscalculia and nonverbal disorders of learning. In Myklebust, H. R. (Ed.), *Progress in Learning Disabilities* (pp. 235–264). New York: Stratton.

Carpenter, T. & Moser, J. M. (1984). The acquisition of addition and subtraction concepts in grade one through three. *Journal of Research in Mathematics Education, 15*(3), 179–202.

Fleischner, J. E., Garnett, K., & Shepherd, M. J. (1982). Proficiency in arithmetic basic fact computation of learning disabled and nondisabled children. *Focus on Learning Problems in Mathematics, 4*, 47–56.

Dowker, A. (2005). *Individual Differences in Arithmetic. Implications for Psychology, Neuroscience and Education*. Hove and New York: Psychology Press.

Garnett, K. & Fleischner, J. J. (1983). Automatization and basic fact performance of normal and learning disabled children. *Learning Disability Quarterly, 6*, 223–230.

Geary, D. C. (1990). A componential analysis of an early learning deficit in mathematics. *Journal of Experimental Child Psychology*, *49*, 363–383.

Geary, D. C. & Brown, S. C. (1991). Cognitive addition: Strategy choice and speed-of-processing. Differences in gifted, normal, and mathematically disabled children. *Developmental Psychology*, *27*(3), 398–406.

Geary, D. C. & Burlingham-Dubree, M. (1989). External validation of the strategy choice model for addition. *Journal of Experimental Child Psychology*, *47*, 175–192.

Geary, D. C., Widaman, K. F., Little, T. D., & Cormier, P. (1987). Cognitive addition: Comparison of learning disabled and academically normal elementary school children. *Cognitive Development*, *2*, 249–269.

Geary, D. C., Brown, S. C., & Samaranayake, V. A. (1991). Cognitive addition: A short longitudinal study of strategy choice and speed of processing difficulties in normal and mathematically disabled children. *Developmental Psychology*, *27*(5), 787–797.

Geary, D. C., Bow-Thomas, C. C., & Yao, Y. (1992). Counting knowledge and skill in cognitive addition: A comparison of normal and mathematically disabled children. *Journal of Experimental Child Psychology*, *54*, 372–391.

Geary, D. C. (1993). Mathematical disabilities: Cognitive, neuropsychological, and genetic components. *Psychological Bulletin*, *114*, 345–362.

Ginsburg, H. P. (1997). Mathematics learning disabilities: A view from developmental psychology. *Journal of Learning Disabilities*, *30*, 20–33.

Goldman, S. R., Pellegrino, J. W., & Mertz, D. L. (1988). Extended practice of basic addition facts: Strategy changes in learning disabled students. *Cognition and Instruction*, *5*, 223–265.

Hiebert, J. & Carpenter, T. (1992). Learning and teaching with understanding. In Grouws, D. (Ed.), *Handbook of Research on Mathematics Teaching* (pp. 65–97). New York: Macmillan.

Hiebert, J. & Lefevre, P. (1986). Conceptual and procedural knowledge in mathematics: An introductory analysis. In Hiebert, J. (Ed.), *Conceptual and Procedural Knowledge: The Case of Mathematics* (pp. 1–27). Hillsdale, NJ: Erlbaum.

Jordan, N. C. & Montani, T. O. (1997). Cognitive arithmetic and problem solving: A comparison of children with specific and general mathematics difficulties. *Journal of Learning Disabilities*, *33*(3), 567–578.

Kirby, J. R. & Becker, L. D. (1988). Cognitive components of learning problems in arithmetic. *Remedial and Special Education*, *9*, 7–16.

Kosc, L. (1974). Developmental dyscalculia. *Journal of Learning Disabilities*, *7*, 164–177.

Montague, M. (1997). Cognitive strategy instruction in mathematics for students with learning disabilities. *Journal of Learning Disabilities*, *30*(2), 164–177.

Ohlsson, S. & Rees, E. (1991). The function of conceptual understanding in the learning of arithmetic procedures. *Cognition and Instruction*, *8*, 103–179.

Ostad, S. A. (1992). Bærekraftige matematikkunnskaper, en funksjon av ferdighet eller forståelse? [Good mathematics knowledge, a function of skills or understanding?]. *Norsk pedagogisk tidsskrift*, *6*, 320–326.

Ostad, S. A. (1997a). Strategic competence: Issues of task-specific strategies in arithmetic. *Nordic Studies in Mathematics Education*, *3*, 7–32.

Ostad, S. A. (1997b). Developmental differences in addition strategies: A comparison of mathematically disabled and mathematically normal children. *British Journal of Educational Psychology*, *67*, 345–357.

Ostad, S. A. (1998a). Developmental differences in solving simple arithmetic word problems and simple number-fact problems: A comparison of mathematically normal and mathematically disabled children. *Mathematical Cognition*, *4*(1), 1–19.

Ostad, S. A. (1998b). Comorbidity between mathematics and spelling difficulties. *Logopedics Phoniatrics Vocology*, *23*(4), 145–154.

Ostad, S. A. (1999). Developmental progression of subtraction strategies: A comparison of mathematically normal and mathematically disabled children. *European Journal of Special Needs Education*, *14*(1), 21–36.

Ostad, S. A. (2000). Cognitive subtraction in a developmental perspective: Accuracy, speed-of-processing and strategy-use differences in normal and mathematically disabled children. *Focus on Learning Problems in Mathematics, 22*(2), 18–30.

Pressley, M., Borkowski, J. G., & Schneider, W. (1990). Good information processing: What it is and how education can promote it. *International Journal of Educational Research, 13*, 857–867.

Robinson, C. S., Menchetti, B. M., & Torgesen, J. K. (2002). Toward a two-factor theory of one type of mathematics disabilities. *Learning Disabilities Research and Practice, 17*(2), 81–89.

Russell, R. L. & Grinsburg, H. P. (1984). Cognitive analysis of children's mathematics difficulties. *Cognition and Instruction, 1*, 217–244.

Siegler, R. S. (1988). Individual differences in strategy choices: Good students, not-so-good students, and perfectionists. *Child development, 59*, 833–851.

Siegler, R. S. & Jenkins, E. (1989). *How Children Discover New Strategies*. Hillsdale, NJ: Erlbaum.

Siegler, R. S. & Shrager, J. (1984). Strategy choice in addition and subtraction: How do children know what to do? In Sophian, C. (Ed.), *Origin of Cognitive Skills* (pp. 229–293). Hillsdale, NJ: Erlbaum.

Svenson, O. & Broquist, S. (1975). Strategies for solving simple addition problems: A comparison of normal and subnormal children. *Scandinavian Journal of Psychology, 16*, 143–151.

Wertheimer, M. (1959). *Productive Thinking*. New York: Harper.

NOTES

1. The *basic facts* of arithmetic are the simple, closed number sentences we use when we compute. These number sentences involve two one-digit addends if they are basic addition or subtraction facts, or two one-digit factors if they are basic multiplication or division facts. Examples of basic facts include the following: $6 + 7 = 13$, $12 - 8 = 4$, $3 \times 6 = 18$, $27{:}9 = 3$. *Basic fact problem solving* is to supply missing sums, addends, products, and factors for these basic facts.

2. The children that were included in the samples of MD children were: (a) registered in the schools' ordinary support services as in need of a special program of mathematics teaching, *and* (b) among the 14% bottom group in mathematics achievement tests taken with a 2 year interval.

8

NUMBER DEVELOPMENT AND CHILDREN WITH SPECIFIC LANGUAGE IMPAIRMENT

RICHARD COWAN[1], CHRIS DONLAN[2],
ELIZABETH J. NEWTON[3], DELYTH LLOYD[4]

[1]*Institute of Education, Department of Psychology and Human Development, University of London, London WC1H 0AA, UK*
[2]*Department of Human Communication Science, University College London, London WC1N OPD, UK*
[3]*Department of Psychology, London South Bank University, London SE1 6LN, UK*
[4]*Department of Psychology, University of Melbourne, Melbourne, Victoria 3010, Australia*

INTRODUCTION

How children develop competence with numbers and why they differ so much in their progress are important questions whether one is concerned with numeracy, the skills and knowledge for dealing with numerical information in everyday life, or mathematics, the sciences dealing with the logic of quantity, shape, and arrangement.

The study of number development in children with specific language impairment (SLI) has the potential to contribute both to the understanding of the factors that influence children's progress generally and to the knowledge base for professionals working with these children.

In this chapter we shall describe some further investigations of the group of children we have previously reported on (Cowan et al., 2005: Donlan et al., 2007). These further studies involved assessing understanding of monetary value, ordinality, and small number quantification.

MONETARY VALUE

Previous work on number in children with SLI (reviewed by Donlan, 1998, 2003) had indicated selective impairments: children with SLI showed impaired procedural skills, particularly in counting, from an early age but less impaired understanding of number, for example counting principles. Our investigations of children with SLI provided ample evidence of the continuing deficit in counting and calculation (Cowan et al., 2005). Our sample of 7- to 9-year-olds with SLI performed substantially below a group matched in nonverbal reasoning and age (AC) and not better than a language match group (LC), who were 2 years younger, on a test of count sequence recall and generation. The SLI and AC groups differed markedly on calculation problems. Only an SLI subgroup attending mainstream schools performed better than the LC group on addition and subtraction and this was limited to problems with sums and minuends less than 10.

In contrast both SLI subgroups were much more successful than the LC group on tests of numerical principles (Donlan et al., 2007). Their position relative to the AC group varied with principle. They performed substantially below their peers on a test of place value knowledge involving real multidigit numbers but did not differ on a commutativity test using 'Martian' numbers. The discrepancy might result from the greater dependence of place value on knowledge of numbers obtained through familiarity with the count sequence. In contrast the commutativity test had been deliberately designed not to involve familiar numbers so that children's application of the principle to addition in general might be assessed.

Another possibility is that commutativity in some form develops much earlier than place value and is less dependent on language. Comparisons of knowledge of principles and strategy use indicate children understand commutativity more than other principles and that understanding of commutativity precedes use of strategies that presuppose it, for example counting on from the second addend (*min*) (Canobi, 2004, 2005; Canobi et al., 1998, 2003). Siegler and Crowley's (1994) study showed preschoolers who were yet to use *min* nevertheless judged it to be smart and differentiated it from illegitimate strategies that resembled it in yielding fast answers.

One early emerging competence that is related to place value is the understanding that the monetary value of a set of coins depends on both denomination and number of coins (Nunes & Bryant, 1996). We constructed a test of children's understanding of monetary value which is derived from Nunes and Bryant (1996)'s tests of relative value.

ORDINALITY

Ordinality is involved in being able to order a set of items and co-ordinate this with seriation of another set (Piaget, 1952) and knowing how to use ordinal number words to label items in a series (Beilin, 1975). Clearly, the acquisition of ordinal number words is likely to be affected by linguistic ability. Seriation seems inherently nonverbal and, indeed, monkeys are suggested to have some ability (McGonigle & Chalmers, 1992). Nevertheless, seriation ability in children appears to be important in predicting number line and number language comprehension in the early years (Kingma, 1984; Kingma & Zumbo, 1987). A previous study (Siegel et al., 1981) found preschoolers with linguistic impairments performed less well on a seriation task than age- and ability-matched controls, even though a nonverbal version was used. Whether this resulted from linguistic or working memory deficit is unknown. We devised three tasks: ordering, where the child arranged a set of objects in order; ordinal labeling, where they had to identify an object in a verbally specified ordinal position; and seriation, where they had to use the position of an object in one series to find the corresponding object in another series.

SMALL NUMBER QUANTIFICATION

Dyscalculia is a specific problem with numbers that can have severe consequences on children's mathematical development. Butterworth (2005) has argued that defects in development of a module specific to small numbers can give rise to dyscalculia. He has drawn on evidence from studies of infant numerosity, animal studies, and neuropsychological cases. Landerl et al. (2004) described the number skills of a group of children identified on the basis of extremely poor performance on mathematical tests. They were nevertheless of normal intelligence and working memory and had no reading difficulties.

Although the language problems of children with SLI are likely to impact on their number development, this does not entail that their language characteristics are solely responsible for their difficulties. We therefore devised a small number quantification task and used data from it to compare the groups and also to reanalyze the data in Cowan et al. (2005) to determine whether small number quantification explained additional variance between children after including the effects of working memory, reasoning, and language comprehension.

The aims of this study are (a) to investigate whether the number skills of children with SLI differ from those of their typically developing peers, matched in nonverbal reasoning, and a group of younger typically developing children matched on language comprehension; and (b) to assess whether small number quantification accuracy accounts for additional variation in number tasks beyond the other influences.

METHOD

PARTICIPANTS

The participants were the 167 children selected through the process described in Cowan et al. (2005). Descriptive statistics concerning the four groups (LC, children with SLI attending special schools, children with SLI attending mainstream schools, and AC) are reported in Table 8.1 (reproduced from Cowan et al., 2005).

EXPERIMENTAL TASKS

Monetary value: This task assessed understanding of monetary value by requiring children to identify which of two cartoon characters had more money using British coins. The size order of British coins used is as follows, from

TABLE 8.1 Descriptive Statistics for the Groups on Nonverbal Reasoning (Raven), Language, Working Memory, and Instruction

Measure	LC[1]		SLI Special[2]		SLI Mainstream[3]		AC[4]	
	M	*(SD)*	*M*	*(SD)*	*M*	*(SD)*	*M*	*(SD)*
Age (in years)	6.0_a	(0.4)	8.2_b	(0.3)	8.2_b	(0.5)	8.2_b	(0.3)
Raven (standard)	106.6_a	(10.9)	102.3_a	(9.1)	103.2_a	(12.3)	105.0_a	(11.6)
Raven (raw score)	18.4_a	(4.0)	23.6_b	(2.9)	24.3_b	(4.8)	25.0_b	(4.5)
Language								
TROG (standard)	94.5_a	(7.2)	80.4_b	(4.9)	80.9_b	(6.5)	101.0_c	(11.6)
TROG (raw score)	11.7_a	(1.7)	11.1_a	(1.4)	11.6_a	(1.7)	16.0_b	(1.8)
Working memory								
Forward span	4.1_a	(0.6)	3.6_b	(0.5)	3.7_b	(0.8)	4.7_c	(0.9)
Corsi span	3.3_a	(0.7)	3.6_{ab}	(0.7)	3.6_a	(1.0)	4.0_b	(0.6)
Backward span	2.2_a	(0.6)	2.2_a	(0.4)	2.2_a	(0.7)	3.0_b	(0.7)
Instruction	4.1_a	(2.0)	3.8_a	(1.8)	7.8_b	(3.1)	11.1_c	(2.3)

Note: Means in the same row that do not share a subscript differ significantly at $p < 0.05$ (Ryan-Einot-Gabriel-Welsch post hoc comparisons). AC, age control group; LC, language control group; SLI, specific language impairment; TROG = Test for Reception of Grammar.

[1] $n = 55$ (8 girls, 47 boys); [2] $n = 11$ (2 girls, 9 boys); [3] $n = 44$ (6 girls, 38 boys); [4] $n = 57$ (8 girls, 49 boys).

smallest to largest: 5p, 1p, 20p, 10p, 2p, and 50p. Following a practice session with feedback, the child received a series of trials. In a trial, each cartoon character had coins of only one denomination. In one subtask, both characters had the same number of coins but these differed in denomination. These assessed the child's understanding that value was independent of size of coin: in five trials, the larger coin was more valuable (e.g. 10p vs 5p), and in six trials, the smaller coin was more valuable (e.g. 2p vs 10p). In the second subtask, the characters differed both in the denominations of coins and in the numbers of coins. These assessed the child's understanding that value was independent of number of coins and single coin denomination. In two trials, the character with the greater number of coins had more (e.g. three 5ps vs one 10p). In six trials, the character with fewer coins had more (e.g. one 10p vs four 2ps). The trials from both subtasks were randomly presented. These items formed a reliable scale with a maximum score of 20 (Cronbach's alpha $= .79$, item-to-scale correlations ranging from .08 to .62). Low correlations resulted from some items being particularly easy with facilities greater than 95%.

Ordering: The ordering task required children to arrange a family of five cartoon squirrels in order of size. The actual size order differed from chronological age: the size order was, from largest to smallest, Daddy, Granddad, Mummy, Grandma (also called Nan), and Baby. Each squirrel was on a separate card. The experimenter introduced them in random order, named them and drew attention to their size. The child was then asked to place the squirrels in size order with the largest on the left. Children who were unsuccessful on the first time were encouraged to try again. If the child was still unsuccessful, the experimenter arranged the squirrels in correct order. Scores out of two were derived by crediting the child with two points if they correctly ordered the squirrels on the first attempt, one point if they succeeded on the second attempt, and zero if they did not succeed on either attempt.

Ordinal labeling: The ordinal labeling task assessed understanding of ordinal number words by requiring children to point to the squirrel in a particular ordinal position. Overall, there were eight items. After asking the child to point to the smallest and largest squirrels, the experimenter asked the child to identify the second, third, and fourth largest and smallest. The order in which these were requested was randomized with the constraint that the correct squirrel was never the same on consecutive trials, for example the request for the second largest was never adjacent to the request for the fourth smallest.

Seriation: This task assessed children's ability to co-ordinate two series. With the squirrels arranged in order of size, the child was shown a series of pictures of items of clothing and asked to identify the item for particular squirrels. Each picture had five items of clothing, identical except in size, for example five pairs of socks. The items were not arranged in order of size on the pictures. The sizes of the items of clothing did not exactly correspond to the sizes of the squirrels to ensure successful matching was based on ordinal position. The experimenter would then point to a squirrel at one end, either Daddy or Baby, and ask the child which would they wear. The second question for a particular item of clothing would be about one of the intermediate sized squirrels (Granddad, Mummy, or Grandma). Overall, there were six types of clothing, and so 12 questions.

Ordinality scale: Items at the endpoints for the labeling and seriation tasks were almost always correctly answered so these items were excluded from the scale that was constructed. The scale comprised the ordering score, the six ordinal labeling items, and the six seriation items that did not involve endpoints. These items formed a reliable scale with a maximum score of 14 (Cronbach's alpha = .71, item-to-scale correlations ranging from .12 to .45).

Small number: Children were asked to judge the numerosity of displays of dots varying in number from three to seven. The displays were presented using a Dell Latitude L400 laptop computer running custom software written in visual basic. Each trial began with the presentation of a 'smiley face' fixation point in the centre of the screen, followed by a blank white screen for 500 m secs. The target display consisted of a number of dots simultaneously presented. Each dot appeared at 1 of 12 fixed locations equidistant from the fixation point. The duration of the display was 150 msecs. After presentation of the target display, a distractor screen of random 'scribbles' was shown for 1000 msecs. The screen cleared and a prompt asked 'How many?' This stayed on the screen until a number was entered via the keyboard. After two practice trials, there were 20 trials, 4 of each numerosity, presented in a fixed random order. The computer recorded the response for each trial. The 20 items formed a reliable scale (Cronbach's alpha = .74, item-to-scale correlations ranging from .07 to .48).

RESULTS

It was not possible to test one child with SLI on the monetary value task. Apart from that, data collection was complete. The groups differed in accuracy on every task and derived scale: monetary value, $F(3,162) = 25.27$, $p < .0005$, $\eta^2 = .32$; ordering, $F(3,163) = 6.68$, $p < .0005$, $\eta^2 = .11$; ordinal labeling, $F(3,163) = 12.41$, $p < .0005$, $\eta^2 = .19$; seriation, $F(3,163) = 10.43$, $p < 0.0005$, $\eta^2 = .16$; ordinality scale, $F(3,163) = 22.03$, $p < .0005$, $\eta^2 = .29$; small number three items, $F(3,163) = 6.24$, $p < 0.0005$, $\eta^2 = .10$; small number four items, $F(3,163) = 4.94$, $p < .005$, $\eta^2 = .08$; small number five items, $F(3,163) = 12.92$, $p < 0.0005$, $\eta^2 = .19$; small number six items: $F(3,163) = 4.03$, $p < 0.001$, $\eta^2 = .07$; small number seven items, $F(3,163) = 3.38$, $p < .05$, $\eta^2 = .06$; small number scale, $F(3,163) = 14.11$, $p < .0005$, $\eta^2 = .21$. Table 8.2 reports task means and differences between groups.

We decided to use the scales for further analysis as they had reasonable reliability. Although the ordinality scale combines both the labeling and the seriation items it does not appear that the position of the SLI groups varies much whether verbal or nonverbal items are used. As Table 8.2 shows, both SLI groups perform worse than the AC group on both tasks and neither group performs better than the LC group.

TABLE 8.2   Number Task Performance by Group

Measure	Maximum possible	LC	SLI Special	SLI Mainstream	AC
Monetary value scale	20	15.62_a (2.78)	15.18_{ab} (4.09)	17.91_b (2.26)	19.18_c (1.32)
Ordering	2	1.42_a (.83)	1.36_a (.51)	1.61_a (.75)	1.93_b (.26)
Ordinal labeling	8	5.35_a (1.48)	5.00_a (1.26)	5.66_a (1.49)	6.79_b (1.28)
Seriation	12	9.44_a (1.44)	9.73_a (1.56)	9.84_a (1.66)	10.96_b (1.45)
Ordinality scale	14	8.40_a (2.52)	8.18_a (2.56)	9.16_a (2.88)	11.82_b (1.85)
Small number					
3	4	2.87_a (1.40)	3.36_{ab} (.81)	3.39_{ab} (.89)	3.68_b (.54)
4	4	2.78_a (1.12)	3.45_{ab} (.69)	2.95_{ab} (1.20)	3.47_b (.85)
5	4	1.27_a (1.01)	1.55_{ab} (1.37)	2.09_{ab} (1.49)	2.68_b (1.17)
6	4	1.04_a (1.05)	$.82_a$ (.87)	1.48_{ab} (1.00)	1.56_b (.91)
7	4	$.56_a$ (.71)	$.55_a$ (.52)	$.59_a$ (.82)	$.98_b$ (.88)
Small number scale	20	8.53_a (3.32)	9.73_{ab} (2.61)	10.50_{bc} (3.68)	12.39_c (2.62)

Note: For all groups, numbers entered are means with standard deviations in parentheses. Means in the same row that do not share a subscript differ significantly at $p < 0.05$ (Games-Howell or Ryan-Einot-Gabriel-Welsch post hoc comparisons depending on heterogeneity of variance).

Table 8.3 shows the zero-order correlations between the background measures and the scales. The first set of multiple regressions were undertaken to determine whether the performance of children with SLI differs from that of their chronological peers (AC group) when relations between performance and curriculum coverage, working memory, receptive grammar, and nonverbal reasoning are taken into account. In the multiple regressions, dummy variables are used which code the SLI Mainstream group as the reference group. The results are summarized in Table 8.4. The regressions were repeated excluding the SLI Special school group, and the estimates of influence of the background measures were very similar.

To assess the contribution of small number ability to explaining variance on number tasks, the multiple regressions reported in Cowan et al. (2005) were rerun with the addition of the small number scale as a predictor. The results are summarized in Table 8.5.

DISCUSSION

The results provide mixed support for the expectations based on previous research. We shall discuss each one separately.

TABLE 8.3 Correlations Between Measures

No.	Variable	1	2	3	4	5	6	7	8	9
1.	Nonverbal reasoning	–	.44	.21	.42	.36	.46	.53	.45	.42
2.	Language comprehension		–	.56	.35	.52	.56	.48	.57	.40
3.	Forward span			–	.18	.46	.28	.26	.37	.27
4.	Corsi span				–	.28	.32	.43	.38	.37
5.	Backward span					–	.45	.37	.45	.39
6.	Instruction						–	.51	.46	.40
7.	Monetary value							–	.55	.45
8.	Ordinality								–	.48
9.	Small number									–

Note: $n = 167$. Nonverbal reasoning is raw score on Raven's. Language comprehension is raw score on TROG. For coefficients greater than .20, $p < .01$; for coefficients greater than .26, $p < .001$.

TABLE 8.4 Summary of Simultaneous Multiple Regression Analyses on Scales

	Monetary value		Ordinality		Small number	
	β	sr^2	β	sr^2	β	sr^2
Nonverbal reasoning	.24**	.03	.19*	.02	.15	
Language comprehension	.14		.23*	.02	.06	
Forward span	.01		.04		.06	
Corsi span	.19**	.03	.12		.17*	.02
Backward span	.06		.12		.15	
Instruction	.08		.06		.05	
AC v SLI (M)	−.03		.11		.02	
LC v SLI (M)	−.19*	.01	.01		−.15	
SLI (S) v SLI (M)	−.21**	.03	−.05		−.04	

Note: $n = 167$. SLI (M) is SLI Mainstream School. SLI (S) is SLI Special School. $R^2 = .46$ for Monetary value, .42 for Ordinality, and .31 for Small number.
   * $p < 0.05$; ** $p < 0.01$.

MONETARY VALUE

The monetary value task was supposed to assess understanding of principles and children with SLI were expected to outperform the younger LC group and possibly approximate the level of the AC group. In fact both SLI groups

TABLE 8.5 Summary of Multiple Regression Analyses of Number Tasks Reported in Cowan et al. (2005) Including Small Number Task as Predictor

	Counting		Addition combinations		Basic calculation I		Basic calculation II		Story problems		Transcoding		Relative magnitude	
	β	sr^2	β	sr^2	β	sr^2	β	sr^2	β	sr^2	β	sr^2	β	sr^2
Nonverbal reasoning	.16*	.02	.04		.26**	.04	.17*	.02	.15*	.01	.15**	.01	.14	
Language comprehension	.22*	.02	.02		.22*	.02	.33***	.03	.28***	.02	.26***	.02	.11	
Forward span	.11		.09		.09		.07		.12*	.01	−.02		−.04	
Corsi span	−.04		.15**	.02	.05		.02		.14**	.01	.03		.15*	.02
Backward span	.12	.01	.09		.13	.02	.18*	.02	.03		.19***	.02	.18*	.02
Instruction	.20*	.02	−.02		−.06		−.08		.11		.20**	.01	.12	
AC vs SLI (M)	.25**	.02	.28*	.02	−.04		−.01		.18*	.01	.17*	.01	.10	
LC vs SLI (M)	.16*		−.21*	.02	−.07		−.09		.03		−.02		−.08	
SLI (S) vs SLI (M)	.04		−.08		−.10		−.16*	.02	−.06		−.05		.05	
Small number scale	.17**	.02	.17*	.02	.18*	.02	.20**	.03	.12*	.01	.14**	.01	.17*	.02

Note: $n = 167$. SLI (M) is SLI Mainstream School. SLI (S) is SLI Special School. Basic calculation I comprises addition and subtraction problems with sums and minuends less than 10. Basic calculation II consists of addition and subtraction problems with sums and minuends above 10 and less than 20. $R^2 = .65$ for Counting, .53 for Addition combinations, .45 for Basic calculation I, .55 for Basic calculation II, .67 for Story problems, .76 for Transcoding, and .50 for Relative magnitude.
$p < .05$; ** $p < .01$; *** $p < .001$.

were less successful than the AC group and only the SLI Mainstream group performed better than the LC group. It may be that variation in task performance reflected differences in calculation skill rather than appreciation of principles.

An alternative is that the presentation of the task caused difficulties for the SLI groups due to the demands it made on visuospatial processing. Corsi spans are supposed to assess the visuospatial sketchpad component of working memory. The SLI samples had lower Corsi spans than the AC group. Corsi span correlated with success on the task, see Table 8.3, and in the multiple regression uniquely accounted for variance, see Table 8.4.

ORDINALITY

Results on the ordinal labeling and seriation tasks bore out expectations based on Siegel et al.'s (1981) study with younger children with SLI. The children with SLI showed deficits compared to age-matched controls on all tasks whether or not these involved ordinal language. Almost all the AC group (53/57) successfully ordered the squirrels on their first attempt. In contrast only a few (4/11) SLI Special group and about three quarters (34/44) of the SLI Mainstream group were right first time. Even when the squirrels were correctly ordered for them, the groups differed substantially in identifying the squirrel corresponding to verbally specified ordinal positions. Whereas most (50/57) in the AC group made two or fewer errors on this verbal task, few (3/11) SLI Special and just over half (25/44) SLI Mainstream achieved similar success. The pattern differed little on the nonverbal seriation task: most (49/57) of the AC group made two or fewer errors but only 25/44 of the SLI Mainstream group did as well. The SLI Special group seemed to do better on this than the other tasks: 7/11 made 10 or more correct responses. The fluctuations of this small group are, however, consistent with random fluctuation.

The multiple regression for this task indicated both nonverbal reasoning and language comprehension uniquely accounted for variance on the overall scale though the amounts accounted for are small (2% each) both in absolute terms and in relation to the overall R^2 (42%). The disadvantage shown by the SLI groups on the seriation task indicates that whatever the seriation capabilities of nonverbal species, human seriation performance derives from linguistic resources. It is certainly more specific than ordering as all three working memory tasks require children to remember orders of stimuli and none of them accounted for as much variation.

SMALL NUMBER

Group differences on this task were small: only the LC and the AC groups differed reliability for every numerosity. SLI group performance was typically between the other groups. In contrast, variation within group was considerable. Despite several substantial zero-order correlations with the other variables, differences in this task were not well accounted for by the variables entered in the multiple regression: the overall R^2 was only 31%. Corsi span made a significant unique contribution.

In the task children saw arrays for a very limited time, 150 msec, and this was followed by a distracting visual display. This was intended to prevent children from counting the objects during or after the presentation. It may be that this manipulation was unsuccessful. Inspecting the times taken by children who were successful indicated that correct answers to five item displays were accompanied by longer response times, typically almost 2 seconds, than those to displays with fewer items, typically less than a second. So there is some uncertainty over the basis for children's success on our small number task.

If the task procedure did succeed in discouraging counting then the processes might be subitizing and estimation. It is unlikely to be just subitizing because even in adults the upper limit is four items (Chi & Klahr, 1975). Also the increase in response times seems to argue against it. Some form of analog-based estimation might underlie success with larger numerosities, such as Huntley-Fenner (2001) argued underlay the success of the children he studied on numerosities between 5 and 11.

Whatever the basis it would seem to be important. In the reanalyses of the data reported in Cowan et al. (2005), small number performance made small but significant unique contributions to explaining variance on each skill.

Finally on many number tasks our samples of children with SLI were performing very much below the level of their peers. Diversity within the samples was considerable with some performing at age appropriate levels but others very much below. It may turn out that SLI is a predictor of maths difficulty as much as it is of reading difficulty. In the US approximately 40% of children with SLI will meet the criteria for reading difficulties (Catts et al., 2002). In contrast only 8% of typically developing children with similar nonverbal ability will do so. As the best estimate of the incidence of SLI in US children is only 7.4% (Tomblin et al., 1997), this does not mean that most children with reading difficulties will have SLI. It does indicate that children with SLI will be disproportionately represented in groups selected on the basis of reading difficulty.

What our work suggests is that it would be a mistake to assume that children with SLI are only at risk for reading difficulties. Some will feature in groups that combine both reading and maths difficulties. It is even possible that others may feature in groups with just maths difficulties. Aram and Nation (1980) found maths skills were even more impaired than literacy skills in adolescents with SLI. Including assessments of linguistic skills in studies of low-attaining groups would help to establish this.

ACKNOWLEDGMENTS

We thank the Nuffield Foundation for funding this project and the staff and children in participating schools.

REFERENCES

Aram, D. & Nation, J. (1980). Pre-school language disorders and subsequent academic difficulties. *Journal of Communication Disorders, 13*, 159–198.

Beilin, H. (1975). *Studies in the Cognitive Basis of Language Development*. London: Academic Press.

Butterworth, B. (2003). *Dyscalculia Screener*. London: Nelson.

Butterworth, B. (2005). Developmental dyscalculia. In Campbell, J. I. D. (Ed.), *The Handbook of Mathematical Cognition* (pp. 455–467). Hove: Psychology Press.

Canobi, K. H. (2004). Individual differences in children's addition and subtraction knowledge. *Cognitive Development, 19*, 81–93.

Canobi, K. H. (2005). Children's profiles of addition and subtraction understanding. *Journal of Experimental Child Psychology, 92*, 220–246.

Canobi, K. H., Reeve, R. A., & Pattison, P. E. (1998). The role of conceptual understanding in children's addition problem solving. *Developmental Psychology, 34*, 882–891.

Canobi, K. H., Reeve, R. A., & Pattison, P. E. (2003). Patterns of knowledge in children's addition. *Developmental Psychology, 39*, 521–534.

Catts, H. W., Fey, M. E., Tomblin, J. B., & Zhang, X. (2002). A longitudinal investigation of reading outcomes in children with language impairments. *Journal of Speech, Language, and Hearing Research, 45*, 1142–1157.

Chi, M. T. H. & Klahr, D. (1975). Span and rate of apprehension in children and adults. *Journal of Experimental Child Psychology, 19*, 434–439.

Cowan, R., Donlan, C., Newton, E. J., & Lloyd, D. (2005). Number skills and knowledge in children with specific language impairment. *Journal of Educational Psychology, 97*, 732–744.

Donlan, C. (Ed.) (1998). *The Development of Mathematical Skills*. Hove, East Sussex: Psychology Press.

Donlan, C. (2003). The early numeracy of children with specific language impairments. In Baroody, A. J. & Dowker, A. (Eds.), *The Development of Arithmetic Concepts and Skills: Constructing Adaptive Expertise* (pp. 337–358). Mahwah, NJ: Lawrence Erlbaum Associates.

Donlan, C., Cowan, R., Newton, E. J., & Lloyd, D. (2007). The role of language in mathematical development: Evidence from children with specific language impairments. *Cognition, 103*, 23–33.

Huntley-Fenner, G. (2001). Children's understanding of number is similar to adults' and rats': Numerical estimation by 5–7-year-olds. *Cognition, 78*, B27–B40.

Kingma, J. (1984). Traditional intelligence, Piagetian tasks, and initial arithmetic in kindergarten and primary school grade one. *Journal of Genetic Psychology, 145*, 49–60.

Kingma, J. & Zumbo, B. (1987). Relationship between seriation, transitivity, and explicit ordinal number comprehension. *Perceptual and Motor Skills, 65*, 559–569.

Landerl, K., Bevan, A., & Butterworth, B. (2004). Developmental dyscalculia and basic numerical capacities: A study of 8–9-year-old students. *Cognition, 93*, 99–125.

McGonigle, B. O. & Chalmers, M. (1992). Monkeys are rational! *The Quarterly Journal of Experimental Psychology, 45B*, 189–228.

Nunes, T. & Bryant, P. (1996). *Children Doing Mathematics*. Oxford: Blackwell.

Piaget, J. (1952). *The Child's Conception of Number*. London: Routledge & Kegan Paul.

Siegler, R. S. & Crowley, K. (1994). Constraints on learning in nonprivileged domains. *Cognitive Psychology, 27*, 194–226.

Siegel, L. S., Lees, A., Allan, L., & Bolton, B. (1981). Non-verbal assessment of Piagetian concepts in preschool children with impaired language development. *Educational Psychology, 1*, 153–158.

Tomblin, J. B., Records, N. L., Buckwalter, P., Zhang, X. Y., Smith, E., & O' Brien, M. (1997). Prevalence of specific language impairment in kindergarten children. *Journal of Speech and Hearing Research, 39*, 1284–1294.

9

THE PERFORMANCE
OF DYSLEXIC AND
NON-DYSLEXIC BOYS
AT DIVISION SUMS

S.A.TURNER ELLIS[1], T.R.MILES[2],
AND T.J.WHEELER[3]

[1]*Formerly of the Universities of Bangor and currently visiting Research Fellow,
University of Chester, Chester CH1 4BJ, Cheshire, UK*
[2]*Professor Emeritus of Psychology, School of Psychology,
University of Bangor, Wales, UK*
[3]*Department of Psychology, University of Chester, Parkgate Road, Chester,
United Kingdom, CHJ1 4BJ, UK*

INTRODUCTION

It is possible for those who are dyslexic to be extremely successful mathematicians (Jansons, 1988). However, there is reason to believe that certain aspects of mathematics cause them problems. This has been found to be true in the experience of practising teachers (Chinn & Ashcroft, 1998; Henderson & Miles, F. 2001) and the various contributors to Miles and Miles (2004). The same conclusion is also supported by research of a more systematic kind. Thus Miles (1993) found that many of the dyslexics whom he assessed had difficulty in comparison with controls over the subtraction and memorization of times tables. Miles et al. (2001) reported data based on the performance of some 12,000 10-year-old children on 72 mathematics items of many different kinds. Those with two or more dyslexia indicators out of a possible four consistently obtained lower scores than those with fewer such indicators despite no differences in scores on the Similarities and Matrices items of the British Ability Scales (Elliott et al., 1983).

Turner Ellis (2002) made a study of both speed and correctness in the carrying out of all four mathematical operations (multiplication, division, addition and subtraction). In the case of multiplication (Turner Ellis et al., 1996) it was found that dyslexic boys, aged between 9 and 16 years (though not the same boys as those in this study) were slower and more error prone than age-matched controls. A paper on subtraction and addition is in preparation; this chapter reports on the results for division.

There is now good evidence that dyslexics are slower than non-dyslexics at operating with and remembering any kind of symbolic information (Miles, 2006) but are unimpaired at 'processing for meaning' and recognizing regularities and patterns (Miles et al., 2006). Since division sums involve operating with and remembering symbols (numerals), our prediction was that the dyslexics in the study would make more errors and be slower than the controls. Also it seemed possible that their weak memorization skills might be compensated for if there were obvious algorithms to help them, such as division by 10 and division by 11. Here, the load on the memory is much less than it is for many of the other tables, since if one is dividing by 10 one simply has to remove the zero, while if one is dividing by 11 the correct answer is there in front of one. It seemed possible, therefore, that the presence of algorithms might lessen the differences between them and the controls.

As we had data relating to three different age bands (see below), we thought it would also be interesting to check if progress was made at a steady rate or if the differences in performance at the different age levels provided evidence of 'spurts' where speed of calculation improved rapidly, and plateaux, where it did not.

The aim of this chapter, therefore, is to provide evidence on the following five questions:

1. Did some division sums present more problems than others?
2. Did the dyslexics make more errors than the controls?
3. Were they slower in carrying out the calculations?
4. Did the existence of an obvious algorithm affect the two groups differently?
5. Does performance improve in a steady fashion with age or are there spurts and plateaux?

PARTICIPANTS, APPARATUS AND METHOD

The participants were 30 dyslexic boys, aged between 9 years 5 months and 15 years 4 months, and 30 non-dyslexic boys matched for age and score on the Raven Standard Progressive Matrices (Raven, 1958). All the children had to be at the 40th percentile or better for their age. A matched pairs design was achieved as follows: each control participant had to be aged within 2 months of their 'pair' if they were older and within 4 months if they were younger; the controls had to have the same score on the Matrices as their 'pair' within two points.

The decision to limit the enquiry to males was made partly on grounds of convenience, given the greater availability of dyslexic males in the general population (Miles et al., 1998) and to avoid any complications which might arise from gender differences.

All the children were holding their own in their school environment and, to the best of our knowledge, were free from any gross physical or emotional disability. They all came from private schools in the south of England and were therefore relatively homogenous in respect of social background. All the schools made provision for dyslexic children.

Because of the differences in age between the oldest and youngest participants and because performance was likely to change over time given the school's general policy of helping dyslexics, it was decided to subdivide the participants into three age bands, (i) young (aged 9 years 5 months to 11 years 4 months), (ii) medium (aged 11 years 5 months to 13 years 4 months) and (iii) old (aged 13 years 5 months to 15 years 4 months).

To qualify as a dyslexic those in the young age band had to have a spelling age on the Schonell S1 spelling test (Schonell & Schonell, 1952) of at least 18 months below their chronological age, or 2 years below chronological age for participants over 13 years of age. All the controls had to have a spelling age at least as high as within 6 months of their chronological age, or a spelling age at least as high as within 15 months of their chronological age in the case of children in the old age band.

A further qualification was specified for being dyslexic: it was necessary to have at least 3.5 positive indicators out of a possible 8 on the Bangor Dyslexia Test (Miles, 1997). In contrast, to qualify as a control it was necessary to have no more than 2.5 positive indicators. Eight items only out of the 10 available on the Bangor Dyslexia Test were used in this research because the remaining two, Subtraction and Tables, were relevant to calculation and their use would therefore have resulted in a circular argument.

By means of suitable technology a particular division sum appeared on a computer screen and the children were asked to type the answer on a keyboard as fast as they could. There were 144 different division sums, presented in random order.

It was decided that if a participant failed to answer within 22 seconds the result should be scored as an error. For purposes of timing, each error was scored as having taken 22 seconds. Although this assumption is a somewhat arbitrary one, it had the advantage of making possible a workable system of scoring for both speed and correctness.

With regard to making comparisons between results where there was and was not an obvious algorithm, it was decided to compare the results for sums involving division by 10 and 11 with results from sums involving division by 7 and 8. We therefore compared the results in the case of $60 \div 10, 70 \div 10, 80 \div 10, 90 \div 10, 66 \div 11, 77 \div 11, 88 \div 11$ and $99 \div 11$ with the results for $42 \div 7, 49 \div 7, 56 \div 7, 63 \div 7, 48 \div 8, 56 \div 8, 64 \div 8, 72 \div 8$. It was hypothesized that the algorithm condition (division by 10 and 11) might be differentially easier for the dyslexics than the non-algorithm condition (division by 7 or 8).

RESULTS

Note that two-tailed tests were used throughout.

1. *Did some division sums present more problems than others?*
2. *Did the dyslexics make more errors?*

Figure 9.1 shows the number of correct responses given by the dyslexics, broken down by divisor and age band. Figure 9.2 provides the same information in respect of the controls.

It will be seen that the dyslexics made more errors overall than the controls and that for both groups some divisors presented more problems than others. These tended to occur when the divisors were 4, 6, 7, 8, 9 and 12. This was true of both groups, though in the case of the dyslexics the effects were more marked. Later in the chapter an analysis will be presented which compares the results when the divisors are 10 and 11 with the results when they were 7 and 8.

Table 9.1 shows the proportion of correct responses for the dyslexics and the controls in each age band (means and standard deviations for the 10 children in each group).

Analysis of variance showed that there is an age effect [$F(2, 54) = 16.930$, $p < 0.01$], a group effect [$F(1, 54) = 25.538$, $p < 0.001$] and an age $\times$ group interaction [$F(2, 54) = 5.536$, $p < 0.01$].

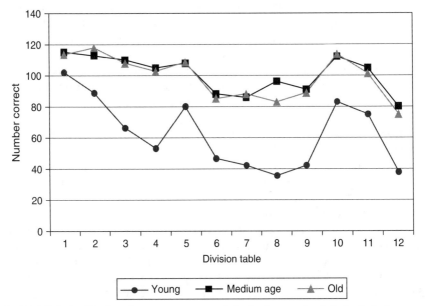

FIGURE 9.1   Number of correct responses made by the three age bands in the dyslexic group.

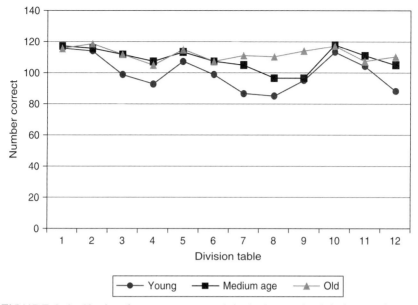

FIGURE 9.2   Number of correct responses made by the three age bands in the control group.

TABLE 9.1   Proportion[1] of Correct Responses for the Dyslexics and
the Controls in Each Age Band

Age	Group	Mean	SD
Young	Dyslexics	0.52	0.23
	Controls	0.83	0.09
Medium	Dyslexics	0.84	0.09
	Controls	0.91	0.08
Old	Dyslexics	0.82	0.13
	Controls	0.93	0.04

[1] The figures are expressed as a proportion so as to make possible a
comparison with addition and subtraction, where the number of sums
involved was not 144 but 150. *Source*: Turner Ellis (2002).

Post hoc tests compared the groups in each age band. The results were young
dyslexics vs young controls ($t = 3.991$, $df = 18$, $p < 0.001$), medium age
dyslexics vs medium age controls ($t = 1.799$, $df = 18$, ns), old dyslexics vs old
controls ($t = 2.546$, $df = 18$, $p < 0.05$).

Thus there were more errors on the part of the dyslexics in the young and old
age bands but not in the medium age band. We will suggest possible reasons for
this in the Discussion section.

3. Were the dyslexics slower?

Table 9.2 gives the mean, standard deviation and median response times in seconds for each group and age band. As a check against the decision to count an error as 22 seconds, medians have also been included.

It can be seen by inspection that there were no major differences between the means and the medians; from this it may be concluded that the decision to count a failed response as 22 seconds was not distorting the results.

Analysis of variance showed the following overall results: there is an age effect ($F(2, 54) = 21.196$, $p < 0.001$), a group effect ($F(1, 54) = 35.913$, $p < 0.001$) and there is an age $\times$ group interaction ($F(2, 54) = 3.604$, $p < 0.05$).

Post hoc tests compared the groups in each age band. The results were young dyslexics vs young controls ($t = 4.673$, $df = 18$, $p < 0.001$), medium age dyslexics vs medium age controls ($t = 2.180$, $df = 18$, $p < 0.05$), old dyslexics vs old controls ($t = 3.289$, $df = 18$, $p < 0.01$).

It will be seen that at all three age levels there are significant differences between the dyslexics and the controls in the time taken to respond. As in the case of correctness, the lack of any increase in speed between the medium age dyslexics and the old dyslexics is puzzling and will be referred to in the Discussion section.

4. Does the existence of an obvious algorithm affect the two groups differently?

In what follows we shall refer to the division by 10 and 11 as the X-condition and the division by 7 and 8 as the Y-condition. Table 9.3 gives the number of correct and incorrect responses in the two conditions.

In the X condition there was a significant difference in the number of correct responses between the young dyslexics and the young controls (Fisher's exact probability test $p < 0.001$) but no difference between the medium age dyslexics and medium age controls nor between the old dyslexics and the old controls ($p > 0.05$). There appears here to be a ceiling effect.

In the Y condition the differences between dyslexics and controls in all three age groups were statistically significant (Fisher's exact probability test: young $p < 0.001$, medium age $p < 0.05$ and old $p < 0.001$).

TABLE 9.2   Mean and Median Response Times (in seconds) and Standard Deviation by Group and Age on Division

Groups	Age band	Mean	SD	Median
Dyslexics	Young	13.90	3.65	13.10
	Medium	7.91	2.51	8.41
	Old	7.58	2.76	7.15
Controls	Young	7.69	2.08	8.01
	Medium	5.67	2.06	5.35
	Old	4.55	0.94	4.79

TABLE 9.3   Number of Correct and Incorrect Responses for the Two Groups and Three Age Bands in the X and Y Conditions

Group	Age band	X-condition correct	X-condition incorrect	Y-condition correct	Y-condition incorrect
Dyslexics	Young	55	25	8	72
Controls	Young	79	1	41	39
Dyslexics	Medium	76	4	46	34
Controls	Medium	77	3	59	21
Dyslexics	Old	77	3	51	29
Controls	Old	77	3	70	10

TABLE 9.4   Mean Response Times (seconds) for the Three Groups and Age Bands in the X and Y Conditions

Groups and age bands	X condition	Y condition
Young age band		
Dyslexics	10.32	20.73
Controls	3.42	14.68
Medium age band		
Dyslexics	4.56	14.19
Controls	3.75	10.51
Old age band		
Dyslexics	3.73	12.30
Controls	2.92	7.81

Table 9.4 gives the results in the case of speed.

Post hoc *t*-tests showed that all six groups (dyslexics and controls, young, medium and old age bands) were slower in the Y condition than in the X condition. The *t*-values and significance levels were:

Young controls	$t = 7.855$,	$df = 9$,	$p < 0.001$
Young dyslexics	$t = 4.607$,	$df = 9$,	$p < 0.001$
Medium age controls	$t = 3.791$,	$df = 9$,	$p < 0.01$
Medium age dyslexics	$t = 6.185$,	$df = 9$,	$p < 0.001$
Old controls	$t = 3.711$,	$df = 9$,	$p < 0.01$
Old dyslexics	$t = 3.910$,	$df = 9$,	$p < 0.01$

In addition the young dyslexics were slower than the young controls ($p < 0.01$ for the X condition and $p < 0.001$ for the Y condition). In the case of the medium age dyslexics and the medium age controls, the differences in the X condition were very small, as was also the case when the old dyslexics were compared with the old controls. In the Y condition the differences between medium age dyslexics and medium age controls and between old dyslexics and old controls were considerably larger; however, although they were in the expected direction they did not reach an acceptable level of significance, with t-values of 1.442 and 1.772 (1.772 is marginally significant if a one-tailed test is used).

5. *Does performance improve in a steady fashion with age?*

Both Tables 9.1 and 9.2 leave us with a puzzling phenomenon: there is no gain in respect of either correctness or speed between the medium age dyslexics and the old dyslexics: the figures for 'proportion correct' were 0.84 and 0.82, while the figures for 'time taken' were 7.91 and 7.58 seconds, respectively.

To gain further understanding we have presented the information in terms of *topographical terrains* shown in Figures 9.3 to 9.8. This is a visual way of showing the level of ease or difficulty, as judged by speed of responding, encountered when working on a particular division table. The six terrains presented have been key-coded with patterns according to mean response time in seconds. The terrain shows the 12 × 12 division grid presented in three-dimensional form. The dimensions represented are the divisor (division table number), quotient and mean response time (in seconds). The higher the terrain, the longer the response time and therefore the harder the division sum.

The terrains have the following properties:

1. *Pattern.* The key-coding pattern indicates the time span within which the response is given. This coding is consistent across groups and age bands. From quickest to slowest response times the patterns are vertical lines, dark shade, white, slant lines and dots. Times given in the coding do not overlap.

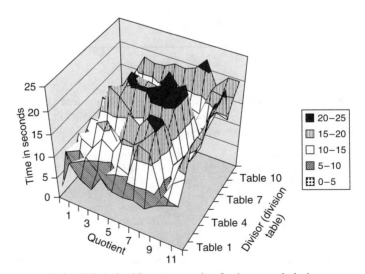

FIGURE 9.3   Mean response time for the young dyslexics.

2. *Plains.* These are flatter expanses of faster response times. A good example of this is found in Figure 9.8 for the old controls and the pattern for this is represented in vertical lines.

3. *Foothills.* These are areas of low-to-middle ground indicating response times of medium value.

4. *Plateaux.* These are flatter expanses indicating division facts, which gained like-timed responses grouped together. Areas of the same pattern show these. A good example of this is seen with response times in the 10–15 seconds in Figure 9.5 with the results for the medium-age dyslexics.

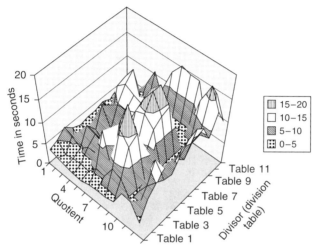

FIGURE 9.4   Mean response time for the young controls.

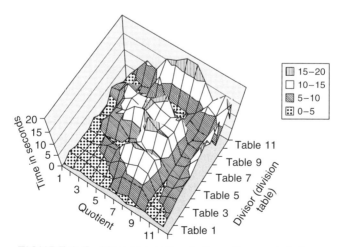

FIGURE 9.5   Mean response time for the medium age dyslexics.

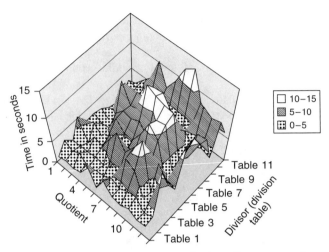

FIGURE 9.6   Mean response time for the medium age controls.

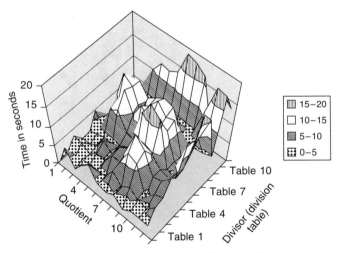

FIGURE 9.7   Mean response time for the old dyslexics.

5. *Valleys.* The valleys in the topographical terrains are tracts of similar lower altitude that run like a track of the same pattern through the hills and mountains. These would indicate particular division tables that evoke similar response times throughout the majority of the division table, such as the ÷10 table. The valley stands out because it is bordered by higher land on either side. Here the adjoining division tables would take the participants longer to answer.

6. *Mountain peaks.* Peaks indicate a sudden climb of difficulty shown by sharp pinnacles of highest ground within an area of the division tables.

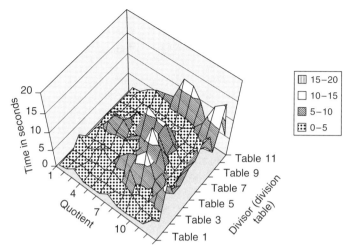

FIGURE 9.8   Mean response time for the old controls.

Inspection of the topographical terrains shows that the progress of the dyslexics, unlike that of the controls, was by no means uniform. Possible reasons for this will be considered in the Discussion section.

DISCUSSION

We are now in a position to answer the five questions posed earlier.

1. Did some division sums present more problems than others?

Not surprisingly, the answer to this question is 'yes'. What emerges from our results is that there appears to be no difference between dyslexics and controls as regards order of difficulty, but that if a task is hard for controls it is *extra* hard for dyslexics. This is a conclusion in respect of dyslexia which may well have wider applications than simply in the area of calculation.

2. Did the dyslexics make more errors than the controls?

The answer is, for the most part, 'yes', though the difference is most marked in the case of those in the young age band.

3. Were the dyslexics slower in carrying out the calculations?

Again the answer is 'yes', with the effect size, as judged by the confidence levels, being greatest among the young age band. That both groups improved with age is not surprising, given that it was policy in all the schools to try to help dyslexics; without such a policy the improvement by the dyslexics could well have been much less. The fact that there was a small but significant inter-action ($p < 0.05$) between age and group confirms that even in a relatively favorable environment progress for dyslexics remains slow. It is also worth noting that the old age-band dyslexics were only as fast as the young age-band controls. In general, it seems that dyslexics improve their performance but do so at a slower pace than controls.

Why, then, given that the dyslexics were matched with the controls on the Raven Matrices, were they more error-prone and slower at division? Our results confirm the widely held view that dyslexics tend to be strong at reasoning and pattern recognition but weak at memorization. Division requires holding a large amount of symbolic material in mind over a significant period of time. This being so, there is less opportunity for knowledge of number facts relating to division (and, indeed, the other mathematical operations) to become automatic; and there is good evidence that, in general, dyslexics need more time than non-dyslexics before skills become automatic (Nicolson & Fawcett, 1990).

In contrast, the easier items on the Raven Matrices require primarily the ability to recognize patterns as similar or dissimilar; the more difficult ones require the ability to detect relationships. Here is an example based on one of the harder items. The patterns presented are circles arranged in a 3 × 3 format, all of them having up to five smaller circles in the form of loops. These loops vary not only in number but also in whether they lie just inside or just outside the main circle. The person being tested has to choose one of the eight figures, the choice depending on the recognition of the combined relationships between number and inside-outside. The patterns are present throughout, which means that no memorization is required; an awareness of numbers up to five is required, although knowing the names of the numbers is unnecessary. In brief, the division task required memorization and automaticity, which are areas of dyslexics' weakness, whereas the Matrices task involves pattern recognition, at which dyslexics are strong.

4. *Does the existence of an obvious algorithm affect the two groups differently?*

Both dyslexics and controls at all ages made fewer errors and were quicker in the X condition than in the Y condition. The effect of the X condition was to narrow the gap between dyslexics and controls. Clearly all children do better when there are algorithms but the advantage to young dyslexics is particularly marked.

Our results provide further confirmation that when dyslexics have the opportunity to use their reasoning powers rather than having to rely on their memories, the limitations arising from their dyslexia are much reduced.

5. *Does performance improve in a steady fashion with age or are there spurts and plateaux?*

In the case of the controls there is a reduction both in error rate and in speed as one progresses from the young age band to the medium to the old. This is not so, however, in the case of the dyslexics. There are, indeed, substantial differences both in correctness and in speed between the young age band and the medium age band, but no significant improvement between the medium age band and the old age band (proportions correct of 0.84 and 0.82 in the case of correctness and 7.91 and 7.58 seconds in the case of speed).

It is hard to be sure of the reasons for these results. One possibility, however, is that not all members of the old age band continue to carry out calculations by hand, and it is possible, therefore, that because of dyslexics basic weakness over calculation, lack of practice may in some cases have caused their skills to have become 'rusty'.

The most striking feature about the topographical terrains is that, while in the case of the controls, scores increase regularly with age, this is not so in the case of the dyslexics. We have already referred to a possible rustiness which may explain the relative lack of difference between the medium age dyslexics and the older dyslexics. But why are the terrains so different when the young dyslexics, aged between 9 years 5 months and 11 years 4 months, are compared with the medium age dyslexics?

It would accord with the experience of teachers that when dyslexics are in a favorable environment the time comes when they 'take off', when 'things click into place' and when they are set to 'get over the hump'. Reading then ceases to be the daunting task which it seemed to be earlier, and the stage is set for further progress. Because of dyslexics' special limitations it seems that they are later than non-dyslexics in gaining the appropriate insights, and that, when they do, they do so in more spectacular fashion. This suggestion is a speculative one, but in view of what we know about dyslexics it seems at least possible.

SOME PRACTICAL IMPLICATIONS

Some of the practical implications of these findings are as follows:

1. Those who teach dyslexics should always allow them plenty of time in which to absorb the information presented; otherwise any dyslexic pupils in the class will 'lose track'.

2. Memorization is much easier if algorithms and other mnemonics can be found.

3. One should not expect progress to take place at an even pace; there may be spurts forward and plateaux. This does not rule out the possibility of further spurts thereafter.

4. Dyslexics can learn correct answers, even though this may take them longer than their non-dyslexic peers. If they fail to do so it is important for the teacher to ask why.

CONCLUDING REMARKS

Success in teaching calculation to dyslexic pupils is possible provided the teacher works systematically and slowly. Moreover teachers should never forget that dyslexic pupils are likely to be strong on logic and pattern recognition but weak at memorization. Setting them to memorize number facts etc. is likely to lead to frustration, whereas showing them logical patterns and helping them to discover these for themselves is likely to lead to success and improvement in self-esteem.

REFERENCES

Chinn, S. J. & Ashcroft, J. R. (1998). *Mathematics for Dyslexics: A Teaching Handbook.* (2nd edn). London: Whurr.

Elliott, C. D., Murray, D. J., & Pearson, L. S. (1983). *The British Ability Scales.* Windsor: NFER-Nelson.

Henderson, A. & Miles, E. (2001). *Basic Topics in Mathematics for Dyslexics.* London: Whurr.

Jansons, K. M. (1988). A personal view of dyslexia and of thought without language. In Weiskrantz, L. (ed), *Thought Without Language.* Oxford: Oxford University Press.

Miles, T. R. (1993). *Dyslexia: The Pattern of Difficulties.* London: Whurr.

Miles, T. R. (1997). *The Bangor Dyslexia Test.* Wisbech, Cambridge: Learning Development Aids.

Miles, T. R. (2006). *Fifty Years in Dyslexia Research.* Chichester: Wiley.

Miles, T. R., Haslum, M. N., & Wheeler, T. J. (1998). Gender ratio in dyslexia. *Annals of Dyslexia, 48,* 27–55.

Miles, T. R., Haslum, M. N., & Wheeler, T. J. (2001). The mathematical abilities of dyslexic 10-year-olds. *Annals of Dyslexia, 51,* 299–321.

Miles, T. R. & Miles, E. (Eds.) (2004). *Dyslexia and Mathematics* (2nd edn). London: Routledge Falmer.

Miles, T. R., Thierry, G., Roberts, J., & Schiffendrin, J. (2006). Verbatim and gist recall of sentences by dyslexic and non-dyslexic adults. *Dyslexia: An International Journal of Research and Practice, 12*(3) 177–194.

Nicolson, R. I. & Fawcett, A. J. (1990). Automaticity: A new framework for dyslexia research. *Cognition, 35,* 159–182.

Raven, J. C. (1958). *Standard Progressive Matrices.* London: H. K. Lewis.

Schonell, F. J. & Schonell, F. E. (1952). *Diagnostic and Attainment Testing.* Edinburgh: Oliver and Boyd.

Turner Ellis, S. A. (2002). *Correctness and Speed of Dyslexics and Non-Dyslexics on the Four Mathematical Operations.* Unpublished Ph.D. thesis, University of Liverpool.

Turner Ellis, S. A., Miles, T. R., & Wheeler, T. J. (1996). Speed of multiplication in dyslexics and non-dyslexics. *Dyslexia: An International Journal of Research and Practice, 2*(2), 121–139.

10

NUMERACY RECOVERY WITH CHILDREN WITH ARITHMETICAL DIFFICULTIES

INTERVENTION AND RESEARCH

ANN DOWKER

Department of Experimental Psychology, University of Oxford, Oxford, OX1 3UD, UK

Up till now, there has been much less research on mathematical development and difficulties than on some other areas of development, such as language and literacy. However, there has recently been an increased emphasis on mathematics in cognitive developmental research (e.g., Baroody & Dowker, 2003; Campbell, 2005; Royer, 2003); in neuroscience (Ansari et al., 2005; Butterworth, 1999; Dehaene, 1997); and in educational policy and practice in the UK and abroad (Askew & Brown, 2001; Kilpatrick et al., 2001).

In particular, there is by now overwhelming evidence that arithmetic is not a single unitary ability at which people are either 'good' or 'bad. This evidence comes from many converging sources, including experimental, educational, and factor analytic studies of typically developing children and adults (e.g., Dowker, 1998, 2005; Geary & Widaman, 1992; Ginsburg, 1977; Lefevre & Kulak, 1994; Siegler, 1988); studies of children with arithmetical deficits (Butterworth, 2005; Dowker, 2005; Geary & Hoard, 2005; Ginsburg, 1977; Jordan et al., 2003; Mazzocco & Myers, 2003; Russell & Ginsburg, 1984; Shalev et al., 1997); studies of patients (Butterworth, 1999; Dehaene, 1997; Delazer, 2003; Warrington, 1982); and functional brain imaging studies (Castelli et al., 2006; Dehaene et al., 1999; Gruber et al., 2001; Rickard et al., 2000).

The broad components of arithmetical ability include counting, memory for arithmetical facts, the understanding of concepts, and the ability to follow procedures. Each of these broad components has, in turn, a number of narrower components: for example, counting includes knowledge of the counting sequence, ability to follow counting procedures in counting sets of objects, and understanding of the principles of counting: for example, that the last number in a count sequence represents the number of objects in the set, and that counting a set of objects in different orders will give the same answer (Greeno et al., 1984; Munn, 1997).

Moreover, though the different components often correlate with one another, weaknesses in any one of them can occur relatively independently of weaknesses in the others. Weakness in even one component can ultimately take its toll on performance in other components, partly because difficulty with one component may increase the risk of the child relying exclusively on another component, and failing to perceive and use relationships between different arithmetical processes and problems; and partly because when children fail at certain tasks, they may come to perceive themselves as 'no good at maths' and develop a negative attitude to the subject. However, *the components described here are not seen as a hierarchy*. A child may perform well at an apparently difficult task (e.g., word problem solving) while performing poorly at an apparently easier component (e.g., remembering the counting word sequence). Though certain specific components may frequently form the basis for learning other specific components, they need not always be prerequisites. Several studies (e.g., Denvir & Brown, 1986) have suggested that it is not possible to establish a strict hierarchy whereby any one component invariably precedes another component.

Many children have difficulties with some or most aspects of arithmetic. It is hard to estimate the proportion who have difficulties, since this depends on the criteria that are used. Moreover, as arithmetical thinking involves such a wide variety of components, there are many forms and causes of arithmetical difficulty, which may assume different degrees of importance in different tasks and situations. It is likely that at least 15% to 20% of the population have difficulties with certain aspects of arithmetic, which are sufficient to cause significant practical and educational problems for the individual (Bynner & Parsons, 1997) though the proportion describable as dyscalculic is much lower.

This chapter is divided into two parts. The first part describes an intervention program, which is based on the findings that suggest that arithmetic is made up of numerous components, and involves assessing and targeting individual children's specific weaknesses. The second part analyses a few specific components of arithmetic, and the relationships between them, in a group of children who were selected for having arithmetical difficulties.

PART 1: NUMERACY RECOVERY SCHEME

The Numeracy Recovery scheme has been discussed earlier (e.g., Dowker, 2001, 2005). It is being piloted with 6 and 7 year olds (mostly year 2) in some First

Schools in Oxford. It was initially funded by the Esmee Fairbairn Charitable Trust; and is currently about to undergo further development and evaluation as Catchup Maths, with funding from the Caxton Trust. Hundred and seventy five children have so far entered the project.

The scheme, as developed up till now, has involved working with children who have been identified by their teachers as having problems with arithmetic.

These children are assessed on nine components of early numeracy, which are summarized and described below. The children then receive weekly individual intervention (half an hour a week) in the particular components with which they have been found to have difficulty. The interventions are carried out by the classroom teachers, using techniques proposed by the researcher.

The teachers are released (each teacher for half a day weekly) for the intervention, by the employment of supply teachers for classroom teaching. Each child remains in the program for 30 weeks, or until their teachers feel they no longer need intervention; whichever is shorter. New children join the project periodically.

COMPONENTS THAT ARE THE FOCUS OF THE PROJECT

(1) Counting Procedures

Arguably the most basic component of arithmetic is the ability to make appropriate use of counting. While most 6 year olds have achieved relatively effortless counting, a significant number have not (Griffin et al., 1994; Yeo, 2003). This may seriously impede their development of arithmetic, both because of the intrinsic logical relationships between counting and arithmetic, and because the effort of counting may distract attention from other aspect of arithmetic (Gray & Tall, 1994; Yeo, 2003).

In the pretest, children are tested for:

  (i) accuracy of counting sets of 5, 8, 10, 12 and 21 objects;
 (ii) rote verbal counting to 10 and to 20.

Intervention

Children are given practice in counting sets of objects, ranging in number from 5 to 25.

(2) Counting-Related Principles and Their Application

[Originally, components (1) and (2) were grouped together on the assumption that very few children as old as 6 or 7 would have difficulty with counting. A higher proportion than expected had such difficulties; so that different components of counting – are here considered separately.]

Most counting principles are acquired before the age of 5 or 6, even in children with some mathematical difficulties. However, the order-irrelevance principle (that counting the same set of items in different orders will result in the same number) is usually the latest of the main counting principles to be acquired

(Cowan et al., 1996); and is sometimes weak even in 6 year olds. Evidence suggests that understanding the order-irrelevance principle is closely related to the ability to predict the result of adding or subtracting an item from a set (Cowan et al., 1996; Dowker, 2005).

In the pretest for the 'counting principles' component, children are assessed on:

(i) The order-irrelevance principle: The children watch an adult count a set of objects, and are then asked to predict the result of further counts:
  (a) in the reverse order;
  (b) after the addition of an object;
  (c) after the subtraction of an object.
(ii) Repeated addition by 1: Children are shown a set of 5 items, and then shown one more item being added, and asked to say, without counting, how many there are now. This is repeated up to 15.
(iii) Repeated subtraction by 1: Children are shown a set of 10 items, and then shown one item being subtracted, and asked to say, without counting, how many there are now. This is repeated down to zero.

Intervention

For the order-irrelevance principle, children practice counting and answering order-irrelevance questions about very small numbers of counters (up to 4), where the numerosity of the set is likely to be obvious to the child. During this practice, the adult makes statements such as, 'It's four this way, and four that way – it's four whichever way you count it!' The child is then given further practice with increasingly large sets.

For repeated addition by 1 and repeated subtraction by 1, children are given practice in observing and predicting the results of such repeated additions and subtractions with counters (up to 20). They are then given verbal 'number after' and 'number before' problems: 'What is the number before 8?', 'What is the number after 14?', etc. They are also given some worksheets devised for the project, including repeated addition and subtraction by 1 from a set of circles. They are encouraged to play 'Number After Dominoes' and 'Number Before Dominoes' (Wynroth, 1986; Baroody, 1992), which are played like dominoes except that the added domino must be the number after (or before) the end item, rather than the same number.

(3) Written Symbolism for Numbers

There is much evidence that children often experience difficulties with written arithmetical symbolism of all sorts, and in particular with representing quantities as numerals (Ginsburg, 1977; Fuson, 1992). With regard to this component, children are asked to read aloud a set of single-digit and two-digit numbers. A similar set of numbers is dictated to them for writing.

Intervention

Children practice reading and writing numbers. Children with difficulties in reading or writing two-digit numbers (tens and units) are given practice in sorting objects into groups of 10, and recording them as '20', '30', etc. They are then given such sorting and recording tasks where there are extra units as well as the groups of 10.

(4) Understanding the Role of Place Value in Number Operations and Arithmetic

This involves the ability to add 10s to units ($20 + 3 = 23$); the ability to add 10s to 10s ($20 + 30 = 50$); and the ability to combine the two into one operation ($20 + 33 = 53$). A related task involves pointing to the larger number in pairs of two-digit numbers, that vary either just with regard to the units (e.g., 23 vs. 26); just with regard to the 10s (e.g., 41 vs. 51); or where both 10s and units vary in conflicting directions (e.g., 27 vs. 31; 52 vs. 48).

Intervention

Children are shown the addition of 10s to units and the addition of 10s to 10s in several different forms: (i) written numerals; (ii) number line or number block; (iii) hands and fingers in pictures; (iv) 10-pence pieces and pennies; and (v) any apparatus (e.g., multilink or unifix) with which the child is familiar. The fact that these give the same answers is emphasized.

Children whose difficulties are more specific to the use of place value in arithmetic may be given practice with arithmetical patterns such as: '20 + 10; 20 + 11; 20 + 12', etc.; being encouraged to use apparatus when necessary.

(5) Word Problem Solving

There is a considerable body of evidence (Hughes, 1986; Mayer, 2003; Riley et al., 1983) that young children often experience difficulty with word problems in arithmetic, even when they are capable of performing the necessary calculations. Indeed, some studies have suggested (e.g., Russell & Ginsburg, 1984) that performance on word problems is one of the tasks that most strongly defines the difference between mathematically normal and mathematically 'disabled' schoolchildren. It is important to take into account the nature of the problems, as their semantic nature has a strong influence on how easily they are solved. For example children tend to find problems involving changes in quantity ('Change' problems) easier than those involving comparisons between quantities ('Compare' problems) (Riley et al., 1983; DeCorte & Verschaffel, 1987).

Pretest

Children are given the Word Problems Test devised by Griffin et al. (1994) for addition and subtraction. This involves the presentation of 'Change' and 'Compare' problems for addition and subtraction and of 'Combine' problems (combining two quantities) for addition.

Intervention

Children who have difficulties in understanding word problems are presented with short addition and subtraction word problems of 'Change', 'Compare' and 'Combine' types (similar but not identical to those used in the assessments). The problems are discussed with them: 'What are the numbers that we have to work with?' 'What do we have to do with the numbers?' 'Do you think that we have to do an adding sum or a taking-away sum?' 'Do you think that John has more sweets or fewer sweets than he used to have?', etc. They are encouraged to use counters to represent the operations in the word problems, as well as writing the sums numerically.

(6) Translation Between Arithmetical Problems Presented in Concrete, Verbal and Numerical Formats

Several people have suggested that translation between concrete, verbal and numerical formats is a crucial area of difficulty in children's arithmetical development. For example, Hughes (1986) reported that many primary school children demonstrate difficulty in translating between concrete and numerical formats (in either direction), even when they are reasonably proficient at doing sums in either one of these formats and has suggested that this difficulty in translation may be an important hindrance to children's understanding of arithmetic.

The *Translation pretest* involves six types of task, for both addition and subtraction. This task will be described in more detail in Part 2. They involve:

(a) *Translation from numerical to concrete*: Where children are presented with sums and are invited to 'show how to do this sum with the counters'.

(b) *Translation from concrete to numerical*: They watch the experimenter perform arithmetical operations with counters and are being asked to write down the sum that the experimenter did.

(c) *Translation from verbal to concrete*: They are presented with word problems, and are invited to 'show me this story with the counters'.

(d) *Translation from verbal to numerical*: They are presented with word problems, and are asked to 'write down the sum that goes with the story'.

(e) *Translation from numerical to verbal*: They are shown written sums, and are asked to 'tell me a story that can go with this sum'.

(f) *Translation from concrete to verbal*: They watch the researcher perform arithmetical operations with counters, and are asked to 'tell me a story to go with what I'm doing here'.

The children's performance on this pretest is looked at in the context of their performance on the Written Symbolism and Word Problem pretests. If the children perform particularly badly on translations that involve numerical material, and also perform poorly on the Written Symbolism pretest, then it is likely that their main problem is with written symbolism. If the children perform particularly badly on translations that involve verbal material, and also perform poorly on the Word Problems pretest, then it is likely that their main problem is with word problem comprehension. However, if they perform uniformly poorly on all parts of the translation pretest, and/or if their performance on the translations involving numerical material is disproportionately worse than their performance on the Written Symbolism pretest, and/or if their performance on the translations involving the verbal material is disproportionately worse than their performance on the Word Problem pretest, then it is likely that the problem is with translation as such.

Intervention

Although the techniques used for some of the other components include elements of translation, the techniques involved in remediating this component focuses specifically on showing that the same arithmetical problem can be represented in different ways. The children are shown the same problems in different forms (problems similar but not identical to those used in the pretest); and are shown that they give the same results. They are also encouraged to represent word problems and concrete problems by numerical sums, and to represent numerical problems and word problems by concrete objects.

They also play 'Same or Different' games, where the experimenter presents a problem in one form (e.g., '6 + 2') and then demonstrates its correct representation (e.g., two counters being added to six counters) or incorrect representation (e.g., two counters being taken away from six counters). They are asked to say whether the second problem is the same or different from the first problem.

(7) Derived Fact Strategies in Addition and Subtraction

One crucial aspect of arithmetical reasoning is the ability to derive and predict unknown arithmetical facts from known facts, for example by using arithmetical principles such as commutativity, associativity, the addition/subtraction inverse principle, etc. (Baroody et al., 1983; Canobi et al., 1998, 2003; Dowker, 1998). For example, if we know that $29 + 13 = 42$, we can use the commutativity principle to derive the fact that $13 + 29$ is also 42.

In the *pretest* to assess this component, children are given the Addition and Subtraction Principles Test developed by Dowker (1998), and described in more detail in Part 2. In this test, they are given the answer to a problem and then asked them to solve another problem that could be solved quickly by the appropriate use of an arithmetical principle (e.g., they may be shown the sum '23 + 44 = 67' and then asked to do the sum $23 + 45$, or $44 + 23$). Problems preceded by answers to numerically unrelated problems are given as controls. The children are asked whether 'the top sum' helps them to do 'the bottom sum', and why. The actual addition and subtraction problems involved vary in difficulty, ranging from those which the child can readily calculate mentally, through those just beyond the child's calculation capacity, to those very much too difficult for the child to solve.

Intervention

Intervention techniques for this component involve training in the use and application of derived fact strategies. The children are presented with pairs of arithmetic problems similar to those used in the pretest. The 'derived fact strategy' techniques are pointed out and explained to them; and they are invited to solve similar problems. If they fail to do so, the strategies are demonstrated to them for single-digit addition and subtraction problems, with the help of manipulable objects, and of a number line; and they are again invited to carry out other derived fact strategy problems.

(8) Arithmetical Estimation

The ability to estimate an approximate answer to an arithmetic problem, and to evaluate the reasonableness of an arithmetical estimate, are important aspects of arithmetical reasoning (LeFevre et al., 1993; Siegler & Booth, 2005; Sowder & Wheeler, 1989).

Pretest

This involves the task previously used by Dowker (1997, 2003), and described in more detail in Part 2. Children are presented with a series of problems of varying degrees of difficulty, and with estimates made for these problems by imaginary characters (Tom and Mary). The children are asked (a) to evaluate 'Tom and Mary's' estimates on a five-point 'smiley faces' scale from 'Very good' to 'Very silly'; and (b) to suggest 'Good guesses' for these problems themselves. Once again, the actual addition and subtraction problems involved vary in difficulty, ranging where possible from those which the child can readily calculate mentally, through those just beyond the child's calculation capacity, to those very much too difficult for the child to solve.

Intervention

Children are given additional 'Tom and Mary' evaluation tasks, and are asked to give reasons for their answers; and further practice in producing their own estimates. This is done under several conditions:

(a) Arithmetical problems similar to those used in the pretest.
(b) Problems with small numbers using concrete objects. It has been found (Dowker, 1997, 1998) that young children perform significantly better on estimation problems involving addition of concrete objects than those involving numerical problems.
(c) Word problems that provide a realistic practical context for estimation.

Children are also encouraged to play 'Twenty Questions' type number-guessing games (cf. Holt, 1966), which involve focussing on the *range* within which a number lies.

(9) Number Fact Retrieval

Although most psychologists, educators and mathematicians agree that memorization of facts is not the essence of arithmetic, knowledge of number facts does contribute to efficiency in calculation (Tronsky & Royer, 2003), and is a significant factor in distinguishing between mathematically normal and mathematically 'disabled' children (Geary & Hoard, 2005; Jordan & Hanich, 2000; Ostad, 1998; Russell & Ginsburg, 1984).

Pretest

This is based on Russell and Ginsburg's (1984) Number Facts Test, which assesses knowledge of basic addition facts. It has been expanded to include some subtraction facts as well.

Intervention

Children are presented with some of the basic addition and subtraction facts (e.g., $3 + 3 = 6$; $6 + 6 = 12$).

As suggested for example by Ginsburg (1977), the main technique is to ask the child to do the same sums repeatedly (during the same session, and in successive sessions), in the hope that the repetition will lead to retention of the facts involved. If the child continues to carry out the same problem over and over again as though it were a new problem, the child is explicitly asked, 'Have we done this sum before?' 'What did we get?' 'Do you think you can tell me what the answer will be, before you work it out.'

They also play 'number games' (e.g., some from Straker, 1996) that reinforce number fact knowledge.

EVALUATION OF EFFECTIVENESS

The children in the project, together with some of their classmates and children are of comparable levels of arithmetical ability from similar schools in the area from other schools, are given three standardized arithmetic tests: the British Abilities Scales Basic Number Skills subtest (1995 revision), the Weschler Objective Numerical Dimension (WOND) Numerical Operations test, and the Weschler Intelligence Scale (WISC) Arithmetic subtest. The first two place greatest emphasis on computation abilities and the latter on arithmetical reasoning. The children are retested at intervals of approximately 6 months.

The initial scores on standardized tests, and retest scores after 6 months, of the first 146 children to take part in the project have now been analyzed. Not all of the data from 'control' children are yet available, but the first 75 'control' children to be retested showed no significant improvement in standard (i.e., age corrected) scores on any of the tests. Moreover, as the tests are standardized, it is possible to estimate the extent to which children are or are not improving relative to others of their age in the general population.

The children in the intervention group have so far shown very significant improvements on standardized tests. (Average standard scores are 100 for the British Ability Scales (BAS) Basic Number Skills subtest and the WOND

Numerical Operations subtest, and 10 for the WISC Arithmetic subtest.) The median standard scores on the BAS Basic Number Skills subtest were 96 initially and 100 after approximately 6 months. The median standard scores on the WOND Numerical Operations test were 91 initially and 94 after 6 months. The median standard scores on the WISC Arithmetic subtest were 7 initially, and 8 after 6 months (the means were 6.8 initially and 8.45 after 6 months). Wilcoxon tests showed that all these improvements were significant at the 0.01 level.

Out of the 146 children 101 have been retested over periods of at least a year, and have been maintaining their improvement.

FURTHER DEVELOPMENT

The project is undergoing further development and evaluation. In particular, a pilot project is currently ongoing, in collaboration with Graham Sigley, Julie Lawes and Wayne Holmes of the Catch Up Trust, to adapt the program (under the title Catch Up in Numeracy) for wider use. Training programs and materials have been developed for use by teachers and teaching assistants; and the program is now being piloted and tested with approximately 240 children in 40 schools in six local authorities. Further expansion of the program is planned. In each school, four children participate fully in the intervention and two are controls. Within the control group, one pupil receives one-to-one support in mathematics, practicing work related to classroom activities, but not the specific targeted program, while the other receives no specific mathematics intervention beyond what is already provided by the school.

The children are given the Basic Number Screening Tests (Basic Number Screening Tests A and B) at the start and end of intervention; and will also be given follow-up tests. So far, results are available for 85 children before and after a 4-month intervention period. The 54 who underwent the targeted intervention showed a mean gain in 'mathematics age' of 8.4 months in the 4-month period. The 19 who underwent matched time intervention showed a mean gain of 5.3 months over the same time, and the 12 who had no intervention showed a mean gain of 4.3 months. An ANOVA showed difference between the targeted intervention group and the controls was significant. The control groups did not differ significantly from one another. Moreover, t-tests showed that the targeted intervention group's improvement was very significantly greater than the 4 months that would be expected just from their increase in age, while neither control group improved significantly more than the expected 4 months.

PART 2: STUDY OF CHILDREN WITH ARITHMETICAL DIFFICULTIES*

The study examined the performance of a sample of children with arithmetical difficulties on three selected components: derived fact strategy use, estimation

---

*At the risk of some repetition, I am giving full details of the tasks used in the study described in Section 2, to avoid the reader's need for constant cross-referencing to Section 1.

and translation, with respect to their arithmetical performance level and perform-ance and improvement on standardized tests. These components were selected because they had already been studied in some detail with unselected groups of children (Dowker, 1997, 1998, 2005). The children were the 146 children who underwent both intervention and retesting in the Numeracy Recovery project described in Part 1.

One of the main aims of the study was to investigate whether there would be a close relationship between scores on the different components, or whether they would be relatively independent. Previous research, as summarized at the begin-ning of this paper, has suggested some functional independence between these components. However, it appeared possible that different components would be more closely linked in children with mathematical difficulties, due to difficulties in one having an adverse effect on development of others, or due to the difficul-ties sharing a common cause.

METHOD AND TECHNIQUES

In order to evaluate the children's competence in addition calculations, a men-tal calculation task was given to each child. It consisted of a list of 20 addition sums graduated in difficulty from $4 + 5$, $7 + 1$, etc. to $235 + 349$. These sums were simultaneously presented orally and visually in a horizontal format. The children's answers were oral.

The sums were as follows:

(1)	6 + 3	(11)	31 + 57
(2)	4 + 5	(12)	68 + 21
(3)	8 + 2	(13)	52 + 39
(4)	7 + 1	(14)	45 + 28
(5)	4 + 9	(15)	33 + 49
(6)	7 + 5	(16)	26 + 67
(7)	8 + 6	(17)	235 + 142
(8)	9 + 8	(18)	613 + 324
(9)	26 + 72	(19)	523 + 168
(10)	23 + 44	(20)	349 + 234

Testing continued with each child until (s)he had failed to give a correct response to six successive items.

The children were then divided into five levels according to their performance on the mental calculation task.

Table 10.1 gives brief descriptions of the levels, and examples of the prob-lems that could and could not be solved at these levels. In practice, only the first three levels were represented in the present group.

DERIVED FACT STRATEGY TASK (USE OF ARITHMETICAL PRINCIPLES)

The children were then given an arithmetical reasoning test involving *use of arithmetical principles in derived fact strategies*. The technique was used of

TABLE 10.1   Levels of Arithmetical Performance in Addition

Level	Problem just within range	Problem outside range
Beginning arithmetic	2 + 2	5 + 3
Facts to 10	5 + 3	8 + 6
Simple facts	8 + 6	23 + 44
Two-digit (no carry)	23 + 44	52 + 39
Two-digit (carry)	52 + 39	523 + 168

giving children the answer to a problem and then asking them to solve another problem that could be solved quickly by using this answer, together with the principle under consideration. Problems preceded by answers to numerically unrelated problems were given as controls. The exact arithmetic problems given varied according to the previously assessed calculation ability of the child, and were selected to be just a little too difficult for the child to solve unaided. Such a set of problems is referred to here, as in earlier studies (e.g., Dowker, 1998), as the child's *base corresponding set*. Children of the highest (three-digit addition) level had no base corresponding set. They were given the same set as the next highest (two-digit addition; no carrying level). These were problems that they might have been able to solve by calculation, and this fact must be taken into account when considering the results obtained from children at this level.

Each child was shown the arithmetic problems, while the experimenter simultaneously read them to him/her. Children were asked to respond orally. The children received three arithmetical problems per principle: on rare occasions, when there was serious ambiguity about the interpretation of their responses, they received a fourth problem.

The principles investigated were as follows, in order of their difficulty for the children:

1. The *identity principle* (e.g., if one is told that 8 + 6 = 14, then one can automatically give the answer '14', without calculating, if asked 'What is 8 + 6?').
2. The *commutativity principle* (e.g., if 9 + 4 = 13, 4 + 9 must also be 13).
3. The *n + 1 principle* (e.g., if 23 + 44 = 67, 23 + 45 must be 68).
4. The *n − 1 principle* (e.g., if 9 + 8 = 17, 9 + 7 must be 17 − 1 or 16).
5. The *addition/subtraction inverse principle* (e.g., if 46 + 27 = 73, then 73 − 27 must be 46).

A child was deemed to be able to use a principle if (s)he could explain it and/or used it to derive at least 2 out of 3 unknown arithmetical facts, while being unable to calculate *any* sums of similar difficulty when there was no opportunity to use the principle.

ESTIMATION TASK

The addition estimation task was that used in previous studies (Dowker, 1997, 1998, 2003). In this study, each child was presented with a set of addition problems within their base correspondence as defined above. Each set included a group of nine sums to which a pair of imaginary characters ('Tom and Mary') estimated answers. Each set of 'Tom and Mary's' estimates included three good estimates (e.g., '7 + 2 = 10', '71 + 18 = 90'); three that were too small; and three that were too large. The children were asked to evaluate each guess on a five-point scale from 'Very good' to 'Very silly', represented by a set of schematic faces ranging from very smiling to very frowning, and were themselves asked to suggest 'Good guesses' to the sums. The Estimation score was the number of reasonable estimates, out of a maximum score of 9, within the base correspondence. Reasonable estimates were defined as those that were within 30% of the correct answer, and were also larger than each of the addends.

TRANSLATION TASK

The children were given tasks involving translations between word problem, concrete and numerical formats for additions and subtractions. The concrete formats involved the use of counters. All six combinations of presentation and response domain were given, as demonstrated below. No sum in any of these translation tasks included a number greater than 10. The order of tasks was varied systematically between participants.

(a) *Translation from numerical to concrete (2 items)*
Children were presented with written sums ("2 + 5 = 7"; "6 − = 4"); and were invited to "show me how to do this sum with the counters".

(b) *Translation from concrete numerical to (2 items)*
They watched the researcher perform arithmetical operations with counters (adding 7 counters to 2 counters; subtracting 6 counters from 9 counters) and then were then asked to "write down the sum that goes with what I did".

(c) *Translation from verbal to concrete (5 items)*
They were presented with word problems and asked to "show me this story with the counters".
Examples of items were:
"Paul had 4 sweets; his mother gave him 3 more; so now he has 7 sweets"
"Peter had 5 buns; he ate 3 buns; so now he has 2 chocolates."
"Farmer John has 7 pigs and 5 cows, so he has 2 more pigs than cows."
(Subtraction: 'Compare' semantic category)

(d) *Translation from verbal to numerical (5 items)*
Children were presented with word problems (similar but not identical to those in ©), and asked to "write down the sum that goes with the story"

(e) *Translation from numerical to verbal (2 items)*

They were presented with written sums ("3 + 6 = 9", "8 − 6 = 2"), and invited to "tell me a story that goes with this sum".

(f) *Translation from concrete to verbal (2 items)*
Children watched the researcher perform arithmetical operations with counters (e.g. adding 5 counters to 3 counters; subtracting 6 counters from 9 counters) and were then asked to "tell a story to go with what I just did with the counters."

CLASSIFICATION OF RESPONSES
TO TRANSLATION TASK

The Translation score was calculated by giving 3 for every fully *complete* response, 2 for every complete response, which involved inverting the operation (e.g., representing the story 'Peter had 5 buns; he ate 3 buns; so now he has 2 chocolates,' as '3 + 2 = 5' rather than '5 − 2 = 3'); 1 for every *incomplete* response and 0 for every *incorrect* response. As the total number of items was 18, the maximum possible score was 54.

Complete responses involved representing the operation: for example, representing the story above by writing '5 − 2 = 3', or putting out a set of 5 counters and removing 2 to leave 3. Incomplete responses involved representing one or more of the numbers within the problem, without showing the operation; for example representing the story above by writing '5 2 3' or '3', or showing 3 counters, or separate sets of 5 counters, 2 counters and 3 counters. Incorrect responses involved the production of incorrect numbers or sums, irrelevant stories or comments, letters of the alphabet, or complete failure to answer.

Results

Table 10.2 gives the descriptive statistics for all the variables for all children.

Of these 146 children, 37 were initially at Addition Performance Level 1 (Beginning Arithmetic); 86 at Level 2 (Facts to 10) and 23 at Level 3 (Facts to 25).

The mean number of derived fact strategies used for addition by the group as a whole was 1.05 (SD 1.13). When children were divided according to their addition performance level, the mean number of derived fact strategies used by children at Level 1 (Beginning Arithmetic) was 0.3 (SD 0.55); the mean number used by children at Level 2 (Facts to 10) was 1.28 (SD 1.17); and the mean number used by children at Level 3 (Simple Facts) was 1.2 (SD 1.06).

By comparison, the mean numbers of derived fact strategies used by unselected children at the same levels (Dowker, 1998) were 0.72 at Level 1; 1.82 at Level 2; and 3.01 at Level 3.

The mean number of reasonable estimates (out of 9) by the group as a whole was 4.23 (SD 2.18). When children were divided according to their addition performance level, the mean number of reasonable estimates provided by children at Level 1 (Beginning Arithmetic) was 3.00 (SD 1.73); the mean number used

TABLE 10.2   Means and Standard Deviations of Test Scores

	n	Mean	Standard deviation	Range
WOND (first score)	175	90.32	10.99	62–123
WOND (second score)	146	92.79	12.34	68–126
WOND improvement	146	2.45	10.9	−23–33
BAS (first score)	175	95.19	11.76	67–123
BAS (second score)	146	100.38	12.45	62–133
BAS improvement	146	5.11	11.87	−25–49
WISC (first score)	175	6.86	2.87	2–17
WISC (second score)	146	8.33	2.5	2–15
WISC improvement	146	1.51	3.13	−8–11
Age at start (months)	175	80.7	6.05	66–97
Addition level	175	1.94	0.67	1–4
Addition derived fact strategies	175	1.05	1.13	0–5
Estimation	175	4.08	2.21	0–9
Translation	175	21.9	9.93	2–47

by children at Level 2 (Facts to 10) was 4.47 (SD 2.28); and the mean number used by children at Level 3 (Simple Facts) was 4.33 (SD 2.16).

By comparison, the mean numbers of reasonable estimates provided used by unselected children at the same levels (Dowker, 1998) were 2.43 at Level 1; 5.4 at Level 2; and 4.95 at Level 3.

The mean translation score of the group as a whole was 22.58 (SD 9.81). When children were divided according to their addition performance level, the mean translation score at Level 1 (Beginning Arithmetic) was 15.33 (SD 7.16); the mean score at Level 2 (Facts to 10) was 24.96 (SD 9.53); and the mean score at Level 3 (Simple Facts) was 25.89 (SD 8.4). The unselected children studied by Dowker et al. (2005) were not divided by performance levels in this way; but the overall average score obtained by 6 year olds was 32.

LACK OF GENDER DIFFERENCES

An analysis of covariance was carried out with gender as the factor, age (in months) as the covariate. The dependent variables were Addition Level, Addition Derived Fact Strategy Score, Subtraction Level, Subtraction Derived Fact Strategy Score, Estimation Score, Translation Score, and the (a) initial and (b) second scores and (c) extent of improvement on all three standardized tests: WOND Numerical Operations, BAS Basic Number Skills and WISC Arithmetic. None of the comparisons proved significant.

RELATIONSHIPS BETWEEN DIFFERENT MEASURES

Table 10.3 shows the correlations between different measures.

In order to investigate the independent contributions of different factors to target measures, entry level multiple regressions were carried out on each of the measures as dependent variable, with the other measures as the predictors.

FACTORS CONTRIBUTING TO SCORES ON COMPONENTS OF ARITHMETICAL PERFORMANCE

An entry method linear multiple regression was carried out with *Addition Derived Fact Strategies* as the dependent variable and Age, Addition Level, Estimation, and Translation as the predictors. None of the predictors proved to be significant.

An entry method linear multiple regression was carried out with *Estimation* as the dependent variable and Age, Addition Level, Addition Derived Fact Strategies and Translation as the predictors. None of the predictors proved to be significant.

An entry method linear multiple regression was carried out with *Translation* as the dependent variable and Age, Addition Level, Addition Derived Fact Strategies and Estimation as the predictors. Age was a significant positive predictor (beta = 3.41; $t = 3.21$; $p < 0.01$) as was Addition Level (beta = 2.6; $t = 2.4$; $p < 0.05$).

Addition Level was included in the analyses because it was a determinant of the precise content of the derived fact strategy and estimation tasks, and it seemed desirable to control for it. As it is an ordinal rather than cardinal score, there could however be doubts as to the appropriateness of its inclusion in a regression. The same analyses were carried out with this variable omitted, and results were identical as regards the significance of the other predictors, with the exception of the regression on Translation. Once Addition Level was removed from this regression, Age continued to be a significant predictor (beta = 0.41; $t = 3.82$; $p < 0.01$), but Estimation also just reached significance (beta = 0.22; $t = 2.04$; $p < 0.05$).

Estimation, and Translation as the predictors. Both Addition Level (beta = 0.37; $t = 3.2$; $p < 0.01$) and Translation (beta = 0.27; $t = 2.13$; $p < 0.05$) were significant positive predictors.

An entry method linear multiple regression was carried out with second WISC Arithmetic score as the dependent variable and first Arithmetic score, Age, Addition Level, Addition Derived Fact Strategies, Estimation, and Translation as the predictors. None of the predictors proved to be significant.

An entry method linear multiple regression was carried out with *improvement in* WISC Arithmetic score as the dependent variable and first Arithmetic score, Age, Addition Level, Addition Derived Fact Strategies, Estimation, and Translation as the predictors. Initial Arithmetic score was a significant negative predictor (beta = -0.81; $t = -7.91$; $p < 0.01$). None of the other predictors proved to be significant.

TABLE 10.3 Spearman Rank Correlations Between the Variables ($*p < 0.05$, $**p < 0.01$) ($n = 146$)

	Age	Addition level	Derived fact strategies	Estimation	Translation	WOND 1	WOND 2	WOND improvement	BAS 1	BAS 2	BAS Improvement	WISC 1	WISC 2	WISC Improvement
Age		0.21**	0.05	0.08	0.29**	-0.21**	-0.22**	-0.02	0.03	-0.15	-0.29**	0	-0.08	-0.05
Addition level			0.33**	0.2	0.43**	0.49**	0.32**	-0.11	0.49**	0.38**	-0.05	0.47**	-0.23**	-0.16*
Derived fact strategies				0.15	0.27**	0.28**	0.09	-0.14	0.34**	0.12	-0.19*	0.25**	0.1	0.05
Estimation					0.3**	0.15	0.32**	-0.02	0.23*	0.15	-0.29**	0.23**	0.18	0.01
Translation						0.23**	0.2*	-0.36**	0.31**	0.2*	0.09	0.43**	0.22*	-0.18*
WOND 1					—		0.54**	-0.34**	0.62**	0.46**	-0.09	0.57**	0.42**	-0.16*
WOND 2					—	—		0.53**	0.51**	0.72**	0.27**	0.44**	0.57**	0.06
WOND improvement									-0.03	0.34*	0.4**	-0.08	0.22	0.23**
BAS 1										0.51**	-0.41**	0.52**	0.44**	-0.1
BAS 2											0.53**	0.37**	0.56**	0.13
BAS improvement												-0.1	0.16*	0.22**
WISC 1													0.39**	-0.6**
WISC 2														0.49**
WISC improvements														

Addition Level was included in the analyses for reasons mentioned above; but as it is an ordinal rather than cardinal score, there could be doubts as to the appropriateness of its inclusion in a regression. The same analyses were carried out with this variable omitted, and results were identical as regards the significance of the other predictors.

DISCUSSION

The children with arithmetical difficulties appeared in general to show some weaknesses in the components investigated: derived fact strategies, estimation and translation, as compared with unselected children in other studies. The groups may not be directly comparable, due to the time lapse and changes in the educational system since the studies of the unselected children; but the figures suggest that the children in the intervention group used on average somewhat fewer derived fact strategies and make fewer reasonable estimates than the unselected children, and that this was especially true of those at the higher addition performance levels. Perhaps children at the higher addition performance levels were only regarded by their teachers as arithmetically weak and needing intervention if they did have additional weaknesses in aspects of arithmetical reasoning. The study of unselected children's translation (Dowker, 2005) did not assess the children's addition performance level; but their translation performance as a group appeared to be somewhat better than that of the children with arithmetical difficulties.

It should be noted, however, that not all children in the latter group performed poorly in the components investigated; that derived fact strategy use and estimation were often quite good; and that their translation performance in particular seemed better than that which would have been predicted by Hughes (1986), who found extreme translation difficulties even in unselected 9 year olds.

Standardized test scores are more related to some specific components of arithmetic than to others. Addition Level was a significant independent predictor of the scores in all tests: not surprisingly, as all the standardized tests emphasized competence at calculation. Neither Estimation nor Derived Fact Strategies was an independent predictor of any test scores. Translation predicted performance in the WISC Arithmetic test, but not in the other tasks. This may be due to the fact that the WISC Arithmetic test places an emphasis on word problem solving, whereas the other tests place greater emphasis on calculation and on reading and writing numbers.

Thus, investigations revealed some general correlations between specific components of arithmetic, but there were few significant independent relationships between these components. It is possible that more such relationships would be found if a larger sample were studied. The results are, however, consistent with the view that arithmetic is made up of many components; that 'there is no such thing as arithmetical ability; only arithmetical abilities' (Dowker, 2005). Indeed, they show rather less relationship between different components than was found in Dowker's (1998) study of an unselected group of children. That study (which did not investigate translation) showed significant independent effects of addition level on both estimation and derived fact strategies, and a particularly strong independent relationship between derived fact strategy use and estimation. By contrast, in the present study, derived fact strategy use and estimation not only did not show an independent relationship; they were not even correlated before other factors were partialled out.

It may be that in a group of children with arithmetical difficulties, there is even less relationship between different arithmetical components than in a typical sample. Perhaps in completely typical mathematical development, different components, though perhaps functionally separable, do inform and reinforce one another in the course of development (as Baroody & Ginsburg, 1986, propose for the development of principles and procedures in younger children, in their 'mutual development' theory). In children with arithmetical difficulties, this integration may not occur to the same extent, either because it is impeded by marked weaknesses in individual components, or because of a failure in the integrative process itself.

However, another possible explanation for any differences found between Dowker's (1998) study and the present one is that the findings are linked to educational changes. There were crucial changes in British mathematics education in 1998–1999, with the introduction of the National Numeracy Strategy (Department for Education and Employment, 1999). There is no transparently obvious reason why the changes in mathematics education at that time should have led to greater dissociation between different components of arithmetic. If anything, one might have expected that the more explicit structure of the mathematics curriculum, and the inclusion of derived fact strategies and estimation in primary mathematics instruction, might have led to the components becoming more integrated with one another. However, curriculum changes sometimes have effects other than the predictable or intended ones. In any case, it is risky to assume that differences in findings between groups are entirely the result of group characteristics, when there are also differences in the instruction that they have received. It would be desirable to compare the children in this group with unselected children undergoing similar mathematics instruction. Such a study is currently underway.

Thus, the findings discussed in this paper strongly support the view that arithmetic is made up of multiple components rather than being unitary; though further research is necessary to establish how the relationships between components vary with ability level and with educational factors.

They also support the view that arithmetical difficulties can be significantly ameliorated by interventions targeting specific weaknesses. There is more research to be done on exactly how such interventions lead to improvement.

Moreover, further investigations are of course necessary to show whether and to what extent specific interventions in mathematics more effective in improving children's mathematics than *other* interventions which provide children with individual attention: for example, interventions in literacy. It is also desirable to investigate whether different approaches to such intervention (e.g., age when intervention starts; degree of intensiveness; degree of individualization; the particular components emphasized) may differ in general effectiveness and/ or differentially appropriate to different groups of children.

The present study also demonstrates the possibilities for bidirectional relationships between research and intervention. The project integrates the implementation and evaluation of the intervention scheme with the investigation of individual differences in, and relationships between, certain selected components of arithmetic. Thus, the intervention project, which was inspired by my earlier research and conclusions about the components of arithmetic, also serves to test theories about these components.

ACKNOWLEDGMENTS

I am grateful to the children and teachers at the schools involved in the research. I thank the Esmee Fairbairn Charitable Trust and the Caxton Trust for financial support.

REFERENCES

Askew, M. & Brown, M. (Eds.) (2001). *Teaching and Learning Primary Numeracy: Policy, Practice and Effectiveness*. Notts: British Educational Research Association.

Ansari, D., Garcia, N., Lucas, E., Hamon, K., & Dhilil, B. (2005). Neural correlates of symbolic number processing in children and adults. *Neuroreport, 16*, 1769–1775.

Baroody, A. J. (1992). The development of preschoolers' counting skills and principles. In Bideaud, J. (Ed.), *Pathways to Number: Children's Developing Numerical Abilities*. Hillsdale, NJ: Erlbaum.

Baroody, A. J. & Ginsburg, H. P. (1986). The relationship between initial meaningful and mechanical knowledge of arithmetic. In Hiebert, J. (Ed.), *Conceptual and Procedural Knowledge: The Case of Mathematics* (pp. 75–112). Hillsdale, NJ: Erlbaum.

Baroody, A. J., Ginsburg, H. P., & Waxman, B. (1983). Children's use of mathematical structure. *Journal for Research in Mathematics Education, 14*, 156–168.

Baroody, A. & Dowker, A. (2003). *The Development of Arithmetical Concepts and Skills*. Mahwah, NJ: Erlbaum.

Butterworth, B. (1999). *The Mathematical Brain*. London: Macmillan.

Butterworth, B. (2005). Developmental dyscalculia. In Campbell, J. I. D. (Ed.), *Handbook of Mathematical Cognition* (pp. 455–467). Hove: Psychology Press.

Bynner, J. & Parsons, S. (1997). *Does Numeracy Matter?* London: Basic Skills Agency.

Campbell, J. I. D. (Ed.) (2005). *Handbook of Mathematical Cognition*. Hove: Psychology Press.

Canobi, K. H., Reeve, R. A., & Pattison, P. E. (1998). The role of conceptual understanding in children's addition problem solving. *Developmental Psychology, 34*, 882–891.

Canobi, K. H., Reeve, R. A. & Pattison, P. E. (2003). Young children's understanding of addition concepts. *Educational Psychology, 22*, 513–532.

Castelli, F., Glaser, D. E., & Butterworth, B. (2006). Discrete and analogue quantity processing in the parietal lobe: A functional MRI study. *Proceedings of the National Academy of Sciences, 103*, 4693–4698.

Cowan, R., Bailey, S., Christakis, A., & Dowker, A. D. (1996). Even more precisely understanding the order irrelevance principle. *Journal of Experimental Child Psychology, 61*, 84–101.

Decorte, E. & Verschaffel, L. (1987). The effect of semantic structure on first-graders' strategies for solving addition and subtraction word problems. *Journal for Research in Mathematics Education, 18*, 363–381.

Dehaene, S. (1997). *The Number Sense*. London: Macmillan.

Dehaene, S., Spelke, E, Pinel, P., Stanescu, R., & Tsivkin, S. (1999). Sources of mathematical thinking: behavioural and brain-imaging evidence. *Science, 5416*, 970–974.

Delazer, M. (2003). Neuropsychological findings on conceptual knowledge of arithmetic. In Baroody, A. & Dowker, A. (Eds.), *The development of arithmetical concepts and skills* (pp. 385–407). Mahwah, NJ: Erlbaum.

Denvir, B. & Brown, M. (1986). Understanding number concepts in low-attaining 7- to 9-year-olds. Part 1: Development of descriptive frameworks and diagnostic instruments. *Educational Studies in Mathematics, 17*, 15–36.

Department for Education and Employment (DfEE) (1999). *The National Numeracy Strategy: Framework for Teaching Mathematics, Reception to Year 6*. London: DfEE.

Dowker, A. D. (1997). Young children's addition estimates. *Mathematical Cognition, 3*, 141–154.

Dowker, A. D. (1998). Individual differences in normal arithmetical development. In Donlan, C. (Ed.), *The Development of Mathematical Skills* (pp. 275–302). Hove: Psychology Press.

Dowker, A. D. (2001). Numeracy recovery: A pilot scheme for early intervention with young children with numeracy difficulties. *Support for Learning, 16*, 6–10.

Dowker, A. D. (2003). Young children's estimates for addition: The zone of partial knowledge and understanding. In Baroody, A. and Dowker, A. (Eds.), *The Development of Arithmetic Concepts and Skills* (pp. 243–266). Mahwah, NJ: Erlbaum.

Dowker, A. D. (2005). *Individual Differences in Arithmetic: Implications for Psychology, Neuroscience and Education*. Hove: Psychology Press.

Fuson, K. (1992). Research on learning and teaching addition and subtraction of whole numbers. In: Leinhardt, G., Putnam, R., & Hattrop, R. A. (Eds.), *Analysis of Arithmetic for Mathematics Teaching*. Hillsdale, NJ: Erlbaum.

Geary, D. C. & Hoard, M. K. (2005). Learning disabilities in arithmetic and mathematics: Theoretical and empirical perspectives. In Campbell, J. I. D. (Ed.), *Handbook of Mathematical Cognition* (pp. 253–267). Hove: Psychology Press.

Geary, D. C. & Widaman, K. F. (1992). On the convergence of componential and psychometric models. *Intelligence, 16*, 47–80.

Ginsburg, H. P. (1977). *Children's Arithmetic: How They Learn It and How You Teach It*. New York: Van Norstrand.

Gray, E. & Tall, D. (1994). Duality, ambiguity and flexibility: A proceptual view of simple arithmetic. *Journal for Research in Mathematics Education, 25*, 115–144.

Greeno, J., Riley, M., & Gelman, R. (1984). Conceptual competence and children's counting. *Cognitive Psychology, 16*, 94–134.

Griffin, S., Case, R., & Siegler, R. (1994). Rightstart: Providing the central conceptual prerequisites for first formal learning of arithmetic to students at risk for school failure. In McGilly, K. (Ed.), *Classroom Learning: Integrating Cognitive Theory and Classroom Practice* (pp. 25–50). Boston: MIT Press.

Gruber, O., Indefrey, P., Steinmetz, H., & Kleinschmidt, A. (2001). Dissociating neural correlates of cognitive components in mental calculation. *Cerebral Cortex, 11*, 350–369.

Holt, J. (1966). *How Children Fail*. New York: Pitman.

Hughes, M. (1986). *Children and Number: Difficulties in Learning Mathematics*. Oxford: Blackwell.

Jordan, N. & Hanich, L. B. (2000). Mathematical thinking in second grade children with different forms of LD. *Journal of Learning Disabilities, 33*, 567–578.

Jordan, N. C., Blanteno, L., & Uberti, H. Z. (2003). Mathematical thinking and learning difficulties. In Baroody, A. & Dowker, A. (Eds.), *The Development of Arithmetical Concepts and Skills* (pp. 359–383). Mahwah, NJ: Erlbaum.

Kilpatrick, J., Swafford, J., & Fundell, B. (Eds.) (2001). *Adding It Up: Helping Children Learn Mathematics*. Washington, DC: National Academy Press.

Lefevre, J. A. & Kulak, A. G. (1994). Individual differences in the obligatory activation of addition facts. *Memory and Cognition, 22,* 188–200.

Lefevre, J. A., Greenham, S. L., & Waheed, N. (1993). The development of procedural and conceptual knowledge in computational estimation. *Cognition and Instruction, 11,* 95–132.

Mayer, R. (2003). Mathematical problem solving. In Royer, J. M. (Ed.), *Mathematical Cognition* (pp. 69–92). Greenwich, CT: Information Age Publishing.

Mazzocco, M. & Myers, G. F. (2003). Complexities in identifying and defining mathematics learning disability in the primary school years. *Annals of Dyslexia, 53,* 218–253.

Munn, P. (1997). Children's beliefs about counting. In Thompson, I. (Ed.), *Teaching and Learning Early Number* (pp. 9–19). Buckingham: Open University Press.

Ostad, S. (1998). Developmental differences in solving simple arithmetic word problems and simple number-fact problems: a comparison of mathematically normal and mathematically disabled children. *Mathematical Cognition, 4,* 1–19.

Rickard, T. C., Romero, S. G., Basso, G., Wharton, C., Flitman, S., & Grafman, J. (2000). The calculating brain: An fMRI study. *Neuropsychologia, 38,* 325–335.

Riley, M. S., Greeno, J. G., & Heller, J. I. (1983). Development of children's problem-solving ability in arithmetic. In Ginsburg, H. P. (Ed.), *The Development of Mathematical Thinking* (pp. 153–196). New York: Academic Press.

Royer, J. M. (Ed.) (2003). *Mathematical Cognition*. Greenwich, CT: Information Age Publishing.

Russell, R. & Ginsburg, H. P. (1984). Cognitive analysis of children's mathematical difficulties. *Cognition and Instruction, 1,* 217–244.

Shalev, R. S., Gross-Tsur, V., & Manor, O. (1997). Neuropsychological aspects of developmental dyscalculia. *Mathematical Cognition, 3,* 105–170.

Siegler, R. S. (1988). Individual differences in strategy choice: Good students, not-so-good students and perfectionists. *Child Development, 59,* 833–851.

Siegler, R. S. & Booth, J. L. (2005). Development of numerical estimation: A review. In Campbell, J. I. D. (Ed.), *Handbook of Mathematical Cognition* (pp. 197–212). Hove: Psychology Press.

Sowder, J. T. & Wheeler, M. M. (1989). The development of concepts and strategies use in computational estimation. *Journal for Research in Mathematics Education, 20,* 130–146.

Straker, A. (1996). *Mental Maths for Ages 5 to 7: Teachers' Book*. Cambridge: Cambridge University Press.

Tronsky, L. T. & Royer, J. M. (2003). Relationships among basic computational automaticity, working memory and complex problem solving: What we know and what we need to know. In Royer, J. M. (Ed.), *Mathematical Cognition* (pp. 117–145). Greenwich, CT: Information Age Publishing.

Warrington, E. K. (1982). The fractionation of arithmetical skills: A single case study. *Quarterly Journal of Experimental Psychology, 34A,* 31–51.

Wynroth, L. (1986). Wynroth Math Program: The Natural Number Sequence. Ithaca, NY: Wynroth Math Program.

Yeo, D. (2003). *Dyslexia, Dyspraxia and Mathematics*. London: Whurr.

NOTE

Some of this material has been reported in Dowker, A. (2007). What can intervention tell us about the development of arithmetric? *Educational and child psychology, 24,* 64–82.

11

MATHEMATICS RECOVERY

AN EARLY NUMBER PROGRAM
FOCUSING ON INTENSIVE
INTERVENTION

ROBERT J. WRIGHT

School of Education, Southern Cross University, NSW Australia

Mathematics Recovery is an intensive intervention program in number learning for low-attaining first-grade students, that is, students typically around 6 years of age. The program aims to advance children's number knowledge to a level at which they are likely to learn successfully in a regular class. Participating students are taught individually in daily sessions of about 25 minutes' duration, for 4 or 5 days per week, for teaching cycles of 12 to 15 weeks' duration. Mathematics Recovery is also an intensive and extensive program of teacher professional development. The main purpose of this chapter is to provide an overview of key aspects of Mathematics Recovery. The chapter does not include a general overview of issues related to intervention to address children's difficulties with mathematics. For a detailed overview of that topic the reader is referred to Dowker (2004).

AN ANECDOTE: THE CASE OF KIM

9 + 7: The setting: Kim is 6 years old and is a first grader participating in a class lesson focusing on early number. In the current phase of the lesson, students are working at their desks, completing a worksheet of exercises involving addition and subtraction in the range 1 to 20. On the worksheet, the tasks are presented in horizontal written format. Kim is currently working on the task 9 + 7.

His task is to work out the answer and to write it to the right of the expression. Kim's class teacher adheres to the principle that counters should be available to students who have difficulty solving these exercises. On his desk, Kim has a pile of blue counters and a pile of red counters. As well, in a horizontal line across each student's desk appears the numerals from '1' to '20' in sequence. Kim's teacher is happy for this numeral sequence to be available to her students in this way because they seem to use it and to enjoy working with it.

Kim's solution: In solving 9 + 7 Kim proceeds as follows. Looking at the numeral sequence on his desk, Kim says each of the number words from 'one' onward in coordination with pointing at each numeral in turn, from '1' onward. When he gets to the numeral '9' he says 'nine' and then stops. He then moves to the pile of blue counters and pulls out a counter, in coordination with saying each of the number words from '1' to '9'. In this way he has made a group of 9 blue counters on his desk. Kim again looks at the numeral sequence and as before, says the number words from '1' onward in coordination with pointing at each numeral in turn. This time he gets to the numeral '7', and says 'seven' and then stops. He then moves to the pile of red counters and pulls out a counter in coordination with saying each of the number words from '1' to '7'. In this way he has made a group of 7 red counters on his desk. At this point Kim combines the two groups of counters (9 blue and 7 red). He now moves each counter in turn in coordination with saying each of the number words from '1' onward. When he moves the last counter he says '16' and then stops. At this point Kim again looks at the numeral sequence and points to each numeral in turn, in coordination with saying the words from '1' onward. When he says '16' he stops and looks intently at the numeral at which he is pointing. He then writes the numeral '16' to the right of the expression 9 + 7.

Discussion: The purpose of the above anecdote is to illustrate difficulties and setbacks that can occur in children's early number learning in the classroom. In order to support Kim in his number learning, his teacher has adopted two well-established practices. One is to make counters available for Kim to use if he so chooses when solving addition tasks. The other is to provide a numeral sequence at the top of his desk. Kim has developed an algorithm for solving written addition tasks involving two one-digit addends. His algorithm as described in the anecdote above consists of seven steps. It is likely that he is quite skilled with this algorithm because he uses it very frequently. Nevertheless, skilfulness aside, because his algorithm is so complex, Kim takes a long time to solve each problem compared with the time most of his classmates take. Kim's teacher might not be fully aware of the intricacies of Kim's solution method. Nevertheless she fully realizes that, although he makes few errors, he takes a relatively long time to solve a set of tasks and persists with his strategy of using counters. Her hope is that, with continued practice, Kim will develop more advanced methods and will no longer need to use counters.

Two observations can be made about Kim's number knowledge and in particular, his solution strategy. First, apparently he cannot or does not directly read numerals such as '7' and '9'. Rather, he uses a strategy of counting along a numeral sequence to generate the name of a given numeral. Second, apparently his strategy for solving the addition tasks involves (a) counting-by-ones; (b) counting-from-one and (c) counting visible items (counters).

Later in this chapter I will return to the case of Kim, and draw on key notions described in the intervening section, to illustrate how approaches in Mathematics Recovery can be applied in Kim's case, and the usefulness of these approaches.

THE LEARNING FRAMEWORK IN NUMBER

For teachers new to Mathematics Recovery (MR), coming to know the Learning Framework in Number (LFIN) is a major and core aspect of their professional learning. In its basic form, LFIN is a set of five tables, each of which contains up to six levels (see Figure 11.1). Each table in LFIN focuses on what is regarded in MR as a key aspect of early number knowledge. And in each table, the levels taken together, constitute a progression of student learning, that is, the levels set out the number knowledge to be acquired progressively by the student. The five tables are referred to as models in the sense that each table models a progression of learning of a key aspect of number knowledge. In a more extended

Stages:
Early Arithmetical Learning

0 – Emergent Counting
1 – Perceptual Counting
2 – Figurative Counting
3 – Initial Number Sequence
4 – Intermediate Number
      Sequence
5 – Facile Number Sequence

Levels
Base-Ten Arithmetical
Strategies

1 – Initial Concept of Ten
2 – Intermediate
      Concept of Ten
3 – Facile Concept of Ten

Levels: Forward Number Word Sequences (FNWS) &
Number Word After

0 – Emergent FNWS.
1 – Initial FNWS up to 'ten'.
2 – Intermediate FNWS up to 'ten'.
3 – Facile with FNWSs up to 'ten'.
4 – Facile with FNWSs up to 'thirty'.
5 – Facile with FNWSs up to 'one hundred'.

Levels: Backward Number Word Sequences
(FNWS) & Number Word Before

0 – Emergent BNWS.
1 – Initial BNWS up to 'ten'.
2 – Intermediate BNWS up to 'ten'.
3 – Facile with BNWSs up to 'ten'.
4 – Facile with BNWSs up to 'thirty'.
5 – Facile with BNWSs up to 'one
      hundred'.

Levels: Numeral Identification

0 – Emergent Numeral Identification.
1 – Numerals to '10'
2 – Numerals to '20'
3 – Numerals to '100'
4 – Numerals to '1000'

FIGURE 11.1   Learning framework in number. Adapted from Wright et al. (2006a, p. 20).

form, LFIN includes not only the five models, but also an extended corpus of pedagogical knowledge about students' learning of these aspects of early number knowledge. A detailed description of LFIN is available elsewhere (see Wright et al., 2006a), including a model of early multiplication and division knowledge also included in LFIN. Because multiplication and division is not a major focus of MR instruction, this model is not further discussed here. The focus here is to give a brief description and some insight into the characteristics and use of LFIN in Mathematics Recovery.

Understanding or knowledge: I use the term 'the child's early number knowledge' to refer to everything that the child knows about early number. In describing what a child knows about early number, I prefer to use the term knowledge rather than a term such as understanding. Thus I would prefer to refer to the child's knowledge of addition, rather than to say that the child understands addition. My difficulty with the latter is that there are many levels on which addition can be understood. What understanding the mathematical notion of addition might mean is very much dependant on the mathematical context. This context can range for example, from one of using counting to add whole numbers in the range 1 to 10, to addition involving decimals or algebraic expressions. So rather than talk about whether the child understands addition or not, and similarly with subtraction and so on, I find it more helpful to try to document as comprehensively as possible, the child's early number knowledge. But what does it mean to do this and how can one go about it?

Domains or aspects: In trying to document a child's early number knowledge, one can list important subtopics that taken together make up the topic of early number. This list might include counting, addition, subtraction and so on. One approach is to think of the task of documenting the child's early number knowledge as analogous to constructing a map consisting of domains in the sense of specific parts or regions that go to make up a larger territory. In accordance with the mapping analogy, the term domains is often used to refer to the subtopics of basic whole number arithmetic. Certainly the process of documenting in detail, the child's current number knowledge is critical in Mathematics Recovery. This emphasis on the detailed documenting of the child's knowledge has its origins in Steffe's constructivist teaching experiments (e.g., Steffe & Cobb, 1988), and in doing so, my preference is to use the term aspect rather than domain to refer to what one might think of as the different subtopics of early number knowledge. The term aspect is used here in the sense of 'a way in which a thing may be viewed or regarded [or] a view commanded' (The Macquarie dictionary, 1981), and is meant to convey the notion that one is taking different views of an object, for example, a mountain. Typically, these different views are not disjoint. Rather, a given number of views overlap in complex ways. Taken together, the aspects can constitute a rich overall portrait of the child's early number knowledge. I use the term portrait in the sense of a verbal picture. Each aspect and the overall portrait are constituted by the observer's interpretation of the child's responses, to groups of inter-related tasks.

Models in the LFIN: Figure 11.1 sets out in brief summary form, five of the models in LFIN. The assessment process in MR is crucial to the teacher's use of LFIN and is described later in this chapter. One important outcome of the assessment is for the teacher to determine the student's current level of knowledge on each of the LFIN models. In this way the teacher builds a profile of the student's current knowledge in early number, across several key aspects. This profile is critical in the teacher's selection of specific instructional topics for the student. For each aspect, the profile specifies the student's current level of knowledge and the next level to be attained. Thus LFIN enables the teacher to determine the new levels of knowledge that are the goal of MR instruction. But LFIN does not set out the specifics of instruction that is, instruction that has the purpose of advancing the student's knowledge in terms of these levels. The specifics of instruction are set out in a second framework referred to as the Instructional Framework in Early Number (IFEN). Thus LFIN is a framework of student's learning and is used in conjunction with the process of assessing and profiling student's knowledge. The instructional framework is closely linked to LFIN but is of a different form because it sets out progressions of specific instructional topics. The instructional framework (IFEN) is overviewed later in this chapter.

FIVE ASPECTS OF THE LFIN

The five aspects of LFIN described here are (a) the Stages of Early Arithmetical Learning (SEAL); (a) Forward Number Word Sequences (FNWSs); (c) Backward Number Word Sequences (BNWSs); (d) Numeral Identification and (e) Tens and Ones.

Stages of Early Arithmetical Learning: The primary and most important model in LFIN is the SEAL. This model is adapted from the work of Steffe (e.g., 1992). This focus of this model is the progression in the ways young children use counting in problem-solving contexts, for example, to figure out how many items in a collection, or to solve simple addition or subtraction tasks. For the purpose of illustrating this progression, three of these stages are explained here and others are explained later in this chapter: The child at the Emergent Stage (Stage 0) cannot correctly count a collection of counters. The child at Stage 3 will typically use counting-on and counting-back to solve simple additive and subtractive tasks. I refer to these as the advanced counting-by-ones strategies. The child at Stage 5 no longer relies on counting-by-ones. Rather, they have a range of facile strategies for solving additive tasks in the range 1 to 20.

Tens and Ones: The model of base-10 arithmetical strategies (Cobb & Wheatley, 1988) focuses on progressions in the ways young children reason in terms of tens and ones, in problem-solving contexts involving two-digit numbers. At Level 1, the child has difficulty reasoning with 10 as a composite unit. For this child, 10 cannot simultaneously stand for one ten and ten ones. At Level 2, the child can reason with 10 as a composite unit, in the context of base-10 materials. At Level 3, the child can reason skilfully with tens and ones, in the absence of any base-10 materials.

FNWSs, BNWSs and Numeral Identification: The models of FNWSs and BNWSs focus on children's facility with number word sequences. This includes saying sequences forward or backward and stating the number before or after a given number. The focus in this case is on the activity of saying the sequence per se rather than using the sequence in counting activity to solve a problem involving counting, adding or subtracting. The model of numeral identification focuses on children's facility in identifying (naming, reading) numerals.

Framework or trajectory?: In LFIN, I prefer the term framework rather than path or trajectory because those terms typically refer to progression of learning along a single path, that is the progressive learning of one topic or domain. Thus use of the term trajectory suggests a single, linear view of learning. The view underlying MR and LFIN is that learning can and should occur concurrently along several paths, the learning along each path has the potential to interact in a supportive way, with the learning along each of the other paths. Thus the student is simultaneously learning several key topics and hopefully, to a strong extent, the learning of each topic is supporting and supported by the learning of each of the other topics.

USING LFIN TO PROFILE STUDENT'S KNOWLEDGE

These models taken together enable the profiling of the child's knowledge. Figure 11.2 shows five examples of such profiles. Figure 11.2 is adapted from Wright et al. (2006b) where this approach to profiling children's knowledge is described in detail and extensive descriptions are provided of the knowledge and strategies characteristic of each profile. With appropriate training, practitioners find this profile approach not only easy to understand but extremely powerful as a model of the progression of early number learning for all learners.

The first column of numbers (0, 1, 0, 0, 0) profiles a student who: (a) is an emergent counter, for example, the child can't correctly count a collection of 15 counters (SEAL = 0); (b) can say the number word sequence from 1 to at least

Model	Examples of Profiles of Student's Knowledge				
Stage of Early Arithmetical Learning (SEAL)	0	1	2	3	5
Level of Forward Number Word Sequences (FNWSs)	1	3	4	5	5
Level of Backward Number Word Sequences (BNWSs)	0	1	3	4	5
Level of Numeral Identification	0	1	2	3	4
Level of Tens and Ones Knowledge	0	0	0	1	2

FIGURE 11.2 Using the LFIN to profile students' knowledge. Adapted from Wright et al. (2006b, p. 67).

10 but cannot, in at least some cases, say the number after a given number in the range 1 to 10 (FNWS = 1); (c) cannot say the words from 10 back to 1 (BNWS = 0); (d) has difficulty identifying (reading) at least some of the numerals in the range 1 to 10 (Numeral Identification = 0) and (e) cannot use notions of tens and ones to reason with two-digit numbers (Tens and ones = 0).

The third column of numbers (2, 4, 3, 2, 0) profiles a student who: (a) is a figurative counter, for example, the child can solve additive tasks involving two screened collections (7 blue counters screened and 4 red counters screened; how many altogether) but will typically count-from-one rather than count-on (SEAL = 2); (b) in the range 1 to 30, can say the number word sequence and state the number word after a given number word (FNWS = 4); (c) is facile with BNWSs in the range 1 to 10, that is can say the sequence from 10 to 1 and can say immediately, the number word before a given number word in the range 1 to 10 (BNWS = 3); (d) can read numerals in the range 1 to 20 but has some difficulty reading numerals in the range 20 to 100 (Numeral Identification = 2) and (e) cannot use notions of tens and ones to reason with two-digit numbers (Tens and ones = 0).

The fifth column of numbers (5, 5, 5, 4, 2) profiles a student who: (a) can skillfully add and subtract in the range 1 to 20 without resorting to counting-by-ones (SEAL = 5); (b) is facile with FNWSs in the range 1 to 100 (FNWS = 5); (c) is facile with BNWSs in the range one to 100 (BNWS = 5); (d) can read one-, two- and three-digit numerals (Numeral Identification = 4) and (e) can reason in tens and ones when adding or subtracting in contexts such as base-10 materials (Tens and ones = 2).

Profile of a typical intervention student: Typically, an intervention student of 6 or 7 years of age would have a profile similar to the first or second column from the left in Figure 11.2. The student's profile might be some combination of the two profiles shown. The level of attainment after successful intervention typically would be similar to the fourth or fifth column or some combination of the two profiles shown.

Origins of profiling number knowledge: LFIN was first used to profile students' knowledge in a research study I conducted in the early 1990s (Wright, 1991, 1994). In that study, three cohorts of students were assessed on three occasions (beginning, middle and end) over the course of a school year. The focus of the study was to document progressions in number knowledge typical of students in the first and second years of school. The study served to document that there was a relatively wide range of levels of number knowledge among children beginning their first year of school and that this range was sustained or increased over the first 2 years of school.

SOME IMPORTANT FEATURES OF THE LFIN

A point made earlier in this chapter is that LFIN takes two forms. First, it can be regarded as the rather bare-boned table in Figure 11.1, consisting of five models with up to six levels in each model. Second, as well as that table of models, LFIN can be regarded as including a corpus of rich observations, descriptions and explanations of children's early number knowledge. A further important point is that LFIN includes particular features relating to ways of conceptualizing and organizing children's knowledge about early number learning that, in many cases are quite distinctive. I highlight these here because I believe doing so has the potential to provide a richer illustration of LFIN and greater insight into its usefulness. The significance of these features usually becomes apparent to professionals as they undertake an extended program of professional development related to MR. But their significance is not necessarily apparent to the person who reads a description of LFIN but might not be working with children and applying LFIN to assessment and instruction related to early number learning.

1. *Counting*: A critical and distinctive feature of LFIN is to hold as important, the distinction between, on one hand, a child saying a number word sequence and on the other hand, a child using counting as a problem-based activity. Thus in LFIN, the term counting is used in the sense developed by Steffe (Steffe, 1992; Steffe & Cobb, 1988; Steffe et al., 1983). In broad terms, we would label a child's activity as counting when they use the number word sequence by ones, in solving tasks such as the following: (a) A collection of 15 counters is placed out and the child's task is to figure out how many items in all. (b) A collection of 8 counters is briefly displayed and then screened and similarly a collection of 4 counters and the child's task is figure out how many in all. (c) A collection of 12 counters is briefly displayed and then screened, and then three counters are removed and screened, and the child's task is to figure out how many remain. Steffe observed that when children are engaged in solving tasks such as these, there is a range of levels of sophistication in the meanings children attach to the number words. A detailed description of this topic is available (e.g. Wright et al., 2006a).

2. *Counting vs. saying a number word sequence*: As described in Point 1 above, in the LFIN the term counting is associated with children's problem-based activity, in a context such as one or more collections of counters which may or may not be screened (concealed). This can be contrasted with tasks that focus specifically on a child's facility with number word sequences per se, such as saying the sequence forward or backward from a given starting point, or saying the word after or before a given number word. I regard this distinction as critically important in early number assessment and instruction. In the topic of early number, a very common assessment task is to ask the child to count forwards or backwards. Historically, the child's activity in this case has been referred to as 'rote counting', and typically, this term is juxtaposed with the term 'rational counting'. My difficulty is that the term 'rote' conjures a notion of relative incompetence that does not necessarily exist. Thus what I find useful is to avoid the dichotomy of rote versus rational counting, and to regard on one hand, relative sophistication of counting, and on the other hand, facility with number word sequences as inter-related but distinct aspects of early number learning

(see Point 1 above). For young children, these are qualitatively different cognitive activities and thus I regard it as important to both observe and document them separately.

3. *Counting-from-one and counting-on*: Typically, models of the development of early number learning highlight the development from counting-all to counting-on in children's problem-based counting activity. Indeed, the progression to counting-on is almost universally regarded as the major advancement in early number learning, in the first 2 years of school. For virtually every child who has participated in Mathematics Recovery, progressing to at least the counting-on stage is a major goal of their intervention instruction. Typically, Mathematics Recovery participants are in their second year of school and their age is in the range 5 to 7 years. Further, the typical MR participant is either at a level that, in other models is referred to as counting-all to solve problems; or is at an earlier point – emergent – where they are unable to count a collection of counters. Thus the MR participant is what Steffe called prenumerical. In short, the progression from very early counting strategies, to having a numerical concept of number, is critically important in the number learning of 4 to 7 year olds. This serves to highlight the potential usefulness of an elaborated model of the prenumerical child's counting activity. And my claim is that LFIN is such a model (see Point 4 below). According to Steffe, the prenumerical child in problem-based activity, counts from one in order to give meaning to the last number word in the count. Further, there are different levels of sophistication in the way children use counting-from-one. Presented with an additive task involving two collections (e.g., 8 counters and 3 counters), the perceptual counter will not be able to solve the task unless both collections are unscreened. Further, the perceptual counter will count-from-one to figure out how many counters in all. By way of contrast, the figurative counter can solve an additive task involving two screened collections, but also will count-from-one rather than count-on. In describing the way prenumerical children solve additive tasks (tasks such as those just described) I prefer to use the term count-from-one rather than count-all because, from my perspective, the critical activity for the child is counting-from-one to give meaning to the last number word in the count. The numerical child, that is the child who counts-on to solve additive tasks, has the notion of cardinality, that is the child has learned 'to attribute cardinal meaning to single number words' (Steffe et al., 1983, p. 29), and this can be contrasted with the child who needs to count-from-one to attribute cardinal meaning to a number word. In my view, the critical behavior of the prenumerical child is counting-from-one rather than counting-all.

4. *An elaborated model of prenumerical counting*: As described in Point 3 above, progression to counting-on and beyond, is a major focus of MR instruction. Steffe's theory of early number development results in an elaborated model of this progression. In Steffe's terms, the typical MR participant is prenumerical, that is emergent, perceptual or figurative (see Point 3). A distinctive characteristic of this model is a coherence across these levels. Each progression in counting is described in terms of a qualitative change in the way the child

ascribes meaning to number words when counting. In Mathematics Recovery, this coherent and elaborated model of early counting activity provides a critical basis for the detailed processes of assessing early number knowledge and planning instruction.

5. *Separate focus on BNWS*: In Point 2 above, I described the distinction in MR between counting as a problem-based activity and facility with number word sequences. Further, I claimed that this distinction is a distinctive feature of the LFIN. My assertion is that (a) the development of facility with number word sequences per se; (b) counting as a problem-based activity and (c) facility with numerals, constitute major areas (or aspects) of number learning of the prenumerical child. Also important is the child's development of facility with ascribing number to spatial configurations of dots, in particular the common spatial patterns of dice, playing cards, etc. Underlying LFIN is the belief that the child's acquisition of not only forward but also BNWSs is important. Thus in LFIN, development of knowledge of BNWSs has a focus separate from that of development of FNWSs. This approach enables one to highlight both the similarities and differences in these two areas. One reason why facility with BNWSs is worthy of a separate focus is because children frequently count back to solve various subtractive tasks, for example: I have 16 counters under this screen and I remove three, how many are left?

6. *Facility with numerals*: Another distinctive feature of LFIN relates to the model of children's developing facility with numerals. Facility with numerals includes inter-related aspects such as identifying numerals, that is, naming or reading numerals, and recognizing numerals, that is, selecting a named numeral from a randomly arranged set of numerals. For example, the numerals from 1 to 10 are arranged randomly on the desk and the child is asked which is the number five. In researching children's learning about numerals I have come to regard numeral identification as a reasonable marker of children's developing facility with numerals. Thus ability to identify or name the numerals in a given range (1 to 10; 1 to 30, etc.) is easily assessed by having the child name numerals displayed one at a time in a random order. Thus in LFIN, on the model of Numeral Identification, the child who can read all of the numerals in the range 1 to 20 (when presented randomly) but cannot read some numerals beyond 20, is at Level 2. Similarly, a child who can read all two-digit numerals but cannot read some three-digit numerals is at Level 3, and so on.

7. *Facility with numerals versus place value*: For LFIN, a point of departure from some other models is to hold the development of facility with numerals quite separate from the development of place value knowledge. This follows from a belief that children can and should develop knowledge of multi-digit numerals long before they develop a sense of place value knowledge, corresponding to those numerals (e.g. numerals to 100, to 1,000, etc.). Models of the development of early number knowledge that couple on the one hand, numeral identification and on the other hand, place value knowledge (sometimes referred to as interpreting numerals), seem to be oblivious to this fundamental point. A beginning

knowledge of place value of two-digit numbers derives from and builds on relatively sophisticated concepts of composite units (tens) and addition. Typically, this knowledge is acquired long after a child has learned to read numerals in the range 1 to 100 and beyond. Related to this, the progression from reading two-digit numerals to reading three- and four-digit numerals is relatively easy because of the very regular pattern beyond 100, in the system of naming numerals. Thus a model of children's development of knowledge of numerals that, at each level, couples reading and interpreting is not useful in MR for at least two reasons. First, a summary statement that a child is at Level 2 (assuming for a moment that this refers to say, the numerals from 1 to 20), leaves unspecified, whether or not the child cannot read or cannot interpret or both, numerals beyond 20, and therefore such a model would lack usefulness as a basis for focused instruction. Second, when naming and interpreting are coupled for each range (1 to 10, 1 to 20, etc.) the obvious response from the point of view of instruction is to teach naming and interpreting concurrently across a given range (e.g., 1 to 100). Such an approach is quite at odds with the belief expressed above, that learning to name numerals should long precede the development of notions of place value. In LFIN, the overriding issues are that (a) children can learn to read numerals (far beyond a range of say 1 to 10 or 1 to 20) at a relatively early age in much the same way as they learn to identify letters and words; (b) children can learn the grammar of the numeral naming system and it is relatively easy for them to extend this to three- and four-digit numbers and (c) learning to read multi-digit numerals in this way, can provide a basis for the later learning of place value.

8. *Facility with numeral sequences*: In the two previous points (Points 6 and 7), a case is argued for the importance of the development of facility with numerals and learning to read numerals in particular, as an aspect quite separate from place value. In MR, emphasis is placed on, not only numeral identification, but also developing facility with numeral sequences. This occurs in the case of assessment tasks that involve arranging numerals (e.g., the numerals 1 to 10, the numerals from 46 to 55) in sequence. Numeral sequences also feature strongly in MR instruction. This is in the form of a setting (instructional device) known as a numeral track, which contains for example, the sequence from '1' to '30' with a lid for each numeral allowing numerals to be displayed or concealed according to the demands of particular instructional tasks. The use of numeral sequences as one important part of instruction seems to result in development of three mutually supportive facilities – number word sequence knowledge, numeral sequence knowledge and numeral identification. Thus instruction involving use of numeral sequences seems to have an important role quite separate from the role of numerals when not presented in an extended sequence.

9. *The inter-relatedness of addition and subtraction*: In LFIN the topics of addition and subtraction are regarded as: (a) closely inter-related with each other and (b) closely inter-related with counting. MR adopts an approach which is common in theories and descriptions of early number learning, that is, to use terms such as additive thinking and additive reasoning to refer the child's

learning of both addition and subtraction. Related to this, learning subtraction is seen as very closely aligned with, and a natural extension of learning addition. Initially, subtraction can be derived from addition by considering an addition situation where, instead of knowing the two addends and having the task of finding the sum, one knows one addend and the sum, and has the task of finding the other addend. This is commonly labeled as missing addend subtraction. Thus a focus on additive thinking as an important topic in early number learning, includes the implicit idea that teaching of addition and subtraction can occur almost concurrently and in a closely inter-related way. In similar vein, terms such as multiplicative thinking and multiplicative reasoning are used to refer to the child's learning of both multiplication and division.

10. *An integrated model of counting, addition and subtraction*: In LFIN, addition and subtraction are regarded as closely inter-related (see Point 9) and taken together are regarded as constituting additive thinking (additive reasoning). Also in LFIN, addition and subtraction are regarded as arising in children's development of increasing sophisticated ways of counting in problem-based activity. Thus in LFIN, counting is not regarded as an aspect separate from or preliminary to addition and subtraction. Rather, counting, addition and subtraction are regarded as one aspect. This coupling of on one hand, counting and on the other hand, addition and subtraction, is a distinctive feature of LFIN. In my view there are two difficulties with the alternative, that is, to separate counting from additive reasoning. First, the child's development of counting is not sufficiently differentiated from the child's development of facility with number word sequences. As described above (Point 2), such a differentiation is important. Second, counting is cast in a very limited (narrow) form, that is, perceptual counting (see above). In this approach the notion of counting is limited to the activity of counting items in a visible collection. This can be contrasted with the notion of counting in LFIN, that is, counting encompasses a progression in the sophistication of the child's use of number word sequences in problem-based situations. This ranges from perceptual counting, to figurative counting, and from figurative counting to advanced counting-by-ones – counting forward or backward in problem-based situations. The critical point to realize is that these problem-based situations are additive and subtractive situations. To say it another way – the child's progression along the path of learning to add and subtract, is one and the same as the child's progression along the path of learning to use counting in more sophisticated ways, to solve additive and subtractive tasks. Alternatively one might say, the development of counting constitutes the development of additive reasoning. The culmination of additive reasoning is when the child progresses from using advanced counting-by-ones (counting-on and counting-back) to additive reasoning that does not involve counting-by-ones. In summary, LFIN has an integrated model of counting, addition and subtraction because the development of counting leads in a seamless way, to additive reasoning. Thus the child's initial concepts of addition and subtraction are the culmination of developing increasingly sophisticated strategies for counting.

PEDAGOGICAL TOOLS

I use the term pedagogical tools to refer to key resources that are used by the teacher in planning, monitoring or administering MR assessment and instruction. The LFIN (see Section 1) is an example of a pedagogical tool. The Mathematics Recovery intervention teacher draws on a set of pedagogical tools for assessment and instruction. The main tools are (a) assessment schedules; (b) the LFIN; (c) the Instructional Framework for Early Number and (d) key topics and instructional procedures. The LFIN has already been described in detail earlier in this chapter. Descriptions of the other pedagogical tools are now given.

ASSESSMENT SCHEDULES

An assessment schedule consists of assessment tasks that are presented to the student during an assessment interview. An assessment interview is typically of 20 to 30 minutes' duration and has the purpose of enabling the teacher to comprehensively document the student's current number knowledge. Documenting number knowledge includes determining the profile (see earlier in this chapter) of the student's early number knowledge and also obtaining specific information about the students' current strategies and facility with number words and numerals. This is referred to as a portrait of the student's number knowledge. Together, the profile and portrait inform the planning of instruction.

Task groups: The assessment schedule consists of a series of task groups. Each task group is a set of closely related tasks that have the purpose of eliciting the student's knowledge of a specific number topic. In the case of each task group, there is flexibility on the part of the teacher, concerning which tasks are presented. For example, as a result of the student's response to an initial task, the teacher might choose to present easier tasks, more difficult tasks, or tasks which are similar in difficulty level. Figure 11.3 exemplifies the notion of a task group. The focus of this task group is the child's ability to state the number word before a given number.

The Instructional Framework in Early Number: The IFEN differs in form from the LFIN but is closely linked to the LFIN. IFEN sets out progressions of instructional topics for Mathematics Recovery. In summary form, this set of

Number Word Before

Say the number that comes just before –.
Example: Say the number just before 2.

(a) Entry task:	24	17	20	11	13	21	14	30
(b) Less advanced task:	7	10	4	8	3			
(c) More advanced task:	67	50	38	100	83	41	99	

FIGURE 11.3 Task group focusing on number word before. Adapted from Wright et al. (2006a, p. 161).

progressions takes the form of a matrix consisting of three strands of instruction and five phases of instruction (see below). The strands of instruction are (a) number words and numerals; (b) counting and (c) grouping. In the cases of the first two of these, extensive descriptions have already been provided in this chapter. The third strand, that is grouping, includes instruction on learning to combine and partition small numbers without counting, and instruction aimed at developing a basis for multiplicative thinking.

Five phases of instruction: Each phase of instruction corresponds to one of the profiles shown in Figure 11.2. Thus the first phase of instruction corresponds to a profile of (a) SEAL Stage 0; (b) FNWSs Level 1; (c) BNWSs Level 0; (d) Numeral identification Level 0 and (e) Tens and ones knowledge Level 0. Similarly, the fourth phase of instruction corresponds to a profile of (a) SEAL Stage 3; (b) FNWSs Level 5; (c) BNWSs Level 4; (d) Numeral identification Level 3 and (e) Tens and ones knowledge Level 0. The profiles shown in Figure 11.2 are intended as exemplars of proximal levels of student knowledge across the five models. In practical terms, a child's profile will not necessarily match precisely with any of the profiles in Figure 11.2. What follows is that a child is not necessarily in just one phase of instruction. For a given child, instructional procedures might be drawn from at least two of the phases.

Key topics and teaching procedures: The matrix of three strands and five phases contains 15 cells (3 × 5). And each of the 15 cells in this matrix gives rise to two key topics of instruction. Thus the IFEN sets out a total of 30 key topics. Each of the 30 key teaching topics is elaborated in a set of teaching procedures. For each key topic, there are typically around six such procedures. In all, there are 182 procedures. The procedures in each key topic typically focus on a set of very specific topics that constitute a progression in instruction or are complementary with each other. Teaching procedures take the form of exemplars for teaching, and include descriptions of the teacher's words and actions, the instructional setting (materials) and notes on purpose, teaching and children's responses. Full details of all of the instructional procedures are available (see Wright et al., 2006b).

ASSESSMENT AND INSTRUCTION

In the previous sections I described and gave examples of the pedagogical tools used in MR. Learning to use these pedagogical tools constitutes a major part of the specialized learning of the MR teacher. Another major part of that learning is to learn the general approach to assessment and the general approach to instruction.

The general approach to assessment: The general approach to assessment in Mathematics Recovery has much in common with the approach called dynamic assessment (e.g. Lidz, 2003) and the clinical interview approach as described by Ginsburg (1997). Nevertheless, the approach used in Mathematics Recovery is distinctive I believe, and I describe it as videotaped, interview-based assessment (VIBA). From the point of view of both teacher and student, this approach differs significantly from the running record approach widely used in early literacy instruction and also used in some instructional programs in early years mathematics. The critical point of difference is that, in MR assessment, the teacher does not record any information during the course of the interview. Rather, the interview is videotaped. Subsequently, the teacher reviews in detail, the videotaped record of the interview, and in doing so, a detailed written record is generated via a standard pro forma corresponding to the interview schedule. The process of generating the written record allows for (a) the categorizing of responses; (b) the recording of correct and incorrect responses and (c) the recording of observations of the child's mathematical behavior and interpretations of that behavior. My experience is that, for the vast majority of teachers who undertake MR specialist training, learning to use the VIBA approach represents a major advancement in their professional knowledge.

THE GENERAL APPROACH INSTRUCTION

The Mathematics Recovery program incorporates a problem-based approach to instruction, that is, the student typically is engaged in solving arithmetic tasks which, for them are quite challenging. At the same time, tasks are carefully selected so that the student has a good chance of success. As well, instruction takes place in a cognitively supportive environment. There is an expectation on the part of the teacher that the student will work hard in attempting to solve the task. At the same time there is an expectation on the part of the student that the teacher will make adjustments to tasks which the student seems unable to solve after an extended period of attempting to solve the task. These expectations are largely implicit, and develop as a consequence of the teacher's instructional approach. Thus instruction in Mathematics Recovery is characterized by: (a) hard thinking; (b) a good chance of success on the student's part and (c) awareness that one is making progress in learning. The experience in the Program is that, by and large, students respond very positively to instruction of this kind.

Instructional tasks used in Mathematics Recovery are selected as being at or just beyond the cutting edge of the students' current knowledge. Alternatively, one could say the instructional tasks are in the student's zone of proximal development in the sense of Vygotsky (Blanck, 1990; Vygotsky, 1978). In this sense, the tasks relate to knowledge that the student is capable of learning when the teacher provides scaffolding (Wood et al., 1976) to support their learning. Task selection in this kind of instruction involves moment to moment judgement and selection on the teacher's part, and this constitutes an important part of the professional learning of the Mathematics Recovery teacher.

Mathematics Recovery instruction for a particular student is based on the results of: (a) a comprehensive initial assessment and (b) on-going observational assessment during the instructional sessions. The initial assessment involves the VIBA and has been described earlier in this chapter. The on-going assessment arises from and is integral to the student's problem-solving activity. In MR, instructional sessions (as well as assessment interviews) are routinely videotaped. This enables the teacher to review the student's responses to her instruction and in particular, the student's advancements and difficulties. As well, videotaped records can be the basis of discussions with the MR instructional leader, as well as colleagues, parents and so on.

The Mathematics Recovery program incorporates an elaborated approach to problem-based instruction. This approach is described via nine guiding principles that are central to the instructional approach, and 12 key elements that further elaborate the approach. The approach also includes a focus on children's responses to problem-based instruction via descriptions of nine characteristics of children's problem solving in the intervention teaching sessions. A detailed description of this approach is available (Wright et al., 2006b, p. 26–31).

The guiding principles (Wright et al., 2006, p. 26–31) are:

1. *The teaching approach is enquiry based, that is problem based. Students routinely are engaged in thinking hard to solve numerical problems which for them, are quite challenging.*
2. *Teaching is informed by an initial, comprehensive assessment and on-going assessment through teaching. The latter refers to the teacher's informed understanding of students' current knowledge and problem-solving strategies, and continual revision of this understanding.*
3. *Teaching is focused just beyond the 'cutting edge' of students' current knowledge.*
4. *Teachers exercise their professional judgment in selecting from a bank of teaching procedures each of which involves particular instructional settings and tasks, and varying this selection on the basis of on-going observations.*
5. *The teacher understands students' numerical strategies and deliberately engenders the development of more sophisticated strategies.*
6. *Teaching involves intensive, on-going observation by the teacher and continual micro-adjusting or fine-tuning of teaching on the basis of her observation.*
7. *Teaching supports and builds on students' intuitive, verbally based strategies and these are used as a basis for the development of written forms of arithmetic which accord with students' verbally based strategies.*
8. *The teacher provides students with sufficient time to solve a given problem. Consequently students are frequently engaged in episodes which involve; sustained thinking, reflection on her or his thinking and reflecting on the results of her or his thinking.*
9. *Students gain intrinsic satisfaction from their problem solving, their realization that they are making progress, and from the verification methods they develop.*

THE CASE OF KIM: CONCLUSION

From the perspective of Mathematics Recovery, the critical first step is to document as fully as possible, Kim's current number knowledge. His solution of the written addition task provides potentially useful insights into his current strategies. Nevertheless, it is not sufficient to conclude on the basis of observing his strategy in solving 9 + 7, that one fully understands his problem and further, one can devise an appropriate instructional response. What is needed now is a comprehensive assessment of key aspects of his number knowledge. In Kim's case at least, the written task of 9 + 7 is of somewhat limited use for diagnosis. There is a sense in which the written addition task conflates several aspects of early number knowledge which are problematic for Kim. These aspects need to be separately examined and understood. The resulting pedagogical knowledge should be the basis of several key hypotheses to be tested in instructional settings with Kim and further refined if necessary. Potentially much more useful, are assessment tasks which are more elemental (in the sense of uncompounded).

One important assessment item for Kim, is that of numeral identification. This involves presenting numerals for Kim to read (name), and presenting them one at a time and not in numerical order. By way of contrast, a task in which Kim is asked to read along a numeral sequence while interesting to observe (extending beyond 20, for example), would not serve to pinpoint Kim's facility with numeral identification. A second important assessment item for Kim involves simple addition and counting tasks presented verbally and with collections of counters. These tasks serve to sidestep Kim's apparent difficulty with reading numerals, and have the purpose of revealing the limit of sophistication of Kim's counting in problem-based activity. When he solved the written task 9 + 7 his strategy resembles what I have called counting forward from one three times. Nevertheless, the counting and additive tasks involving counters can lead to a determination of whether Kim is at the perceptual, figurative or counting-on stage, as described earlier in this chapter. Also important is to assess Kim's facility with forward and BNWSs as also described earlier.

The purpose of the approach to assessment just described is to comprehensively document Kim's current early number knowledge. When that is completed, an initial plan for instruction can be developed.

TEACHER DEVELOPMENT

Teacher development is a key ingredient of the Mathematics Recovery Program. The overview given here will draw on the teacher development program used in the US, the country in which MR is most extensively used. The program of teacher development is both intensive and extensive. Teachers new to MR undertake a year-long training program with an accredited MR leader. This involves (a) an initial 5-day training program usually taken in the summer break; (b) over the course of the school year, an additional 5 days of training and a minimum of three one-day, follow-up cohort meetings and (c) a minimum of three one-on-one coaching sessions with an MR leader. Each teacher is required to (a) conduct pre- and post-assessments with at least 10 students, and using MR assessment schedules and (b) complete 100 hours of one-on-one MR instruction.

The 5-day initial phase focuses on an introduction to the LFIN and involves (a) practicing assessment interviews and (b) using the LFIN in the process of analysis of videotaped records of assessment interviews. Typically, this process of learning is undertaken by a cohort of up to 12 teachers. Teachers work in triads to practice and administer the task groups on the assessment schedule, learning key steps in the process, for example, when to administer more advanced tasks. During this period, the instructing leader makes extensive use of video-based resources which exemplify (a) the ways in which assessment tasks are administered and (b) the range of student responses to the assessment tasks.

During the first 4 weeks of school, the teachers conduct assessment interviews with at least 10 students and analyze the videotaped interviews. The next phase of the training program focuses on learning to apply the results of assessment in the planning of instruction. This includes an introduction to the IFEN, and the planning and administering of appropriate instructional procedures. Again, video-based resources are used extensively to exemplify aspects of MR instruction. The teachers now undertake teaching cycles with an initial cohort, typically four students, taught individually four or five times per week for teaching cycles of 12 to 15 weeks. The objective of the instructional program is for the student to attain a level at which they can learn successfully in their classroom. As each student graduates from the intervention program a new student takes their place in the cohort of four students receiving instruction.

During the course of the school year, there are two main avenues of support and further learning for the new MR teacher. First, three one-day cohort meetings will be scheduled across the school calendar. The schedule for these meetings focuses on each MR teacher presenting an overview of their instruction with at least one of their students. The teachers use video excerpts to illustrate students' advancements and on-going and persistent difficulties or challenges that arise in the course of the teaching cycle. The intention is that these one-day cohort meetings result in significant professional development in a collaborative and supportive environment.

A second major avenue of support and further learning are one-on-one coaching sessions, typically of 2-hour duration and provided by the leader to each teacher in the cohort. At least three such sessions are held with scope for additional sessions in the case of teachers whose learning of the MR program has progressed at a slower rate than is typical. The sessions involve the leader observing an instructional session, and include pre- and post-conferences which focus on detailed aspects of both planning for and delivering MR instruction. Analysis of instruction involves the use of a rubric constructed from the nine guiding principles (listed above) and the 12 key elements of MR instruction which are referred to earlier.

BRIEF HISTORY

The Mathematics Recovery intervention program was initially developed in the 1990s, in New South Wales, Australia. Development was via a 3-year research project funded by the Australian Research Council. The development project was undertaken in partnership with regional school systems. These systems contributed in a major way, to the funding of the project via allocation of significant portions of participating teachers' time. The development project involved 20 teachers in 18 schools and approximately 200 participating first-grade students.

MR in the US: The program was first used in the US in 1995. The initial use of the program was in school districts in the south-eastern region. In the period since 1995, the program has been used in school districts in approximately 25 states, and the program has extended to most regions of the US. In the last 10 years, as part of the development of the program, an extensive network of specialist MR leaders has been developed. One of the main roles of MR leaders is to provide new implementations of MR in either the school district in which they are located or in school districts other than their own and which are new to Mathematics Recovery. School districts using Mathematics Recovery typically will monitor progress of their participating students via existing state testing regimes. In many cases the outcomes of the program as indicated by participating students' performance on state tests, have resulted in extensions of the program to other districts in the same state or to districts in other states. Most recently the program has been used by a national center focused on improving literacy and mathematics learning in the primary years (kindergarten to year 4), in a tradition-ally under-served population. As well, the program has been used in a state-wide initiative involving 40 schools, and focusing on mathematics intervention in the early years of school. Currently the program is the focus of a 2 year, nationally funded evaluation study focusing on student outcomes and teachers' learning.

The program was first used in England in 1996. The initial use was in three local education authorities in the north-west. In the period since 1996, use of the program has extended to other local education authorities in England and Wales. As well, the program has been used extensively in Scotland and most recently on a national scale in Ireland. The program has also been used in Canada and The Bahamas, and most recently there are plans to use the program in at least one country of language other than English. In Australia, key components of Mathematics Recovery, including the LFIN, the approaches to assessment and instruction, and the approaches to teacher development have been adapted as a major initiative focusing on classroom instruction across all attainment levels. This adaptation has been and continues to be widely used in Australia and New Zealand. In many of its implementations, use of the program has been extended to intervention for second- and third-grade students. Finally, a current project (2004–2008) is being undertaken to extend the scope of the program by the development of an additional range of pedagogical tools aims specifically at 8 to 10 year olds (third- and fourth-grade levels).

SOURCES OF ADDITIONAL INFORMATION

The overview presented above is complementary to two early overviews of Mathematics Recovery (Wright, 2000, 2003). As well, I am the first author of three books on early number learning. Collectively these contain much of the detailed information on Mathematics Recovery pedagogy. The current versions of these three books were all published in 2006. Because this can result in confusion, a short explanation about the focus and content of each book is provided here. The focus of Wright et al. (2006a) is a detailed explanation of assessment in Mathematics Recovery and includes the assessment schedules, the LFIN and the general approach to assessment. The focus of Wright et al. (2006b) is a detailed explanation of Mathematics Recovery instruction and includes the IFEN, details of key topics, extensive descriptions of exemplar teaching procedures and a detailed description of the general approach to instruction. Wright et al. (2006c) focuses more broadly on assessment and instruction in early number and is oriented to general classroom instruction. This book serves very well as an introduction to or primer for the other two books.

REFERENCES

Blanck, G. (1990). Vygotsky: the man and his cause. In Moll, L. C. (Ed.), *Vygotsky and Education: Instructional Implications and Applications of Sociohistorical Psychology* (pp. 31–58). Cambridge: Cambridge University Press.

Cobb, P. & Wheatley, G. (1988). Children's initial understandings of ten. *Focus on Learning Problems in Mathematics*, *10*(3), 1–24.

Dowker, A. (2004). *What Works for Children with Mathematical Difficulties (Research Report RR554)*. Oxford: Department for Education and Skills.

Ginsburg, H. P. (1997). *Entering the Child's Mind: The Clinical Interview in Psychological Research and Practice*. Cambridge, UK: Cambridge University Press.

Lidz, C. S. (2003). *Early Childhood Assessment*. Hoboken, NJ: John Wiley & Sons.

Steffe, L. P. (1992). Learning stages in the construction of the number sequence. In Bideaud, J., Meljac, C., & Fischer, J. (Eds.), *Pathways to Number: Children's Developing Numerical Abilities* (pp. 83–98). Hillsdale, NJ: Lawrence Erlbaum.

Steffe, L. P. & Cobb, P. (with E. von Glasersfeld) (1988). *Construction of Arithmetic Meanings and Strategies*. New York: Springer-Verlag.

Steffe, L. P., von Glasersfeld, E., Richards, J., & Cobb, P. (1983). *Children's Counting Types: Philosophy, Theory, and Application*. New York: Praeger.

The Macquarie Dictionary (1981). Sydney: The Macquarie Library.

Vygotsky, L. S. (1978). *Mind in Society: The Development of Higher Psychological Processes*. Cambridge, MA: Harvard University Press. (Original work published 1934.)

Wood, D., Bruner, J., & Ross, G. (1976). The role of tutoring in problem solving, *Journal of Child Psychology and Psychiatry and Allied Disciplines*, *17*, 89–100.

Wright, R. J. (1994). A Study of the Numerical Development of 5-year-olds and 6-year-olds. *Educational Studies in Mathematics*, *26*, 25–44.

Wright, R. J. (1991). What number knowledge is possessed by children entering the kindergarten year of school? *The Mathematics Education Research Journal*, *3*(1), 1–16.

Wright, R. J. (2000). Professional development in recovery education. In Steffe, L. P. & Thompson, P. W. (Eds.), *Radical Constructivism in Action: Building on the Pioneering Work of Ernst von Glasersfeld* (pp. 134–151). London: Falmer.

Wright, R. J. (2003). Mathematics Recovery: A program of intervention in early number learning. *Australian Journal of Learning Disabilities*, 8(4), 6–11.

Wright, R. J., Martland, J., & Stafford, A. (2006a). *Early Numeracy: Assessment for Teaching and Intervention* (2nd edn.). London: Paul Chapman Publications/Sage.

Wright, R. J., Martland, J., Stafford, A., & Stanger, G. (2006b). *Teaching Number: Advancing Children's Skills and Strategies* (2nd edn.). London: Paul Chapman Publications/Sage.

Wright, R. J., Stanger, G., Stafford, A., & Martland, J. (2006c). *Teaching Number in the Classroom with 4- to 8-Year-Olds*. London: Paul Chapman Publications/Sage.

12

MAKING INTERVENTION IN NUMERACY MORE EFFECTIVE IN SCHOOLS

MARGARET HASELER

Specialist Teacher, Personalised Learning Team, London Borough of Bromley, Bromley, BR1 3UH, UK

INTRODUCTION

This chapter will briefly describe the most common intervention programmes in numeracy currently adopted in English schools and considers their merits. It will then discuss the conceptual difficulties most commonly seen in pupils and will argue that because of the nature of these difficulties, numeracy intervention programmes should be targeting pupils primarily in Key Stage 1. Finally, it will consider some resources commonly used in classrooms and suggest alternatives which the author believes address the above difficulties more effectively. These observations have not been based on any primary research, but are rather an accumulation of the author's experiences in teaching maths in a variety of primary and secondary schools in both inner and outer London.

Any search for material on teaching special needs pupils will produce far more on teaching literacy skills than on numeracy skills. An obvious explanation for this is that literacy skills are considered to be the gateway to all learning. Why this is so is not clear – possibly literacy skills are considered, quite understandably, to be the gateway to all learning and consequently of more importance than numeracy skills. There is also the social element – When was the last time you heard anyone admit that they can't read? I would guess that this has rarely happened whereas many people freely admit to being poor at maths. Anecdotal evidence also suggests that many primary school teachers and a majority of learning support assistants feel more confident in teaching literacy than numeracy.

Happily, in recent years, we have seen an increase in research on the causes of maths difficulties and how to deal with them, although we still have a long way to go if we are to catch up with literacy research. The advent of the Numeracy Strategy (now called the Renewed Framework) in English schools has transformed maths teaching in both primary and lower secondary schools, especially for less confident teachers.

And while government statistics show that achievement levels in maths have been improving steadily, they are still below the levels of achievement in literacy. In 2007, percentages of pupils in local authorities gaining the expected Level 4 at the end of Key Stage 2 ranged from 70% to 88% in English and between 66% and 84% in maths (DCSF, 2007). A more worrying statistic concerns the percentage of pupils who at the end of Key Stage 1 achieved level 2C but by the end of Key Stage 2 had not made the expected 2 levels of progress. In 2007, this figure was 2% in English but in maths, it was 7%. (DCSF, 2008) Why did more than three times the number of pupils not reach the expected level in maths? Is it because of the importance placed on literacy skills over numeracy skills so that intervention in literacy was seen as a higher priority? Or if the pupils did receive numeracy intervention in Key Stage 2, are we to conclude that literacy intervention programmes are more effective than numeracy intervention programmes?

CURRENT INTERVENTION PROGRAMMES

Many schools arrange for pupils with mathematical difficulties to have regular *withdrawal sessions* away from the classroom with either a learning support assistant or a special needs teacher. Pupils are usually taught in groups in order to maximise staff resources and time but can also be taught on an individual basis. The content for these sessions can vary but usually follows either a published programme written specifically for pupils who are not achieving age expected goals or a programme devised by the school.

The Renewed Framework (formally the Numeracy Strategy) has produced a range of intervention programmes designed to help pupils achieve age expected goals. These have been categorised at three levels:

1. Effective differentiation within the classroom or quality first teaching, designed to ensure that all children are included in the daily mathematics lesson (Wave 1 support);
2. Springboard programmes for years 3, 4, 5, 6 and 7, aimed at pupils just below age expected levels (Wave 2 support); (DfES, 2000)
3. 'Supporting children with gaps in their mathematical understanding' is for pupils in Key Stage 2 who continue to have significant difficulties despite Wave 1 and 2 interventions (Wave 3 support). (DfES, 2005)

As Wave 1 intervention takes place within the classroom and is considered to be part of the daily mathematics lesson, it may not be regarded as an intervention programme per se. This chapter will refer to only Wave 2 and 3 interventions which are seen to be additional to the daily mathematics lesson. *Wave 2* 'Springboard' (DfES, 2000) programmes run for up to 20 weeks for groups of pupils and most are designed to be provided mainly by a teaching assistant with some input from a class teacher. Programmes consist of a series of lessons which follow the format of the Numeracy Hour lessons and focus on topics which are known to cause particular difficulty for pupils. In contrast, *Wave 3* support 'Supporting children with gaps in their mathematical understanding' (DfES, 2005) is not time limited and does not follow the usual lesson format, but consists of a number of short tasks or 'spotlights' which focus on very specific areas of difficulty. Both Wave 2 and Wave 3 materials are scripted, making them accessible and easy for any member of staff to deliver.

All of the maths intervention programmes mentioned above are aimed at pupils in Key Stage 2. This is in contrast to literacy intervention programmes which target pupils as early as year 1. It is interesting to note that although independent organisations such as the Fischer Family Trust have developed an early intervention programme for Key Stage 1 pupils in literacy, to date, they do not have an equivalent in numeracy. (Fischer Family Trust, 1999)

Currently, the only published intervention programme specifically aimed at Key Stage 1 pupils is the *Mathematics Recovery Programme* (Wright et al., 2000), which has originated in Australia and is based on the principles of early intervention.[*] It relies on a rigorous initial assessment to identify pupils' difficulties and ongoing assessment through teaching and observation, supported by a bank of graded tasks. Teaching is on an individual daily basis for 12–14 weeks. As the emphasis is on ongoing diagnostic observations, a considerable amount of training is required to implement it, depending on the knowledge and experience of the member of staff. It involves a thorough knowledge of the early stages of mathematics learning as well as an understanding of how to assess pupils' mathematical difficulties. Such training is costly and time consuming and many schools are reluctant or unable to invest in it. However, anecdotal evidence shows that time and resources spent undertaking such training brought significant benefits, as both teachers and support assistants were able to transfer the skills learned to a wider group of pupils. This has had a positive effect on general classroom practice.

Where no published programme is being used with groups or individuals, the content of the sessions can vary according to the adult taking the session but is often linked to recent work done in the daily mathematics lesson. While this can make for a more individual 'personalised' learning programme, the quality of teaching can vary enormously, according to the experience and expertise of the adult.

---

*Two other intervention programmes are currently in the pilot stage – Numeracy Recovery and Elite Maths – but at the time of writing these are not yet available to all schools.

THE DIFFICULTY WITH MATHS

Much has been written about the reasons why mathematical skills are harder to acquire than literacy skills. For one thing, Maths is a more abstract subject so by its very nature will be more difficult to master. Other reasons why particular children will have difficulty in learning maths include:

- *Low cognitive ability*: any abstract subject will be difficult for those with low cognitive ability.
- *Specific learning difficulties such as dyslexia, dyscalculia, dyspraxia, ASD, speech and language and ADHD*: Children with any of these conditions often find particular aspects of maths difficult.
- *Behaviour difficulties/absence from school through truancy or illness*: Mathematical skills are progressive and cumulative. Furthermore, these skills are interrelated. Interruptions in schooling for whatever reason will impact on subsequent progress.
- *Poor or inconsistent teaching*: In recent years, the need to adapt teaching techniques to accommodate the different learning styles found in classrooms has become more widespread. Unfortunately, this is still more common in literacy than in numeracy. Added to this, there is a wide variation in mathematics teaching abilities, even within one school, so some children suffer from an inconsistent approach.

While we cannot eradicate all of the above causes, we can certainly do something to minimise their effects and many schools work very hard to achieve that. Unfortunately, many maths difficulties are not identified until Key Stage 2 – hence the Renewed Framework's Wave 2 and 3 interventions. In the past, this was partly due to the assessment process which took place at the end of Key Stage 1. An analysis of questions on any of the previous Key Stage 1 SATS papers will show that a child could gain enough marks to achieve an age appropriate level without developing many of the strategies necessary for successful computation. Because of this, early misconceptions were not always apparent. Although in recent years, more emphasis is now put on teacher assessment at the end of Key Stage 1, I would argue that because schools tend to use one of the previous Key Stage 1 tests to inform part of their teacher assessment, some judgements may still be misleading.

From my experience in assessing and working with pupils who have maths difficulties ranging from just below to severely below age expected levels, there are several particular problems which frequently arise. These are:

- Lack of memorised number facts;
- An insecure concept of place value;
- Difficulty carrying out multi-step procedures;
- Difficulty solving word problems.

Children can have one or more of these problems (and others, as well!) and the reasons can vary according to the particular difficulties of the individual child. Of the four identified, the first two – number facts and place value – both feature heavily in Key Stage 1. In fact, children are expected to have memorised many addition and subtraction facts by the end of Key Stage 1 as well as having an understanding of the place value of 2 digit numbers. A discrepancy in either often leads to use of inefficient calculation strategies and insecure methods later on. It is also reasonable to assume if insecure methods of calculations and/or poor number fact recall is evident, a child is likely to struggle with both word problems and multi-step procedures as an even greater burden will be placed on the working memory. There may of course be other reasons why some children have difficulties with solving word problems or multi-step procedures, such as a speech and language impairment or organisational difficulties.

Much of the teaching which takes place in Key Stage 2 assumes a proficiency in number fact recall and place value, building on the skills acquired in Key Stage 1. As these skills are progressive and cumulative, if some of the earlier building blocks have been missed, the impact on subsequent maths achievement will be significant. To extend the building metaphor, if some of the foundation blocks are missing, the wall will have some weak spots. If only a few blocks are missing, the wall may remain relatively stable but the more layers added to the top, the greater the chance of the wall becoming unstable. If enough foundation blocks are missing, the wall will collapse after only a few layers. Early identification and intervention would therefore seem to be a crucial step in helping children with mathematical difficulties and I would argue that this should take place primarily in Key Stage 1.

MAKING INTERVENTION MORE EFFECTIVE

Ann Dowker (2004) identified a number of important points in relation to numeracy intervention programmes:

- Children's arithmetical difficulties are highly susceptible to intervention.
- Individualised work with children who are falling behind in arithmetic has a significant impact on their performance.
- Although intervention can take place at any age, it is desirable that programmes should focus on early intervention in order to prevent difficulties from becoming entrenched.
- The time spent does not have to be great in order to be effective.

My own teaching experience would heartily support those points and I would also suggest three more:

1. Professional development is an important component in an effective intervention programme.
2. Intervention programmes should be an integral part of the maths curriculum
3. Using effective equipment makes a significant difference to a successful outcome.

PROFESSIONAL DEVELOPMENT

One of the disadvantages in my view of the Renewed Framework intervention programmes mentioned above is often considered by schools to be an asset, namely the fact that they provide scripted lessons. This may lead schools to expect that any member of staff can run Springboard (Wave 2) or Wave 3 groups with minimal training as long as they have the folder of lessons. While this may seem acceptable on the surface, problems can arise when pupils do not respond as expected to the teaching strategies or techniques employed in these lessons. In most cases, the strategies are a repetition of what will have occurred in the daily mathematics lesson, but at an earlier level. This may be sufficient for pupils who are behind due to previous absences or inconsistent teaching but will not necessarily help pupils whose difficulties arise for other reasons. Training is an important part of the Mathematics Recovery programme but in my opinion is crucial to any successful intervention programme. Staff, whether they are qualified teachers or learning support assistants, need to have an understanding of the importance played by the early building blocks in developing mathematical concepts. This knowledge is essential if we are to successfully analyse the child's difficulties and remediate effectively. Intervention is more effective if there is the opportunity for ongoing assessment through observation, which in turn informs the next step of any teaching programme.

Staff also need to be aware of how specific learning difficulties such as dyslexia or dyspraxia can affect the development of mathematical skills, and not just reading and writing skills. A child with co-ordination difficulties may have missed opportunities to practise counting in the early years so may not have developed one to one correspondence. Dyslexic children will often have problems memorising number facts and will need to develop strategies to compensate for this.

INTERVENTION AS AN INTEGRAL PART OF
THE MATHS CURRICULUM

Published programmes such as Springboard follow a series of lessons which do not always fit with the topics being taught in the classroom. Because of this, children who have been taught effective strategies in an intervention programme may not have the opportunity to put these into practice immediately in the classroom if the class mathematics lesson has moved on to a different topic. The programme by its very nature cannot fit in with the numeracy lesson in class – if it does, it moves on too quickly and the children face their original problem: no time to practise and consolidate what has been learned. In cases where pupils do not follow a published programme and the class teaching informs the intervention programme, this also leads to a fragmented approach, with the same consequences. When the strategies or skills being targeted in the intervention programme are not followed up in class, the child defaults to previous ineffective and time consuming strategies. Teachers and teaching assistants involved in supporting special needs children know that repetition and consolidation are keys to success. Careful attention needs to be paid to the content of any intervention programme so that it is an integral part of the child's whole mathematics curriculum, not just an 'add-on'. An intervention programme should identify the child's mathematical difficulties through a detailed initial assessment and subsequent ongoing diagnostic observations. This information should in turn inform some of the differentiated teaching which takes place in class, so pupils use part of the daily mathematics lesson to practise the necessary skills. This coordinated approach to intervention will ensure that difficulties are targeted and effective strategies are regularly practised by creating suitable opportunities for consolidation within the maths lesson. The format of the Wave 3 materials and the Mathematics Recovery programme are both more suitable to this way of working.

An additional difficulty with 'ready made' programmes is that they dictate how each topic is taught, regardless of the child's particular difficulties. A Springboard lesson on using number facts to develop effective strategies for calculations does not uncover the reason why a pupil has difficulty remembering number facts or why he/she fails to employ them in a meaningful way. This information is important because we may need to adapt our teaching style or adopt a different approach if we are to help that particular pupil overcome their difficulties. There is greater flexibility with Wave 3 materials, which includes some suggestions on what to do if a pupil gives an incorrect response. However, these materials are more often than not being used without an initial in depth analysis of the pupil's difficulties. Because of this, problems may not be 'tracked back' to an early enough level, so early misconceptions are in danger of being overlooked.

EFFECTIVE EQUIPMENT

If we are to intervene effectively in Key Stage 1 to prevent difficulties from becoming entrenched, then the two areas mentioned earlier need to be tackled, namely, lack of memorised number facts and an insecure concept of place value. If children are secure in both of these areas by the end of Key Stage 1, many of the subsequent difficulties can be avoided. I believe that both problems can be tackled in the same way by helping children to develop a strong visual image of number. The key to successful visual imagery is the resources or equipment used.

First of all, let us explore the concept of visual imagery. Subitising is the ability to know how many units there are without counting (Mandler & Shebo, 1982) and this is a skill which Brian Butterworth believes our brains are hard-wired to do from infancy (Butterworth, 1999) with 4 as the maximum number of objects possible for most adults. Because they can subitise, children quickly develop a 'sense' of the numbers up to 3 or 4 once they start matching the counting names with the relevant numerosities. As the counting range is extended and counting skills become more proficient, children begin to develop an understanding for the remaining numbers, particularly up to 10. Yeo (2003) uses the term 'number sense' to describe the intuitive feel for numerosities and numbers, stating that it is generally acknowledged that good number sense plays 'a significant role in children's general ability ... to make confident progress in the early stages of primary school number-work.' Butterworth (2005) suggests that progress in arithmetic is dependant on developing 'an increasingly sophisticated understanding' of numerosities and an 'increasing skill in manipulating' them.

Butterworth's research identifies the inability to subitise as one of the characteristics of being dyscalculic. This affects the development and understanding of numerosities, causing severe mathematical difficulties. In this respect, dyscalulics could be described as having very little number sense, or even none at all. Only a small minority of children with maths difficulties are dyscalculic but there are other children who, although able to subitise, still have not developed 'good' number sense. Admittedly this will not be nearly as severe as those with dyscalculia and, in common with many such learning difficulties, will be on a continuum.

What has prevented these children from developing good number sense? The answer may lie in the way numbers have been presented to them. Young children are given many opportunities to match numerals to collections of objects – the symbol 4 matches 4 buttons. In this way, we teach children how each numeral relates to the number it represents. We assume that once a child can identify how many there are in a set by counting and matching it to the correct numeral, they have 'understood' that number and have formed an image of that number. However, things are not so simple. Being able to count four objects does not in itself tell us much about the number 4 and how it is constructed, other than it contains four units. There is certainly nothing in the symbol we use (4) to tell us anything about the number either. It is in itself an abstract symbol. What we need is a visual image for the number 4 in our minds. Luckily our ability to subitise may help us here but this is more difficult, if not impossible, for higher numbers. Yeo remarks that children with poor number-sense often have a 'very poor "fuzzy" sense of quantities and numbers between 5 and 10 and above' (Yeo, 2003). In other words, they have not developed a strong visual image of those numbers. Because of this, Fuson and other writers in the education field believe that we should build on the brain's natural ability to subitise by introducing to young children number representations using instantly recognisable patterns (Fuson, 1992; Sharma, 1981; Yeo, 2003).

Representing numbers in pattern form helps children to see each number as a whole with several different components. In this way, children will not only have a mental picture for each number but will also understand how each is constructed. From this comes an appreciation of how numbers relate to each other, particularly those on either side – for example, that 4 is one more than 3 and one less than 5. They will also learn that 4 can be subdivided into subsets 2 + 2 as well as 3 + 1. So if you take 1 away from 4, you will get 3. If you take 3 away from 4, you will be left with 1 and so on. At some point, they will discover that if you have 2 lots of four, you will get 8. The ability to flexibly split 4 into different subsets is the basis for calculating and inherent in this skill is the relationship between addition and subtraction. By building up a strong visual image of each number and seeing how that number relates to other numbers around it, we have helped ourselves to learn some addition and subtraction facts, as well as learning the very important and useful concept about the relationship between addition and subtraction. We know these facts because we understand the links between the numbers. We do not have to rely on our memory to recall the facts. For children who have weak memories – which incidentally includes the majority of special needs children I have met, including those with a specific learning difficulty – this is very powerful.

Children who have a weak visual image of number see each number as just a collection of ones – this limits their understanding and ability to manipulate numbers in an efficient way. Seeing numbers as random collections of ones leads to 'ones-based' counting strategies to solve calculations, which is both time consuming, inefficient and open to error.

How can we help children develop good visual images of number? A glance through any major educational catalogue will show a bewildering array of equipment available to support mathematics teaching and it is important here to distinguish two types of resources, 'manipulative or concrete' and 'pictorial'. The former is generally taken to mean something that can be physically picked up and manipulated, such as cubes, counters, beads – in other words a real life representation of number. Pictorial resources include number lines, number squares and place value cards, as they all use the abstract symbols for number rather than the real life representations. Where children are given pictures of beads, cubes, counters or indeed any other object depicted on a worksheet, card or book to help them, these would also be considered pictorial. Both types are to be found in classrooms up and down the country with those in the manipulative category being commonly used in early Key Stage 1, while the pictorial resources are to be found in upper Key Stage 1 and lower Key Stage 2. Although it is generally accepted in the teaching profession that a multi-sensory approach to any learning is best – seeing, doing, hearing and saying – one finds a wide variation in how schools use their maths equipment throughout the key stages. Furthermore, I have found that many pupils with maths difficulties have had limited access to manipulative (as opposed to pictorial) resources or in some cases none at all. Thus, it seems reasonable to suggest that these pupils may have fared better if they had access to manipulative apparatus, especially in the early stages of mathematical development. There is no doubt that the introduction of the Renewed Framework (formerly the Numeracy Strategy) has encouraged teachers to use a variety of resources to aid understanding. However, if we are to effectively help children with mathematical difficulties, we need to be more discerning in the resources we choose and to be clear about the fundamental differences between manipulative and pictorial resources. Number lines and place value cards are excellent pictorial resources but due to their abstract nature will not provide a visual image of number. Children need opportunities to work with manipulative resources first to build up visual images before moving on to pictorial resources.

Choosing *appropriate* manipulative resources is our next task. Most Key Stage 1 classrooms are equipped with manipulative resources such as linking cubes and Base 10 materials and these are commonly used both for addition and subtraction calculations and for demonstrating place value. Let us take the example of Ben faced with solving the calculation 4 + 3. He might be encouraged to get 4 cubes and then get 3 more and count to find the total.

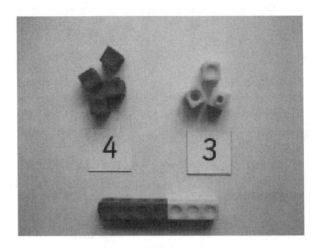

At first, he would count all of the cubes once he had set out each subset. We would then encourage him to count on from one of the numbers, preferably the larger one. These are considered good strategies. He may then progress to carrying this out on a number line, or counting on using his fingers. However, the process is still the same – Ben has learned that in order to solve an addition calculation, you need to be able to count. At some point in this process, we expect Ben to memorise that 4 + 3 is 7 – for some reason we think that by having lots of practice in counting sets of cubes, somehow the number facts will be absorbed, memorised and recalled the next time he needs them. Some children make this leap but many children like Ben do not. If for whatever reason children do not make this leap in year 1, when memorising a certain amount of number facts is expected, they have already started to fall behind in maths.

Let us look now at Amy. She can count to 20 and her teacher is introducing place value to her by using Base 10 equipment to show that 10 unit cubes are the same as a 10 stick. The teacher places the 10 unit cubes together in a line so that Amy can see that it is indeed the same as the 10 stick.

Unfortunately, for some reason, Amy is not sure about this so she always counts the 10 stick each time she uses it. Teachers reading this will be only too familiar with the children like Amy, who despite being shown how 10 unit cubes match a 10 stick, carry on counting the sections in the 10 stick as if by some strange twist of fate, one day it might equal 10 but another day, it might not! There may be a number of reasons why Amy is not sure. Perhaps she is having difficulty seeing 10 as a whole group because she is accustomed to seeing it as a random collection of ones. Perhaps she simply keeps forgetting how many unit cubes there were in the first place – after all, you can't tell by just looking that there are 10 cubes in the pile there could be 8 or 9 or even 11. As long as Amy is unsure of the value of the 10 stick, subsequent work on using Base 10 to show 2 digit numbers will always be compromised for her because her concept of 10 as an important group in our number system is insecure.

Children like Ben and Amy have similar problems – their image of numbers is weak so they resort to the only thing they can confidently do and that is count to get the answer. Eva Grauberg (1998) says that some children lack grouping strategies because there is a 'primary weakness in perceiving structures' which in turn is responsible for a 'weakness in using structures'. Such children may have difficulty in appreciating our number system where grouping in tens is crucial to how we record magnitudes. Others may have problems seeing the relationship of component parts to the whole. For example, understanding that 8 can be made with 2 and 6 or 3 and 5 or even two sets of 4.

Sharma (1981) believes that children who only experience number representations in linear or non-uniform visual clusters continue to use ones based counting strategies long after they are appropriate. Equipment like linking cubes or Base 10 present numbers either in a linear form as in a 'stick' or non-uniform visual clusters as in a random group. This limits their usefulness in helping children develop visual imagery. Cubes linked together to show numbers over 5 are not immediately recognisable and the child has to resort to counting again. As regards Base 10, until children meet the 10 stick (usually when they begin to learn about partitioning 2 digit numbers), 10 (and most of the numbers below) is just a random collection of ones which you have to count each time, mainly because it is too big to subitise. What follows then is an insecure concept of teens numbers because the image of 10 itself is not a secure one.

Dice patterns are one of the most common number 'shapes' available to children and most children can tell which number is represented by each pattern of dots. However, dice patterns are limiting in their ability to provide a useful visual representation of number. For one thing, the patterns for 3 and 4, although instantly recognisable, do not easily relate to each other – the shapes of each pattern are not linked. In other words, it is not obvious that 4 is one more than 3.

Patterns for 7, 8, 9 and 10 are not commonly used and are also not consistent, as can be seen from these two patterns to represent the number 8.

Effective resources in maths are therefore those which promote a strong visual image of number in a *structured* way where the relationships between each of the numbers is obvious.

Two particularly effective models of number representation which fulfil the criteria for strong visual imagery are:

- *Numicon* shapes which represent numbers up to 10 in arrays of 2. The shapes 1–10 when set out in order form a staircase pattern with the odd numbers providing the 'steps' up. This mainstream resource was originally based on the number patterns devised by Catherine Stern and then further developed by practising teachers using government research money. The Numicon system promotes a multi-sensory approach to teaching maths and also places an emphasis on children understanding and using mathematical language.

- *Ten frames* which use our ability to subitise for numbers up to 5 and for the numbers 6–10, use 5 as a benchmark. So 6 is seen as 5 + 1, 7 as 5 + 2, 8 as 5 + 3 (or 10 − 2) and 9 as 5 + 4 (or 1 less than 10) and 10 as 5 + 5. Ten frames are one of the resources used throughout the Mathematics Recovery programme and similar images have also been suggested in a few Wave 3 'spotlight' activities.

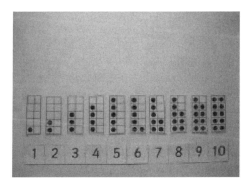

The image of 5+ numbers can also be seen elsewhere:

- In a 10-bead string using 2 colours of beads, 5 in one colour and 5 in another colour. While this is useful to depict the numbers up to 10, the 100 bead string which has alternate decades in 2 different colours, is not as versatile for showing numbers above 10.

Showing 8 on a 10 bead string

Showing 26 on a 100 bead string

- In the tallying system which represents numbers in groups of 5. I have found this useful with some secondary school special needs pupils who may have found other structured apparatus too infantile.

For both Numicon and ten frames, each number up to 10 has a particular pattern and is therefore instantly recognisable. Because the patterns are consistent with each other, the relationship between each number is clear. It is generally accepted that memorising number facts in order to develop effective strategies for calculations is a particular stumbling block for pupils with mathematical difficulties. Weak memories for number facts can be supported by the visual images provided by structured apparatus. By depicting numbers through the imagery of pattern, we are exploiting one of children's strengths: their love of pattern. By providing a visual image of each number up to 10, addition and subtraction facts can be seen and understood and as such do not rely on memory for recall. For example, Ben would be less likely to resort to counting if he was familiar with Numicon shapes – he would put a 4 shape and a 3 shape together and he would recognise that he had made a 7 shape. Or if his visual image of number was based on the ten frame model, he would know what shape would be made if he added 3 more counters to his 4 frame.

Eventually, he would be able to manipulate these images in his mind.

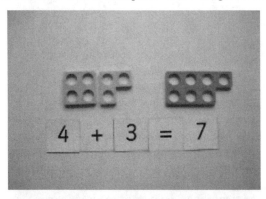

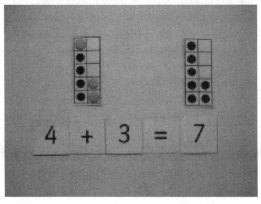

Numbers over 10 are also quickly recognised by their component parts. 16 has a 10 shape and a 6 shape – no counting required. 26 is two 10 shapes and a 6 shape.

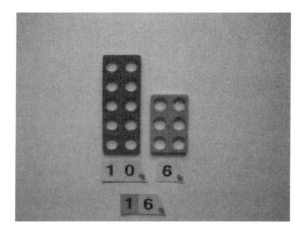

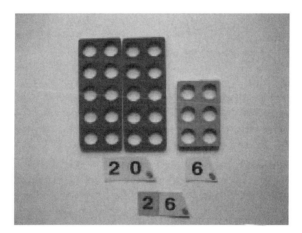

Representing numbers in this way provides a strong basis for understanding place value. Because Amy would know the image for 10 either through the ten frame or through the Numicon shape as soon as she could count to 10, she would know its value without having to count so her image of teens numbers would include 10 as their base, providing a strong foundation for her developing concept of place value. In turn, she would also be more confident in applying the number facts up to 10 that she has learned to bigger numbers, thus developing effective strategies for calculations.

Although resources like Numicon and ten frames provide a more useful visual image of numbers, it is important to emphasise that a child's visual image of number should not be confined to one representation. Because our experiences of number come from many sources, children need to see numbers represented in different ways, in different contexts and most importantly in how they relate to real life. However, in choosing particular equipment to support children's developing mathematical concepts in key areas such as place value and calculations, it is important to understand what we want the equipment to do and how some equipment, because of its limitations, can lead to misconceptions.

It is also important to remember that however 'good' we believe the equipment to be, it will only be of value to pupils if it is used by suitably trained staff who understand the rationale behind it.

CONCLUSION

By providing intervention at an earlier age and ensuring we help children to develop a strong visual image of number, we may be able to prevent a significant number of children from falling even further behind when they move from Key Stage 1 to Key Stage 2.

REFERENCES

Butterworth, B. (1999). *What Counts – How Every Brain Is Hardwired for Maths*. New York: Focal Press.

Butterworth, B. (2005). The development of arithmetical abilities. *Journal of Child Psychology and Psychiatry*, 46(1), 3–18.

Department for Children, Schools and Families (DCSF) (2008): *Making Good progress in Key Stage 2 English*

Department for Children, Schools and Families (DCSF) (2008): *Making Good progress in Key Stage 2 mathematics.*

Department for Children, Schools and Families (DCSF) (2007). *National Curriculum Assessment at Key Stage 2 in England 2007.*

Department for Education and Science (2005) *Supporting Children with Gaps in Their Mathematical Understanding.* DfES1168-2005G

Department for Education and Science (2000): *Springboard Material, Years 3 – 7.* DFEE0151/2000

Dowker, A. (2004). *What Works for Children with Mathematical Difficulties?* Research Report No 554. Nottingham: Department for Education and Skills.

Fischer Family Trust (1999). *ELS Programme.*

Fuson, K. (1992). Research on learning and teaching addition and subtraction of whole numbers. In Leinhardt, G., Putman, R. and Hattrup, R. A. (Eds.), *Analysis of Arithmetic for Mathematics Teaching*. Hillsdale, NJ: Erlbaum.

Grauberg, E. (1998). *Elementary Mathematics and Language Difficulties*. London: Whurr.

Mandler, G. & Shebo, B. J. (1982). Subitising: An analysis of its component processes. *Journal of Experimental Psychology: General*, 11, 1–22.

Sharma, M., (1981). *Visual Clustering and Number Conceptualisation*. Math Notebook, volume 2, number 10. Published by Center for Teaching/Learning of Mathematics

Wright, R., Martland, J., & Stafford, A. (2000). *Early Numeracy: Assessment for Teaching and Intervention*. London: Paul Chapman.

Yeo, D. (2003). *Dyslexia, Dyspraxia and Mathematics*. London: Whurr.

Details about the Numicon system, including the teaching programmes can be obtained from: Numicon Ltd., 12 Pine Close, Avis Way, Newhaven, East Sussex, BN9 0DH www.numicon.com.

Ten frames can be bought from: Smartkids UK Ltd., 5 Station Road, Hungerford, Berkshire, RG17 0DY www.smartkids.co.uk.

AFTERWORD

HELPING CHILDREN WITH NUMERACY DIFFICULTIES IN SCHOOL

A TEACHER'S NOTES

JILL HANNINGTON

St Ebbes' Primary School, Oxford, UK

Mathematics intervention programs have become increasingly necessary, particularly in the past 10 years, or so it seems. My experience of nearly 30 years as a teacher has led me to consider mathematics intervention programs as very important.

Recently, Ann Dowker asked me to put together my view of intervention programs in primary schools, which gave me reason to reflect on the past 30 odd years!

The importance of such interventions has been increasingly emphasized recently, because of concern to find an antidote to problems arising from children in danger of underachieving, i.e., not reaching the 'national expectations' for the end of a key stage.

Since the introduction of the national curriculum there now seem to be several 'best fit answers' to gaps in children's learning – or at least those not likely to achieve these goals or targets set to maintain a school's elevated position in the league tables. Before the establishment of an official National Numeracy Strategy (NNS) in the UK, schools relied on a combination of strategies to teach mathematics: 'gut feelings', experience and 'hard sell' from publishers as to which 'Maths Scheme' suited their school. This often resulted in a mixture of several approaches; making it difficult to actually pinpoint where children were experiencing difficulties.

One good result of the National Numeracy Strategy has been the unification of the key objectives loosely linked to age, making it slightly easier to diagnose where a student might be having difficulties. Solving the problem then becomes the next issue. In school, once the issue was identified we would then either take a child a step back in the key objectives or match a 'Springboard' (government-sponsored small-group intervention program) to suit the child's needs.

The next dilemma is when, how, and who should work with identified students. Working in the groups at the same time as the math lesson in the class, worked in some cases, but only if children were not missing the introduction of a topic. Withdrawing groups of children with difficulties and working at a different time (extra math) has also worked. Giving some of the tasks for homework, provided the student has been clear about what to do, has also worked.

The dilemma for teachers is always when and who should supervise, in effect teach these students. Often it comes to teaching assistants who may not have the confidence or indeed the expertise to 'teach'. In such cases, the teacher needs to find the time to organize the class to leave with a teaching assistant whilst they themselves teach the intervention group.

In schools we have found the Wave 3 material, recently introduced by the Government for individualized interventions, excellent for diagnosing and tracking back to where problems may have initially began. When we find time to plan with one of our experienced and confident Teaching Assistants in Mathematics using the Wave 3 intervention materials, we find that this is the most successful, whether used as a pre-teaching lesson, or with a small group working alongside the whole class but using the materials separately under the support of the Teaching Assistant. Such materials are also used to give as homework or as the basis of a lesson; tracking back to revise and reinforce earlier learning; or as an additional supplementary approach to teaching a mathematical strategy.

Note: For further information about the details of the Springboard and Wave 3 materials, and the ways in which these may be used in schools, the reader may refer to information on the British government's 'Standards Site' website:

www.wave3.org.uk/pages/downloads/pns_wave3_108305_pub.pdf
www.standards.dfes.gov.uk/primary/features/mathematics/intervention/
    springboard
www.standards.dfes.gov.uk/primary/features/inclusion/wave3feature/-

INDEX